# GOD, WHAT'S
# MISSING?

*Going
to Church
and Still
Empty*

# CAROL PEET

Destiny Image® Publishers
Shippensburg, PA

**Destiny Image**® **Publishers, Inc.**
**P.O. Box 310**
**Shippensburg, PA 17257-0310**

*"Speaking to the Purposes of God*
*for This Generation and*
*for the Generations to Come"*

ISBN 10: 0-7684-2333-3
ISBN 13: 978-0-7684-2333-4

For Worldwide Distribution

Printed in the U.S.A.

This book and all other Destiny Image, Revival Press, MercyPlace, Fresh Bread, Destiny Image Fiction, and Treasure House books are available at Christian bookstores and distributors worldwide.

1 2 3 4 5 6 7 8 / 09 08 07 06

For a U.S. bookstore nearest you, call
**1-800-722-6774.**

For more information on foreign distributors, call
**717-532-3040.**

Or reach us on the Internet:
**www.destinyimage.com**

When we started this journey of marriage, we thought we knew so much, but as a few years went by, we came to realize we knew so little. Times got hard as we found ourselves traveling through a dark forest of doubts, confusion, misunderstandings, and disappointments. Yet I never doubted your love for me, and you always accepted (without intimidation) and encouraged (without competition) God's call on my life. As the trees of our forest have given way to the light of God's truths, we have made the miraculous and wonderfully mysterious discovery that our journey has become a great adventure. Thank you for asking me to travel with you. I love you.

# Contents

# Foreword —
## Mark Hanby

When Carol mentioned to me that she was writing a book about personal and spiritual relationships between men and women and asked if I would do the Foreword, I agreed without hesitation. I know Carol Peet. She and her husband, Richard, have been in a precious "father/son" relationship with me for many years, and I have the highest regard for her knowledge and revelation concerning scriptural and spiritual matters.

I knew that Carol would offer a fresh approach for dealing with the festering conflict that continues to be one of the greatest challenges of the 21st Century—the sanctity of marriage and the family structure. Never in the history of the world has there been such a battle for the minds and souls of those who seek Godly relationships. This unrelenting attack includes the fight for equality between male and female gender; fueled by misconception and encouraged by ancient theory. In the midst of this we ask God, "What is Missing?"

I know that Carol would obviously begin where all of us should begin—the garden—in the beginning. If we don't know where we have come from, we cannot possibly know where we are going. I therefore expected that the forthcoming manuscript would gloriously confirm our accepted historical biblical record of creation of the male and female and the divine relationship structure between them.

When I opened the FedEx and looked at the title, *God What's Missing?*, I had a feeling that Carol was taking a different tack in writing this book than most books on marriage. The weight of my commitment to do the Foreword for the book you now hold in your hand was compounded when I read some of the first lines of the book: "God did not create Eve to wash Adam's clothes—they didn't wear clothes!"

As I read on into the depths of *God, What's Missing?*, I became more and more aware of the presence of God whispering to me that our past doctrinal position on this extremely important subject has not ever settled the matter nor assuaged the tide of relational destruction throughout the ages.

The subject, *God, What's Missing?*, at first glance seemed somewhat threatening and revolutionary. But it soon became a pool of clear water with refreshing new ideas and insight into the heart of God concerning our most sacred human and divine connection— "Love."

Carol refuses to water down the issues and fearlessly makes some very bold statements about subjects we most often avoid. She has, however, offered these with abundant love and grace.

Having read and reread the manuscript, *God, What's Missing*, it has become abundantly clear to me that Carol Peet has tapped a powerful spiritual source that washes over our complicated theological boundaries, skillfully revealing the dynamics, responsibilities, differences, and uniqueness of the male and female. This is obviously not just another "spiritual self-help" read.

While you may not agree with every idea or proposal set forth in this book, you can not deny its powerful spiritual inspiration. Remember that true revelation is always viewed as unorthodox and change is the most difficult and blessed word in redemption.

Open your heart and as you read *God, What's Missing?* and remember what I have so often said…"tradition always dies screaming."

Dr. Mark Hanby
Founder, Mark Hanby Ministries
Author, *You Have Not Many Fathers*

# FOREWORD —
*Richard Peet*

Men, have you ever said, "I just cannot understand my wife," or "It's just a woman thing"?

Women, have you ever said, "My husband just won't listen, talk, or express himself"?

Studies have shown that over 50 percent of all marriages end in divorce. Why? It is simple: We are such a self-centered people. We lack understanding of what a relationship really is. For most people, everything centers on themselves—*their* fears and insecurities, and what they think they really want and need to be happy. Yet in all their striving, they still don't feel secure, nor are they happy. But, I challenge you to ask, *God, What's Missing?*

There are so many false teachings in the world today regarding the role of women in the Kingdom of God. Where does it say that God created the woman to see to Adam's needs? Adam, as God created him, did not lack for anything. He and his wife were fed, sheltered, and provided for by God. Just think, they walked with God in the cool of the garden.

God created man in His image—both male and female. God did not create one to be a servant to the other, but both to be an equal, significant part in becoming what God intended in man. Men, we need to get off our self-proclaimed pedestals. We are not given any greater authority or a closer position to God than the woman.

*God, What's Missing?* is a book that will help both men and women to understand each other. Many men and women are unfulfilled in their lives and in their marriages; there is more to life than just earning a living, collecting material things, and acting as a physical playmate. Many people feel unimportant as individuals and as a married couple. They feel less than what God created them to be. It is time for each of us to look beyond what has been defined as "normal" to see the intensions of God that far exceed daily coping.

After seeing, understanding, and applying the truths in this book, I discovered a whole new relationship with my wife. God has given Carol a new, but old, revelation so profound, and yet so simple. By applying these revealed truths, both men and women will come into a greater understanding of who they are individually, become better equipped to grasp purpose and move into destiny, and start a reformation in their marriages.

As long as I have known Carol, she has been a seeker of God's heart and has battled many roadblocks in her quest to become the woman God created her to be. Like many women, Carol has been put down, criticized in her efforts to know God, and just outright ostracized for being a confident, outspoken woman of God. She has been a Bible teacher for 40 years, but only recently has God opened doors to the greater public for her to share the truths that He has brought through her.

Carol and I have been married for 37 years and are still working on our marriage, discovering God's role for each of us and learning how to function in those roles. We have three fine sons who love their wives and challenge them to be what God desires for them. We all have walked the walk of which Carol teaches.

I am very proud of Carol's sensitivity to God's Spirit and honored that she has asked me to write this Foreword. I have had the privilege of being one of the first recipients of the revealed truths God has shown Carol through the years, and as a result, I am different—and I like it. I still don't claim to know all the answers about male/female relationships, but I know by experience that this book opens the door to find answers. If both male and female readers will open their hearts and minds to hear, it will become a heart-healing and life-changing experience that will answer the question, *God, What's Missing?*

Judge Richard Peet

*So God created man in His own image; in the image of God He created him; male and female He created them. Then God blessed them, and God said to them, "Be fruitful and multiply; fill the earth and subdue it; have dominion..."* (Genesis 1:27-28a).

God did not create Eve to wash Adam's clothes. They didn't wear clothes. God did not create Eve to cook Adam's meals. They ate from the trees in the garden. God did not create Eve to clean Adam's house. They didn't live in a house. God had a much higher plan and purpose in the way He brought Eve forth and presented her to Adam. The plan for this book is to bring women and men out of the darkness of the dead, carnal, gender mentality and into the light of God's plan and purpose.

*chapter one* | THE DREAM

It was a cave. The depth and true spaciousness of it could not be seen because the only light was the natural sunlight that managed to penetrate from the entrance. At the opening was a massive, cold, iron-bar gate, suggesting a place of imprisonment. The whole place wreaked with an atmosphere of coldness, dreariness, and even despair.

This apparent prison was full of women, not children or young girls, but women of marital age. They all exhibited the same demeanor which reflected the coldness and dreariness of their environment. They were expressionless and lifeless with little movement and no apparent interaction, almost like zombies. There was an air of acceptance and resignation. One standing outside could easily see a few women standing near the gate of iron bars, while many others could be seen throughout the massive deathlike space as far as the light could penetrate. And although they could not be seen, it was known that many more women had found a place back in the deep, despairing darkness.

There was a male gatekeeper or jailer, who was the only man inside the prison. Yes, he was stationed *inside* the gate and possessed the only key to the gate. It seemed the women's acceptance and resignation was so complete that the thought of overtaking the jailer and escaping their prison was never considered. This was the way it was supposed to be.

Near the end of the day, a mass of men equal to the mass of women locked in the cave began making their way to the cave. They were full of life and animation, interacting with each other in the manner that men interact. Each of them was coming to collect his wife, for it was the appointed time for her to join him and to do and to be what was expected. Thus began the evening ritual.

As the men approached the cave, the jailer unlocked the gate, and each woman, like an automaton, began filing out of the cave to join her man. She knew what was expected of her. Some would experience some pleasantness. Others would experience some brutality. Some would experience perversion. Yet, there was no fear—just acceptance and resignation in varying degrees. The acceptance and resignation overrode the dread, so there was not even a thought of refusal or objection. This was her time to be with her husband and then she would return to the cave.

There appeared no maliciousness in the men. This was just normal, the way love and marriage was supposed to be.

Patsy Gates, my faithful friend and coworker in ministry for many years, had this dream. She believed it was from God and had something very significant to say to us. At the time she shared the dream with me, she did not know the interpretation or the understanding of what God wanted to communicate.

Patsy and I had been going through some hard years together, and we sought the Lord for something we felt missing from our lives. We both were married to men we loved and had the children we always wanted, but we were not happy in the lives we found ourselves living. Something was wrong, but whose fault was it? Of course, we didn't want to blame ourselves, but in some degree, we did anyway. Still, it was all too easy to blame everything else and mostly you know who—the husband.

When God finally brought Patsy and me to the maturity level that we could take the blame off everything and everyone, including ourselves, He began to give us some answers. Even though we were going through this time together, the answers God gave were given to us individually in personal ways. Every woman needs to hear God in her own personal way. There are some things she will never see and some changes she can never make based on what others know and say. There were times when Patsy and I would share what God was showing one of us by His Spirit through His Word. Patsy describing her dream to me was one of those times.

In a time alone, I began to think on Patsy's dream, and God opened to me the understanding. Then I heard, "This is the gender mentality that rules in the church and the world."

## INTERPRETATION OF THE DREAM

The cave is a place deep in the earth and represents earthly or worldly mentality. When Adam and Eve disobeyed God and ate from the forbidden tree, death was released in the earth. As a result, the earth with its world mentality became the lowest place of existence for living human beings. What is of the earth is death. Christian believers are *in* the world, but are no longer *of* the world. Even though we are still in the world, God has called us through Jesus Christ to walk in the Spirit (see Rom. 8:1), to be transformed in our minds (see Rom.12:2), and to be seated with Him in heavenly places (see Eph. 2:6). We are to live in a God mentality, not an earth mentality. "*Set your mind on things above, not on things on the earth*" (Col. 3:2). This cave in the dream relates primarily to marriage, but also represents an underlying mentality that invades every arena where men and women interact.

The jailer is the carnal mind. *"For to be carnally minded is death, but to be spiritually minded is life and peace. Because the carnal mind is enmity against God; for it is not subject to the law of God, nor indeed can be. So then, those who are in the flesh cannot please God"* (Rom. 8:6-8). Webster defines carnal as "of the flesh; material; worldly." Any life system or way of thinking the carnal mind creates or devises can only produce death. When the carnal mind interprets the words of God, the result is still death because it cannot know the true mind of God. It is an enemy of God and His thoughts.

We can see by the example of the Pharisees and leaders in Jesus' time that, acting out of their carnal minds, they added to the laws of God, dumping a heavy burden on the people in their desires to obey God. " *'Woe to you, scribes and Pharisees, hypocrites! For you are like graves which are not seen, and the men who walk over them are not aware of them.' Then one of the lawyers answered and said to Him, 'Teacher, by saying these things You reproach us also.' And He said, 'Woe to you also, lawyers! For you load men with burdens hard to bear, and you yourselves do not touch the burdens with one of your fingers'* " (Luke 11:44-46). That's what the carnal mind does. It creates a belief structure that binds us to its rules. In the church, that belief structure can be based on Scripture, but it twists and perverts it from God's original intent. The Bible says that God has given five positions of leadership to the church, which include the pastor, for the equipping of the saints to do the ministry (see Eph. 4:11-12). Religion has twisted it to mean the pastor does the ministry while the saints take care of the church. In the world, the belief structure can be based on nothing more than what is perceived as a "good" idea. "Teachers are educated and better trained to teach morality and sexuality to our children." Sounds like a good idea, but who gets to set the rules on morality and sexuality? The parents or the educators? Whatever it is based on, it still comes with its rules of right and wrong, and everyone who lives with a carnal mind will live by the rules. If some can't live up to the rules or don't like the rules, they will just create their own rules, again using their carnal mind.

The important point is that we see belief structures can be and are created by human thought and reason. By the time a child starts school, he or she already has their own self-written mental encyclopedia and dictionary. What has been recorded in these mental "books" is what they have learned, all their experiences, and the resulting conclusions they have made. Information is added regularly as the child continues in his life experiences. It includes everything children (and later, adults) have come to believe about themselves, their lives, how they are to relate to people and the world around them, and expectations of self and others. The way they think and assess new information is now based upon their created "belief structure."

When understanding the carnal mind, we can recognize our potential of having perverted belief structures. Having a perverted belief structure simply means we believe some lies and have some unreal expectations. We believe things that do not conform to or agree with reality from God's perspective and His truths. We believe them to be the truth, or else we wouldn't believe them. Because we believe them to be the truth, we bind ourselves to them regardless of the consequences, and we obligate others to them. Because we believe them to be right, we cannot see the enemies or lies in them.

Fear is probably the strongest influence in how we build our belief structure. We create a mental atmosphere where we can survive in the midst of what we fear. We don't just fear things that can harm us physically; we also fear the emotional pain that comes from rejection. So we form our "reality" into something that fits how we can cope, except it is then no longer reality. It's a belief structure with an unstable foundation of lies.

Harry is really not an athlete and has come to the conclusion in his belief structure that he doesn't have much going for him other than his intellect. He has judged his mental abilities as his only real, positive asset. When he met his wife, he concluded that she fell in love with him only because of his intellect. We can see the dangerous, shaky foundation of lies he has already built into his marriage relationship. Now, anytime his wife disagrees with him, he becomes defensive needing to protect what has become his identity. Hiding under all of his outward reactions is the fear that if he fails her mentally, she will no longer love him.

I have a daughter-in-law whose parents divorced when she was very young. When her mother remarried, her biological father, because of the difficult and limited conditions of his life at the time, relinquished his children to be adopted by their step-father. Soon the biological father became essentially non-existent in presence and conversation. Through the ensuing years, when just happening to hear a comment or see a photograph, my daughter-in-law created a concept of who and what her biological father was. For example, in the photograph she saw, her father was holding a drink, and from that he became, in her belief structure, an alcoholic or at least had a drinking problem. Recently, because of all God has done in her life, she contacted him in hopes of retrieving the lost relationship, and found him not to be those things she had believed. She had created them. The problem is what she had put herself through, facing and dealing with the person she had created, not the real man. There was a man out there in the world with whom she still felt a connection and perhaps never really stopped loving. Thinking about him as she had created him to be, had caused unnecessary conflicting emotions that were difficult for her to handle.

There are many people, not just in the world but also in the church, who believe, "God helps those who help themselves." It sounds and feels so right and is so easy to believe. But it is a lie from the pit of hell that has been accepted as truth by the carnal mind in its belief structure. It robs Christians from the free gift of grace, especially when they need it the most. When they face hard times, they find it impossible to rest in God's faithful provisions. They strive and strive to do this and to do that, hoping they will become worthy enough for God to come help them. What is the truth? God helps those who fall flat on their face, totally broken, admitting that they are utterly helpless and need what only a loving God can give.

Expectations that the carnal mind creates in our belief structure can be vicious enemies. The husband is expected to be just like Daddy, but he isn't, so there is something "wrong" with him. The sons are expected to go to college and begin professional business careers, but one wants to race cars and the other wants to grow flowers, so something is "wrong" with them. The wife is expected to take care of her husband and everything else; she is expected to make his life better (easier); but she wants to get involved in and complicate his life, so what's "wrong" with her? We end up making the circumstances and the people our enemies because they don't conform to our expectations. If you kill the real enemy—the carnal expectation, your life becomes a lot easier.

So, in the dream, the jailer is the carnal mind operating in the belief structure it has created. It is the jailer, the carnal belief structure, that controls the gate and who goes in and out. And both women and men accept it without objection, even though there is no life in it. It has been agreed mentally that this is the way it is supposed to be. And so it is, day after day.

Because the jailer, the carnal belief structure, stands inside the gate with the key, the women can easily overpower him, or change their thinking and let themselves out; but they never consider it. The men can also change their thinking and refuse to send their wives back to the cave, but they likewise never consider it. They are mentally in agreement. It is not that they don't have a choice to agree or disagree. Rather, they have never seen the possibility, much less the legality, of having another choice.

The men appear to be content with how it is, but *contentment* does not always mean *fulfillment*.

The jailer is a male (male-dominated carnal thinking) and the prisoners are women. Even though the women appear to be the victims, their acceptance and resignation play a part in establishing the perversion of this gender mentality. They can easily leave this place. So why don't they? Because in their carnal mind and thinking, they *need a man* in order to exist. And that is what they are doing—existing. (We will speak to this subject at length later in the book.)

From the very beginning when God *put enmity between satan and the woman and between his seed and her Seed,* (see Gen. 3:15), satan's plan has been to keep women ignorant of who they are as God made them; therefore, they remain ignorant of the great potential God has put within them. Satan knew that God's plan was for the woman's Seed to destroy him, so he became a hater of women. He played on and used male ego as a tool to accomplish his plan. Of course, ultimately he was after her Seed (the Christ) and still is after her Seed (the sons of God).

It is important to note that each woman relates to the jailer or the carnal mind in a personal way. Any day when the gate is opened, any woman who has the "right mind" to do so, can walk away and not come back.

The darkness in the cave represents an ignorance and not knowing who women are as God intended them to be. Darkness is the lack of light. Light means seeing and understanding. Therefore, ignorance is a lack of seeing and understanding or a lack of knowledge. Women are intelligent and know how to do many things well. They can wash clothes, cook meals, clean house, care for children, do jobs outside the home, and please a husband. But they are still ignorant of who they really are as God made them and intended them to be. They are still ignorant of the potential and spiritual greatness He has put within them. God did not create Eve to wash Adam's clothes. They didn't wear clothes. God did not create Eve to cook Adam's meals. They ate from the trees in the garden. God did not create Eve to clean Adam's house. They didn't live in a house. God has a much higher plan and purpose in the way He brought Eve forth and presented her to Adam. And it is the plan for this book to bring women and men out of the darkness of the old gender mentality and into the light of God's purpose.

In the dream there are different intensities of light and darkness, which represent different levels of knowledge resulting in corresponding levels of dread. The women who stand near the gate have more knowledge while the women who stay in the deep darkness have less. Even though many of the women have been used, misused, and abused, the same acceptance and resignation bind them in their ignorance. Whatever knowledge they do have is not enough knowledge to know they can be free from the bondage of a dead gender mentality.

Men, generally speaking, have the freedom to spend their whole day in the sunlight, coming and going and doing what is in their hearts to do with no imposed limitations or boundaries. They are free to have and to live the full expression of their individual lives. Yes, there can be various individual men and even groups of men who because of certain circumstances find limitations and boundaries imposed upon them, but not simply because they are men. For instance, financial difficulties can limit a man's ability to function the way he wants to, and in some countries, political powers can bring oppression upon its people. In other cases, a man can allow self-imposed limitations and boundaries, which come from his own carnal thinking. But, again, these things don't come upon them just because they were born male.

*In the dream, their darkness came at evening time when they went to the cave to get their wives.* In the dream, the man's relationship with his wife is only a nighttime relationship. Nighttime is darkness, and darkness is ignorance or lack of knowledge. In this case, the wife is just a hireling, someone compensated for doing her duty. *"After all, he does make a living and provides food on her table, clothes on her back, and a house to live in."* The husband who has only a nighttime relationship with his wife is in darkness, lacking understanding of who she is and what marriage is, as God intended it to be.

The sameness of the women in the cave during the daytime is a picture of the sameness that has been expected of women generation after generation. There are certain behaviors and duties that have always been expected of married women: clean the house, cook the meals, wash the clothes, etc. Consequently, these expectations have disregarded a woman's giftedness, her abilities, her desires, and how she may be motivated. Often there is no consideration that she could have purpose and destiny beyond being a wife and mother. (*Let me be quick to say being a wife and mother is the greatest purpose a woman can have,* but she is not limited in that regard. And certainly, those women who choose not to marry or have children are not to be diminished in the greatness of their purpose.)

I was a school teacher before I married and taught for three more years after I married. I quit teaching when we were about to have our first child, and I wanted to stay home to care for him. Within five years, we had two more children. I loved being a wife and would have never chosen my single years over being married. I loved my children. I loved being a mom. But I did *not* love the mundane, repetitious tasks that I had to face day after day. I believe few women do. I would often say: A man gets to choose, for the most part, what he does every day. He has the potential to do what's in his heart to do if he takes his opportunities. But the days of a woman are dictated by the fact that she is a woman, she is married, and has children. I have felt stuck in this gender mentality. Today, I believe God wants to show us something different.

So it is the carnal mind that devises the way of life, which is depicted in the dream. And it is the carnal mind's belief structure that keeps both women and men bound to a lifestyle of marriage that is lifeless with limited, if any at all, fulfillment.

When all this information was laid before me and I understood the dream, I grieved. This gender mentality has robbed both women and men of the greatness God had intended when He instituted marriage in the Garden of Eden. I was angered that satan and the carnal mind could take so few Scriptures in light of the whole Bible and become so powerful. I was overwhelmed with the huge mountainous aspect of it and wondered how we could ever get over it. But I was also encouraged because as I mentioned before, I was on a journey to find the truth, to find what was missing from my life.

Now that we have identified the gender mentality created by the carnal mind, let's continue on to see the power of its affects in our world today and then discover the gender mentality that comes from the mind of Christ, the living Word, as revealed by His Spirit.

| # IN THE BEGINNING

The beginning is always a good place to start. Refreshing our background knowledge and understanding is perhaps a good idea at this point. It is mostly information you may already know, but it brings you, the reader, to the same launching pad from which I wish to develop the concepts I have learned. So please hang in there with me for the next few pages.

The greatest Artist of all, the supreme Creator, had spoken into existence five days filled with lights and water and earth and plants and trees and living creatures. Then came the sixth day when He was nearly finished with the work He had so meticulously planned. It was a work and a plan that reached far beyond what the human eye could see, what the human mind could understand, and what the human heart could conceive; yet, it was the place where the human being was to dwell. And God said that "it was good."

Now, all that God had spoken was in place and poised, waiting for the crowning glory of all that was to be made.

*And God said, Let Us make man in Our image, after Our likeness: and let them have dominion over the fish of the sea, and over the fowl of the air, and over the cattle, and over all the earth, and over every creeping thing that creepeth upon the earth. So God created man in His own image, in the image of God created He him; male and female created He them. And God blessed them, and God said unto them, Be fruitful, and multiply, and replenish the earth, and subdue it: and have dominion over the fish of the sea, and over the fowl of the air, and over every living thing that moveth upon the earth* (Genesis 1:26-28 KJV).

The triune God made man in Their image and after Their likeness. God created (formed) man: *male* and *female*. What name did God give to the female? Adam called the female "woman" (see Gen. 2:23), and he named the woman "Eve" (see Gen. 3:20).

*This is the book of the generations of Adam. In the day that God created man, in the likeness of God made He him; male and female created He them; and blessed them, and called their name Adam, in the day when they were created* (Genesis 5:1-2 KJV).

God named the woman "Adam" or "man." Adam was the male Adam or the male man. The woman was the female Adam or the female man.

Just as God stated no difference in their names, He also declared no difference in what they were instructed to do in the earth.

*And God blessed them, and God said unto them, Be fruitful, and multiply, and replenish the earth, and subdue it:*

*and have dominion over the fish of the sea, and over the fowl
of the air, and over every living thing that moveth upon the
earth* (Genesis 1:28 KJV).

She, too, was to subdue and have dominion. In fact, God
gave the commission to a joined-together male and female in a
union that we call marriage. He didn't give it to the Church, and
He didn't give it to government. The only place where God dif-
ferentiates between the male man and the female man is when
He speaks of how they are to function in their personal relationship together.

In the present day, many of us have traveled across the
country and have had to use a map to find our destination and
not get lost. Sooner or later, we drive through a large city where
there can be several highway changes. Even if we look at a
statewide map, we may wonder how we are ever going to find our
way, especially with all the traffic we can encounter in a city. To
receive more detailed instructions, we can go to a corner or along
the side of our map and find a blown-up picture of the city that
shows in much greater detail the highways and exchanges. Likewise, the account of the creation of man in Genesis chapter 2 in
relationship to the account in chapter 1 gives us a greater
detailed picture of the process through which God created the
male man and the female man.

*And the Lord God formed man of the dust of the ground,
and breathed into his nostrils the breath of life; and man
became a living soul* (Genesis 2:7 KJV).

The Master Creator reached down into the earth He had
created and from it He formed man. There is a part of man that
is earth in origin. Then God breathed into the nostrils the breath
of life. There is another part of man whose origin is God. When
the breath of God joined with the formed earth, man became a
living soul. Just as God is triune in nature, He made man triune
in nature. He made man in the "likeness" of Himself. Man had a
body made from the dust of the earth; he had a spirit that came

from the breath of God; and he had a soul with mind, emotions, and will. We could say that man comes from two worlds—the earth world and the spirit world. Soon, the living souls would be confronted as to which world they would serve.

*And the Lord God took the man, and put him into the garden of Eden to dress it and to keep it. And the Lord God commanded the man, saying, Of every tree of the garden thou mayest freely eat: but of the tree of the knowledge of good and evil, thou shalt not eat of it: for in the day that thou eatest thereof thou shalt surely die. And the Lord God said, It is not good that the man should be alone; I will make him an help meet for him. And out of the ground the Lord God formed every beast of the field, and every fowl of the air; and brought them unto Adam to see what he would call them: and whatsoever Adam called every living creature, that was the name thereof. And Adam gave names to all cattle, and to the fowl of the air, and to every beast of the field; but for Adam there was not found an help meet for him. And the Lord God caused a deep sleep to fall upon Adam, and he slept: and he took one of his ribs, and closed up the flesh instead thereof; And the rib, which the Lord God had taken from man, made he a woman, and brought her unto the man. And Adam said, This is now bone of my bones, and flesh of my flesh: she shall be called Woman, because she was taken out of Man. Therefore shall a man leave his father and his mother, and shall cleave unto his wife: and they shall be one flesh. And they were both naked, the man and his wife, and were not ashamed* (Genesis 2:15-25 KJV).

In the first three chapters of Genesis when Scripture uses the words "the man," it is referring to the one male man. The use of the article "the" identifies man as a single person. The term "man" without "the" includes both the male man and the female man. It can be said that "man" means mankind. And it is true that Adam and Eve made choices representative of all mankind, but in the garden events "man" meant the one male man and the one female man—Adam and Eve.

Therefore, it is the man, the male man, who was to tend the garden and keep it. He was to keep the garden safe, productive, and fruitful. It was to the man that God gave the commandment not to eat from the tree in the middle of the garden. And it was about the man that God said it was not good to be alone (see verses 15-18).

Many years ago, I read an article that said the word translated "rib" in Genesis 2:22 actually means "*a side.*" I did not record the source because at the time I was not expecting to write a book on this subject. I was just searching for my own identity. However, as a reference, Strong's Concordance also states "a side" as the meaning. I feel very strongly that "a side" is more accurate than "a rib." Let me explain.

God does not exist in time. Time is a section of space that God created to accomplish a purpose. He placed mankind and our world into that section of space; therefore, everything about our lives is governed by time: days, seasons, growth, age, etc. However, "*Jesus Christ is the same yesterday, today, and forever*" (Heb. 13:8). God is not governed by time. He is eternal. He can be in our past and in our future at the same time. We don't know anything different from time so we cannot conceive how this is possible. It goes beyond our finite minds. "*But Jesus looked at them and said to them, 'With men this is impossible, but with God all things are possible'* " (Matt. 19:26).

In God's dimension of eternity that is not governed by time, Adam and Eve didn't come first; Jesus dying for His Bride came first. Jesus was slain from the foundation of the world (see Rev. 13:8). Genesis 3:22a says, "*And the Lord God said, Behold, the man is become as one of us, to know good and evil*" (KJV). There was only one of the Godhead who knew both good and evil intimately or experientially, and that was Jesus on the cross when He became sin. He was called the "last Adam" because His finished work was not manifested in time until after the time of the first Adam.

Therefore, on God's calendar of events not ordered by time, Adam and Eve came after Jesus' work was finished, which made Adam and Eve a type and shadow of what was to come or to be later manifested in the realm of time. Adam, called the first Adam, was a type of Christ who was called the last Adam. Eve was a type of the Bride of Christ who is the Church.

(The Old Testament is full of types and shadows revealing to mankind things that were to come and be established through the sending and giving of God's Son, Jesus. Because our minds are so limited to the time and space in which we live, God has given to us examples through these types and shadows to help us at least begin to understand the vastness and greatness of His purposes toward us and for us.)

Jesus, on the cross, was in the deep sleep of death when a Roman soldier took a spear and opened His side. From His side, the side of the living Word (the Word made flesh), flowed blood and water. Where does the Bride of Christ come from? It is those who have been redeemed by the blood of the Lamb and cleansed by the washing of the water by the Word.

*In Him we have redemption through His blood, the forgiveness of sins, according to the riches of His grace* (Ephesians 1:7).

*Husbands, love your wives, just as Christ also loved the church and gave Himself for her, that He might sanctify and cleanse her with the **washing of water by the word**, that He might present her to Himself a glorious church, not having spot or wrinkle or any such thing, but that she should be holy and without blemish* (Ephesians 5:25-27, emphasis added).

It was not a rib that came from Jesus' side. It was His life flow that gushed forth. It was what He could not live without as a man. It was important and prophesied in Psalms that Jesus' bones would not be broken. *"For these things were done that the Scripture should be fulfilled, 'Not one of His bones shall be broken' "* (John 19:36). God would have broken a bone if he had taken a rib from Adam's side, which would have made Adam inconsistent in being the type and shadow of the last Adam.

God wasn't realizing or acknowledging that He had made a mistake when He said, "It is not good for the man to be alone." The female man, Eve, was not just an afterthought. God knew what He was doing, and He had reason and purpose in it. The female man was very much present in Adam from the very beginning. At the appointed time, God put the male man into a deep sleep and took from him a side, the female man, Adam's bride.

God gave the male man *"a helper comparable to him"* (Gen. 2:18b). *Helper* simply means *helper*. It is the "comparable to him" that makes this helper unique. Years ago in my search for identity, I had spent months reading, researching word meanings, and meditating on these Scriptures. I would pray, "Father, I have got to see what You saw in Adam when You said it was not good for him to be alone." At that time, I was frustrated over my inability to see and understand, and I was feeling so dead of purpose as a woman. I thought that if I knew why Adam should not be alone, I could better see my purpose. One day I was relaxing in a bathtub of stimulating hot water, once again meditating and going through it all in my mind. And once again, I met a dead end. As I was getting out of the tub, drying off, and not really thinking about anything, I heard these words clearly shoot through my mind, "Look for your answer in Eve." Of course, it only made sense! Who and what she was, was exactly what Adam needed, so it would be "good." With great excitement and hope, I began looking.

So who and what was Eve other than being female? She was a physical being. Although she was very much like Adam, there were significant differences. (Hey, reader, I hear you chuckling.)

Contrary to Henry Higgins' question, "Why can't a woman be like a man?" in *My Fair Lady*, Adam needed a helper that was like him, but had just the right amount of complementary differences so that they could fit together. "Become one" is the way God put it. And when this is accomplished to its ultimate expression, the result is procreation, *fruitfulness*, and *multiplication*. Fruitfulness and multiplication was part of God's commission to man in Genesis 1:28a, "*Then God blessed them, and God said to them, 'Be fruitful and multiply....'* " Mankind has gotten a hold of this concept and has carried it out quite well throughout the generations. We have seen it and understood it in the *physical* dimension, but the physical dimension is not the only dimension where man was to be fruitful and multiply. Sex and having babies is only one fifth of the five-dimensional relationship that God intended to happen in a marriage.

The male man and the female man were to be fruitful and multiply in *every aspect of their beings and capabilities—physically, mentally, emotionally, socially, and spiritually*. In so doing they would replenish the earth, subdue it, and take dominion. In every ability and capability, there was seed to bear fruit. This meant more than just having babies.

We must recognize that one alone cannot multiply. One times zero is zero. It takes two. God did not tell the male and female to add. One plus one is two. He told them to multiply. One times one is *one*. "*Therefore a man shall leave his father and mother be joined to his wife, and they shall become **one** flesh*" (Gen. 2:24, emphasis added). When the sperm of the man penetrates the egg of the woman, they become one. The result is multiplication. The one cell grows and then multiplies. One times two is two. Then it grows and multiplies again. Two times two is four. It grows and multiplies again. Two times four is eight. And so on until it comes into a full manifestation of a whole new creation.

This dimension of multiplication is given to marriage. One person alone with all of his or her gifts, abilities, and talents can do great exploits, but cannot enter into the dimension of multiplication. Adam and Eve were *designed* by God to enter into and live in the dimension of multiplication.

Eve was also a *mental* being, and the same principal applies: alike with differences. Adam needed someone outside of himself to stimulate greater mental possibilities. Rather than criticize and make fun of how she functioned mentally, he was to appreciate her differences and receive them as part of himself. They were to fit together mentally. The result would not be "two heads are better than one." The multiplication result would be greatness. *One can chase a thousand and two can put ten thousand* (not two thousand) *to flight* (see Deut. 32:30).

Eve was an emotional being. God gave Adam the ability to go to war, to make difficult decisions, and execute unpleasant tasks. The male man can put his feelings aside to do what he has to do, whereas the female man was not so made. The normal, healthy female is never void of feeling. She feels a situation first and then processes it mentally. This is how God made her, and He said it was "good." And God made the male and female to perfectly fit together emotionally. When their differences are valued, accepted, received, and learned, the multiplication process is activated, and the result is greatness.

Eve was a *spiritual* being. The male can know God and relate to God in only the way a male can. Likewise, the female can know God and relate to God in only the way a female can. They are different, and God made it that way. Once again, the differences are to fit together, not to accomplish a whole, but to ignite the multiplication process that is unlimited in the heights, the depths, and the breadths that God can be known and experienced. God instructed both Adam and Eve to subdue the earth and take dominion. Multiplication is essential to accomplish the great task.

Eve was a *social* being designed to interact with another through communicating, working, and playing. The process of the male man and the female man accepting and receiving each other socially gives access to the other four dimensions of relationship. Communication is essential to relationship at any level in any dimension.

When God formed Eve and presented her to Adam, they were already two whole individuals—healthy, strong, and capable in spirit, soul, and body. They were *not* needy in the sense that they needed the other to be who they were. Adam was a complete man. He didn't need Eve to make him more of a man. Eve was a complete woman. She didn't need Adam to make her more of a woman. They needed each other to enter into the multiplication dimension so that they could fill and subdue the earth and take dominion.

God gave Adam and Eve bodies that were so physically well constructed that it took hundreds of years for them to die after the judgment of death was released in them. Regarding their mental beings, Adam and Eve had sound minds using 100 percent of their brain capabilities. Scientists today say mankind uses only about 10 percent of its brain capacity. In addition, because they had not (yet) been exposed to the victimizing power of sin, they were emotionally whole. Nothing was out of order; therefore, they had no lack of security, acceptance, and value. God had provided an environment that was complete for them to live in without need. I repeat—they were *not* needy.

In this environment, Adam and Eve simply *enjoyed each other* as they worked and played together. Because they were not needy, they were free from the responsibility of the other's needs. They did not need the other to make them complete in themselves.

Because Eve was taken out of man (see Gen. 2:23), she was Adam's other part in the multiplication equation, which in turn, made Adam her other part. Adam was to "know" his wife in every area there was to know her, not just physically. First Peter 3:7 says that husbands are to dwell with their wives with knowledge. As each one's other part, Adam and Eve began to search out the other—physically, mentally, emotionally, socially, and spiritually, causing them to experience new dimensions of themselves. They were "life-magnets" attracting and pulling the best out of the other, unearthing new and greater potential. There was great joy and fulfillment from interacting and communicating with each other through these five avenues of relationship. They didn't just get acquainted with each other; they learned and experienced each other as part of themselves. This is what it means to become *one*, and when it happens between husband, wife, and God, the result is *greatness*.

Adam and Eve were to put to use and make productive every aspect of the capabilities God had given to them with no boundaries other than not eating from the tree of the knowledge of good and evil. They were not just free to, but commanded to express and explore every idea and talent that surfaced from the depths of their beings. The first male and female man were free from all the restrictions, limitations, boundaries, and judgments that we find ourselves living under in today's world. Religion, tradition, prejudice, culture, and customs all have a part in telling us how we are to live. In other words, they were free to fully express themselves physically, mentally, emotionally, socially, and spiritually without any inhibitions. They never had to consider if something were appropriate, if something they said sounded stupid, if they would be laughed at, or if they would be rejected. They didn't even have a sin nature at this time to complicate their lives. Adam and Eve lived under only one law: Don't eat from the tree in the middle of the garden.

They actually lived in the place where the great omniscient Teacher came to walk with them in the cool of the day. Unfortunately, their life together in the Garden of Eden was to be short-lived.

## THE TREE OF LIFE

To date, I have found nothing to indicate that Adam and Eve had any knowledge or revelation of the tree of life. There were two trees in the midst of the garden; and they were told *not* to eat from the one, but it appears they were not told *to* eat from the other. It was just never mentioned. Since Jesus is our New Testament Tree of Life, we now have knowledge and revelation of the tree of life in the garden. Jesus is and was then the Tree of Life. Had they eaten from the tree of life, they would have received the Seed of the Tree and become partakers of the nature of the Tree, which was God's divine nature. They already were created in His image and likeness; after eating of the tree, they would also have acquired His nature and lived forever (see 2 Pet. 1:2-4; Gen. 3:22).

We Christians who know and experience a living God cannot comprehend how other peoples and cultures could worship and cling to an image or an idol that is dead through and through. What good is an image without life in it? When God created man in His image and after His likeness, He made him as a container in which to put His life. God created man as a place for Him to dwell. *"Do you not know that you are the temple of God and that the Spirit of God dwells in you?"* (1 Cor. 3:16). It is not that man is to be worshipped, but a living God has put Himself into living vessels or images to show Himself and express Himself. We are not to be God. We are earthen vessels made to contain God and let Him live His life through us. *"But we have this treasure in earthen vessels, that the excellence of the power may be of God and not of us"* (2 Cor. 4:7). This should speak volumes to us and cause us to take a moment to try to grasp the awesomeness of it and thank Him for such a privilege.

It has been stated that Adam and Eve were not needy. They were not needy as a man and as a woman, but perhaps there was a need they were experiencing without really knowing or understanding what it was. As dwelling places for God to live, they remained empty. As God came and walked with them in the cool of the day, was He waiting for them to eat from the tree of life? For God never forces Himself into human vessels; He waits for a heart that is prepared and ready and longing for Him.

Throughout time, whatever God has asked man to do, He has never intended man to do it apart from Him. God has always planned and intended to be the empowerment of all that mankind accomplished in the earth. So when God told the male man and the female man to be fruitful and multiply; to fill the earth and subdue it; and to have dominion; functioning in the multiplication dimension alone was not to be enough. It would take both the multiplication dimension and the indwelling life and power of the living God.

I believe Adam and Eve felt in some way the lack of this power. Even though they didn't know what it was, they were looking for it. These were highly intelligent and capable beings surely able to make right decisions, so there had to be something inside of them reaching out for something beyond them. We know it was in the tree of life. But before they discovered it, satan met them at the tree of the knowledge of good and evil.

So why didn't God tell Adam about the tree of life? In searching for an answer to this question, the last Adam comes to mind. Before He was released into His ministry, *"Jesus was led up by the Spirit into the wilderness to be tempted by the devil"* (Matt. 4:1). *"Though He was a Son, yet He learned obedience by the things which He suffered"* (Heb. 5:8). When going through hard times, times of suffering, we can do one of two things: We can resent it, saying, "Why me?" and become angry and bitter, or we can run into God, accepting the reality of our suffering, put our pain into His hands, and let His love comfort our hearts and minds. If we choose to run into God, something very extraordinary happens. We fall deeper and more passionately in love with Him, and that love commands obedience.

If the first Adam was a type and shadow of the last Adam, then he too would need to have been tempted by the devil. It was Jesus' great love and passion for His Father and the great enabling power of the Holy Spirit that caused Him to hold fast, and after not eating and drinking for 40 days and nights declare,

*"It is written, 'Man shall not live by bread alone, but by every word that proceeds from the mouth of God' "* (Matt. 4:4).

The first Adam did not have the indwelling power of the Holy Spirit, and he also had not been without food and water for 40 days and nights. But because Adam did have Almighty God come visit with him in the cool of the day, surely he had the same love and passion for His Creator that Jesus had for His Father. Or maybe not. There was nothing for him to have suffered to cause him to know the deeper, more passionate love that results in obedience.

Man was created with the ability to choose to return God's love. Love originates from God, but He gave man the ability in his free will to choose to love. God does not *force* man to love Him. It is obvious when we read the Bible that God wanted a family. He calls Himself the Father and calls us His children, His sons and daughters. He has a Son, Jesus, and identifies the Church as the Son's Bride. It is the love for each other that makes a family a family and not just a group of people living in the same house together.

Forced love is an oxymoron. Love has to be free or it loses the very nature that makes it love. If God had created man without the ability to choose to love, then man would have been robotic in nature. I know that there is not much else in this world that blesses a mother's heart more than to hear one of her children, on his or her own volition, say, "I love you, Mom." If we are created in His image and after His likeness, then we know what it does to the heart of God when we say, "I love You, Father."

How do we know what is real love? By what it does when tested. We see it in Jesus when He was tempted by the devil. On the other hand, it was missing when Adam was tempted by the devil. *"If you love Me, keep My commandments"* (John 14:15). *"This is love, that we walk according to His commandments"* (2 John 6a). Adam didn't have the love to obey one commandment.

Surely, it is legal to say that only when man is free to choose not to love, is he really free to choose to love. God didn't want a robotic family, so He made provision to restore a people who would know the difference and choose to *"love the Lord your God with all your heart, with all your soul, and with all your mind"* (Matt. 22:37).

*chapter three* | THE TEMPTATION

*Now the serpent was more cunning than any beast of the field which the Lord God had made. And he said to the woman, "Has God indeed said, 'You shall not eat of every tree of the garden'?" And the woman said to the serpent, "We may eat the fruit of the trees of the garden; but of the fruit of the tree which is in the midst of the garden, God has said, 'You shall not eat it, nor shall you touch it, lest you die.' " Then the serpent said to the woman, "You will not surely die. For God knows that in the day you eat of it your eyes will be opened, and you will be like God, knowing good and evil." So when the woman saw that the tree was good for food, that it was pleasant to the eyes, and a tree desirable to make one wise, she took of its fruit and ate. She also gave to her husband with her, and he ate. Then the eyes of both of*

*them were opened, and they knew that they were naked;*
*and they sewed fig leaves together and made themselves cov-*
*erings. And they heard the sound of the Lord God walking in*
*the garden in the cool of the day, and Adam and his wife hid*
*themselves from the presence of the Lord God among the*
*trees of the garden* (Genesis 3:1-8).

I t was in this environment of "good" that satan, in the nature
and character of a serpent, approached Eve and with a question began to set her up for the temptation. *"Has God indeed*
said, 'You shall not eat of every tree of the garden'?"

It is in Eve's answer to satan's question that we recognize it
was likely Adam who had given her the instructions not to eat
from the one particular tree. She then added to what God had
commanded Adam. Adam could have told her something like,
"God said we could eat from all the trees in the garden except that
one in the middle. He said that if we eat from that tree, we will die,
so don't even touch it." It's obvious they both knew and understood the instructions. I wonder if they really understood dying.

*Then the serpent said to the woman, "You will not surely die.*
*For God knows that in the day you eat of it your eyes will be*
*opened, and you will be like God, knowing good and evil." So*
*when the woman saw that the tree was good for food, that it*
*was pleasant to the eyes, and a tree desirable to make one*
*wise, she took of its fruit and ate* (see Gen. 3:4-6).

I have tried many times to put myself in Eve's place, hoping
to get a glimpse of what was going through her mind when making her decision to eat the fruit. It is difficult because I see
through a sin nature, but she had no sin nature (yet). So, to
acquire any kind of understanding, we need to get it from the
facts as the Bible relates them.

We must first start with the fact that Eve was deceived (see
Gen. 3:13; 1 Tim. 2:14). Deception does not mean rebellion. For
instance, suppose that parents instruct their child not to get into

a car with a stranger. Then one day after school, a stranger approaches the child and says, "I am your mommy's friend. She is sick and asked me to pick you up and take you home." If the child gets into the car, is it rebellion? No. It is disobedience, but not rebellion. The motive of the heart was not to rebel. The disobedience came through deception.

Eve was deceived and she disobeyed, but she was not being rebellious against God. Did she want to be like God? This is something I do understand. I want to be like God. I want my eyes opened to see beyond my understanding, and I want to be wise. Yet, she was already like God, created in His image and after His likeness. But as we discussed earlier, there was something missing. If the motive of her heart was not to rebel, perhaps she was reaching out for something she thought she needed, only to be deceived. This may not have been rebellion, but it was spiritual adultery.

Any time we turn elsewhere for something that legally belongs to God, it is spiritual adultery. Even if what she was wanting was more of God, she turned to an illegal source to get it. Christians do it all the time. They may believe in God and know they are Heaven bound, but they trust in man's ability, whether their own or others, to survive in life. The world is full of self-help books and seminars that many people, including Christians, devour, seeking after things that don't satisfy.

So why was Eve deceived? She *let the senses of her eyes appeal to her feelings and made a choice that overrode the instructions or the law that God had given.* Look at Genesis 3:6 again: "*...the woman saw that the tree was good for food, that it was pleasant to the eyes....*" We do this all the time, don't we? We know what God says, and we want to please Him. Yet we allow information that complicates the issue to *come in through our senses and stir our feelings.* Do we then go back to what we know God says, or do we disobey?

*"She also gave to her husband with her, and he ate. Then the eyes of both of them were opened, and they knew that they were naked...."* So Adam was there with Eve, yet he wasn't deceived. Why didn't he stop her, or at least try? Once she ate, what were his options? Eve didn't take the fruit, wrestle him to the ground, and cram it down his throat. He was still in a free state to make a "good" or right choice.

If Adam would have acted in the nature and character of the last Adam after whom he was a type and shadow, he would have stepped between his bride and God, threw his arms open wide, and said, "Father, forgive her. She didn't know what she was doing. Blame me. I take full responsibility. It is my sin, no longer hers."

## ABOUT ADAM

*Skyler Smith, my birth brother and a significant part of our ministry wrote the following. He says it well.*

Adam stood in silence as he watched Eve eat from the tree that God had clearly said, "Do not eat." Scripture says that Adam was with Eve and that she gave the fruit to him and he ate (see Gen. 3:6). Having the access to God that they had in their sinless state was still not enough for them to do the right thing. It is important for us to gain all the understanding we can from this situation because Adam's act of disobedience affected his relationship with God, with Eve, and with his environment. And this is the situation in which we find ourselves. Our relationships with God, spouse, and environment are often troubled, if not a mess.

According to Romans 5:14 (NIV), Adam was a pattern of the One to come, Jesus, the last Adam. Reading Philippians 2:5-10 we see the pattern Jesus set.

*Let this mind be in you which was also in Christ Jesus, who, being in the form of God, did not consider it robbery to be equal with God, but made Himself of no reputation, taking the form of a bondservant, and coming in the likeness of men. And being found in appearance as a man, He humbled Himself and became obedient to the point of death, even the death of the cross. Therefore God also has highly exalted Him and given Him the name which is above every name, that at the name of Jesus every knee should bow, of those in heaven, and of those on earth, and of those under the earth.*

Seeing the words "form" and "likeness" used in this Scripture reminds us of how the first Adam was "formed" and made in the "image" and "likeness" of God. And the "cross" is often referred to as a "tree." *Both Adam and Jesus died at a tree.*

Adam had also been given a name above every name that existed in the earth at the time. He too was named by God and given the authority to name all the other life creatures. As Jesus was given dominion over three areas—things in heaven, on earth, and under the earth—so Adam was given dominion over the fish of the sea, over the fowl of the air, and over every living thing that moves on the earth.

There may not have been much written about the man, Adam, but there is a complete Bible written on the last Adam, Jesus the Christ, who was to have been the pattern of Adam's choices. So looking at the last Adam we can gain understanding as to what happened in the Garden of Eden.

Let us continue our comparison of Adam to the pattern of Jesus in Philippians. Adam became *disobedient* unto death at a tree, but Jesus became *obedient* unto death, even the death of the cross (tree). Jesus humbled Himself and became obedient. *Obeying God is humility.*

Adam, on the other hand, must not have humbled himself or he would have responded the same as Jesus, which would have led to obedience and ultimately *life*, not death. If he didn't choose humility, then what part did pride play in Adam's actions at the tree? Proverbs 16:18 states, *"Pride goeth before destruction, and an haughty spirit before a fall"* (KJV). Surely Adam lifting his thoughts or his will above the thoughts and will of God should have qualified as a haughty spirit.

Who knew better about pride than that serpent, the devil? He knew all about wanting to be like the Most High. Establishing his will above the will of God and being lifted up in pride resulted in his fall from Heaven (see Isa. 14:12-14). He, being the father of lies, must have been planting his own seed in the mind of Adam, and the fruition came when Adam went to the point of no return; he chose to eat the fruit.

Why was it that nothing happened when Eve ate? There is no mention of shame or nakedness or anything changing until the first Adam ate. Then both their eyes were opened. To help us understand, let's first look at the example of Moses.

Moses was not allowed by God to enter the Promised Land because he had disobeyed God. God had been miraculously providing the Israelites water from a rock, which represented a type of Jesus who was to come. Jesus is the Rock of our salvation and from Him flows living water that makes us whole. The second time Moses approached the rock for water, he was instructed by God to only speak to it, not strike it as he did the first time. Because he was angry at the people for grumbling, Moses decided to strike the rock instead of speak to it—and he did it twice. Disobeying God and striking the rock broke the pattern of Christ who was only *once* and for all to be smitten (see Heb. 9:28, Num. 20 6-12). Breaking the pattern of Christ was serious enough to keep Moses from ever entering the earthly Promised Land.

When Adam ate from the tree of the knowledge of good and evil, he broke the pattern of the last Adam. Eve was consistent with her pattern, the Church. She had sinned by disobeying God's law which put her in need of a Savior and redemption. Adam, for a brief moment after Eve ate, was still in his sinless state, still like his pattern, Jesus, who was sinless. He was positioned to and could have given his life for her.

The last Adam did it for His Bride. He died for her, taking the responsibility of what *she* did upon Himself. He humbled Himself to become obedient to save His Bride. He who knew no sin became sin. The Bride is still the Bride as long as the Bridegroom fulfills His (his) instructions.

Let me remind you that Jesus was also faced with temptation to eat something that His Father had not instructed Him to eat. We tend to focus only on the work of Jesus on the cross in bringing salvation to mankind. Indeed, it was the point of no return; it was the point in time when Jesus said, "It is finished!" Nothing can change what was done at the cross and its great importance. But it is also true that every step Jesus took on His path to become the Tree of Life, every act of obedience to what He saw from His Father was crucial and meant the difference of redemption coming to His Bride or not. *Everything!* Learning obedience through the things He suffered, being baptized by John the Baptist, and being tempted by the devil was only the beginning. With that in mind, did Jesus do these things to elevate Himself or His ministry, or to bring His Bride back into perfection?

As Skyler so clearly explains, the first Adam failed in following the pattern of the last Adam and became one who also needed a Savior and redemption. Was it rebellion? Knowing the right thing to do, he made a free choice of his will to disobey. He lifted his will above the will of God. That is rebellion.

I have read excerpts written by Bible scholars, who lived during the last two centuries, who thought Adam had already started his descent toward his fall before God formed Eve. That is why God stated it was "not good" about Adam being alone. To this date, I personally have not seen sure evidence of this in Scripture. In Genesis chapter 1 when God created man, male and female, He called them "good." In chapter 2, He does not say that Adam was no longer "good." He says that Adam being alone was not "good." Yet for Adam to so easily and knowingly disobey God, he surely had to have been entertaining illegal thoughts. Perhaps he had had prior encounters with lucifer.

We have identified both pride and rebellion present in Adam—the same causes for which lucifer fell from his great position in glory. But for Adam, God had a plan.

Before the temptation, Adam and Eve were naked and were not ashamed. Now their eyes were opened, and they knew they were naked and were ashamed. They covered themselves, and they hid themselves. Shame causes fear, and fear causes hiding. We understand that, don't we? We all do it. Even though we put up a front and say, "I'm not afraid." We have all kinds of secrets, and we play all sorts of games to keep our true selves hidden so no one really knows who or what we are. And we hide from God, balancing ourselves noncommittally on the fringes of what is going on spiritually, because we are *afraid* of what He sees in us and what He might expect from us. Adam was foolish in choosing his thoughts over God's known order, and mankind inherited it.

*Then the Lord God called to Adam and said to him, "Where are you?" So he said, "I heard Your voice in the garden, and I was afraid because I was naked; and I hid myself." And He said, "Who told you that you were naked? Have you eaten from the tree of which I commanded you that you should not eat?" Then the man said, "The woman whom You gave to be with me, she gave me of the tree, and I ate"* (Genesis 3:9-12).

God confronted the male man with the question, *"Have you eaten from the tree of which I commanded you that you should not eat?"* Why would God ask such a question when He already knew what had happened? He was giving Adam another choice. There was a right answer, and there were wrong answers. What would have been the right answer? "Yes,

God, I disobeyed You and ate from the tree. I was wrong. I repent and ask You to please forgive me." What would have been the result of giving a right answer? We can only speculate, and that would accomplish nothing. What we do know for sure is that our God is a forgiving God whose forgiveness is full of redemption and restoration.

Instead, Adam gave a different answer. He *blamed* his wife, and he *blamed* God. Adam's answer (paraphrased) goes something like this, "It's this woman's fault because she gave me the fruit, and it's Your fault, God, because You put this woman in my life." If he was going to blame, why didn't he blame the real culprit—satan? Even though satan, likewise, didn't cram the fruit down Adam's throat, he was, however, the originator and the instigator of the temptation. Adam knew he was to rule all the creatures on the earth and to keep or guard the garden. This "keep" is the same word as the angel was to "keep" or guard "the way of the tree of life" in Genesis 3:24 (KJV). To blame satan would also be admitting to his failure of keeping the garden. Now instead of following the pattern of Christ, he established a new pattern of hiding and blaming. Adam established a new pattern for his sons, generation after generation, to follow. Job commented in Job 31:33, "*If I have covered my transgressions as Adam, by hiding my iniquity in my bosom....*" Adam did not repent. He hid.

God then confronted the female man. "*And the Lord God said to the woman, "What is this you have done?' The woman said, 'The serpent deceived me, and I ate'* " (Gen. 3:13). Eve did tell the truth by mentioning the real enemy. Satan did deceive her. However, was she admitting or blaming? I do have reason to believe that she was admitting and repenting. We will return to this subject a little later.

## JUDGMENT, CURSE, OR CAUSE AND EFFECT

It would be wise before going any further to understand the differences between judgment, curse, and cause and effect because all three were put into action as this drama for the ages was being played out on the magnificent stage of nature in the Garden of Eden created by the Master Designer. However, this drama was not playacting. It was so powerfully real that its effects would reach far beyond—even to the moment you are reading these words on this page, and even to eternity. It was a drama that was surpassed only by the One on the cross.

We find throughout the Bible that God is very consistent in speaking His *judgment* up front. In other words, before the person or people committed acts of disobedience, of idolatry or rebellion, God let them know the judgment He would execute as a result. For example, in Deuteronomy 28:1-2, God tells the Israelites, "*Now it shall come to pass, if you diligently obey the voice of the Lord your God, to observe carefully all His commandments which I command you today, that the Lord your God will set you high above all nations of the earth. And all these blessings shall come upon you and overtake you, because you obey the voice of the Lord your God.*" He continues on to identify the blessings. Then He says in Deuteronomy 28:15, "*But it shall come to pass, if you do not obey the voice of the Lord your God, to observe carefully all His commandments and His statutes which I command you today, that all these curses will come upon you and overtake you.*" He also identifies the curses. Contrary to what the world knows and believes, God is a perfect and righteous Judge who deals with His people up front and doesn't sneak around their backs ready to pounce on them with judgments and curses according to His whims.

*And the Lord God commanded the man, saying, "Of every tree of the garden you may freely eat; but of the tree of the knowledge of good and evil you shall not eat, for in the day that you eat of it you shall surely die"* (Gen. 2:16-17). So what was God's "up-front" judgment for eating the fruit from the forbidden tree? They would die! They knew it from the beginning. And true to His word, the day they ate, they died.

The first result of death was that mankind died spiritually. The spirit part of man came from God when He breathed into man's nostrils. It was the spirit part of man that connected him with God. Man's spirit wasn't just like God; it was a part of God, and it enabled man to know God. The soul of man, made up of his mind, his will, and his emotions, was subject to and served the spirit. The spirit and the soul of man were one and functioned in unity.

When mankind died spiritually, they lost their spiritual connection with God and with God's spiritual realm. Their spirits didn't actually die as we think of death, but the spirit lost its rightful place in the beings we call human, and it lost its life-giving power to lead the living soul. *An invisible veil fell and separated their spirit from their soul.* They were left to their own humanness with their own human resources, which, without the corralling and guiding function of the spirit, are more like animalistic instincts fighting for survival. They were left to the creations and devices of the carnal mind. Mankind became responsible for their own survival.

Mankind's soul took on evil, following a path of wickedness that would ultimately end in eternal death, totally separated from God without any potential of restoration. This is what I call the *"death process."* It is the second result of death that started in the garden with mankind, and today it starts with each individual the moment we are conceived. We are born under this curse of death, and we are born with the sentence of death hanging over our heads. This death not only affects our soul, but it also robs the body of its life-sustaining power until it ends up rotting, returning to dust, with just a mark of remembrance over a grave, which is the third result of death.

Thank God! He did not leave us in this place of death. He had already put a plan into action before He spoke creation into being.

God cursed satan and then He cursed the ground. *Curse* in the Strong's Concordance means "to execrate: bitterly curse."

Webster's Dictionary defines it "to call evil down," and it defines execrate "to denounce scathingly; to loathe; abhor."

We really don't like to use these words when talking about God. We would rather talk about Him as gracious and loving. But that's because we don't always understand God's love. God said that everything He created was "good," and it all had its place and function in the order God intended. So when God curses something, it falls out of order and loses its place and function, and it alters God's original intent. It becomes subject to evil.

God does not curse according to His whims. God's curse comes as a result of the choice of man, not the choice of God. A father tells his young son, "Don't go out into the street. Those big cars that go by can hurt you. You stay on the grass where it is safe. If you go into the street, I will spank you." Of course, spankings are not curses, but it illustrates the point that the consequence of a spanking is dependent upon the choice of the son. A spanking could save his life.

*Everything* God does is rooted in love and is for purpose—even curses. And all of His purposes are to lead man to one final destination—eternal life. Thank God for *"Christ has redeemed us from the curse of the law, having become a curse for us (for it is written, 'Cursed is everyone who hangs on a tree')"* (Gal. 3:13). It is God's desire that all men be saved. Of course, a man's will can strive with and resist God all the way to hell. The final destination will always rest with the individual.

Webster defines *cause* as anything producing an *effect* or result. If you put ice in a glass of water, it will make the water cold. Ice is the cause and cold is the effect. If you jump into the water, you will get wet. Jumping into the water is the cause and getting wet is the effect. If sin is released in an environment that is good, it will spoil the good. Sin being released is the cause and good being spoiled is the effect.

Adam and Eve ate from the tree of the knowledge of good and evil. Now mankind lives with its effects. What they thought would make them wise didn't make them wise, nor did it make them able to discern and know the difference between good and evil. Mankind calls what is good, bad and what is bad, good (see Isa. 5:20). When Adam and Eve ate, they took in them the seed and the nature of the tree. As God's creation, they had known **good** intimately. Their Creator had declared they were good (see Gen. 1:31). Then through the act of disobeying God's law, they came to know *evil* as intimately as they had known the good. Genesis 3:22a says, "*Then the Lord God said, 'Behold, the man has become like one of Us, to know **good** and **evil**'*" (emphasis added).

Adam and Eve or mankind eating and taking in the seed and the nature of the tree was the cause. Because evil was in the nature of the tree, the effect of eating was that evil began its work in their mortal bodies (see Rom. 7:5) and was passed on in the heritage of man from one generation to another, except it abounded or increased with each generation (see Matt. 24:12).

A simple example of the difference between *judgment and cause and effect* follows: A father plans to attend a business meeting at a large municipal airport with someone who is passing through. His 10-year-old son, totally fascinated with airplanes, wants to go along. Dad is not sure it's a good idea because he won't be able to keep his attention on his son. But upon the son's insistence, the father relents, saying, "I will take you this time, but you must do what I say. If you do not follow my instructions or give any amount of resistance, it will be a very long time before I take you with me again." The *judgment* for disobeying: The son will not be given another opportunity to go with Dad for a long time.

When the father and son get to the airport, Dad gives the instructions, "Stay right here and watch the planes. Don't move from this area. I will be sitting at those tables. Don't move out of my sight." In a while, the son spies a plane that for the most part is out of view from his vantage point. Perhaps if he moves to the next set of windows, he can see it better. He discovers that he can see it better, but still not well enough. In a few minutes, after he makes a couple more attempts to better see the plane, the boy gets turned around and goes in a wrong direction. Now he is lost.

We already know the judgment that will result: He won't be going with his father again for a long time. But what are the effects that will be experienced and even suffered that the father never intended and would have wanted to spare his son? The most immediate effect is fear that quickly grows into sheer terror. What earlier appeared to be common people getting on and off airplanes have, in the boy's mind, turned into kidnappers and terrorists. Once he is found, other resulting effects will be a dad who is upset, disappointed, and who has lost trust in his son. It is possible for effects to live far beyond judgments.

In summary, judgments are up-front, before-the-fact declarations by God of the inescapable consequences of disobedience. Curse is God releasing something from His order making it vulnerable to evil. Effects are the chain reactions that result from choosing to disobey God. Now we should be able to see more clearly what was happening and what was going to happen as God confronted satan, the woman, and the man in the garden.

## TO THE SERPENT

*So the Lord God said to the serpent: "Because you have done this, you are cursed more than all cattle, and more than every beast of the field; on your belly you shall go, and you shall eat dust all the days of your life. And I will put enmity between you and the woman, and between your seed and her Seed; He shall bruise your head, and you shall bruise His heel"* (Genesis 3:14-15).

Satan or lucifer, as he was named, was one of the archangels and held high rank in the spirit realm. But he was lifted up in *pride* and *rebelled* against God (see Isa. 14:12-16). As a result, he was exiled to the earth realm. Jesus said He saw satan fall as lightning through the skies (see Luke 10:18). The name, lucifer, means shining one. Since Jesus used lightning as the metaphor for satan's fall, it would appear that he had some celestial shine about his nature.

Lucifer, before the creation of man, had already faced his judgment for what occurred in the heavenly realm. There would be no savior providing redemption for him. Now, God in the garden cursed him to his belly and to eat dust. Whatever still remained of lucifer and his shining nature of heavenly origin was stripped from him. He lost his celestial shine and was bound to the earth realm.

What dust would satan eat? *"Be sober, be vigilant; because your adversary the devil walks about like a roaring lion, seeking whom he may devour"* (1 Pet. 5:8). Mankind is made of dust (see Gen. 3:19). As stated earlier, man came from two worlds. Part of them was made from the dust of the earth, and part of them came from the breath of God. It was when they were tempted that they chose which world they would serve. They chose the earth world and became fodder for the devil. Thank God for His promise in Genesis 3:15 of a Savior who had already defeated satan and would, at the appointed time, manifest it in the earth world.

When Adam ate the forbidden fruit, sin became generational. He received the seed of sin, and it would be passed through his bloodline from generation to generation. He could no longer give pure seed. It would be the woman whom God would use to bring salvation to what had been lost. It would be the woman who would birth the Destroyer of satan's kingdom, and satan hated her. Woman became his enemy. Because we live on this side of the cross, we know the fulfillment of this prophecy in verse 15. Jesus on the cross was bruised but not defeated or destroyed, and satan's head or power was crushed.

Every person who connects to the promise of the Savior can be freed from the victimization of earth mentality where satan eats daily. It is not appetizing for satan to sink his teeth into those who are living in the righteousness of Jesus and walking in the Spirit.

According to the parable of the sower in Matthew 13:3-30, seed can also represent a message. From that fateful event in the garden to the present day, there has been an ongoing war between satan's seed or message, which is propagated by the carnal mind, and woman's Seed or message, which is Jesus, the living Word. Even though the power of satan's message was crushed on the cross at Calvary, satan can continue to trespass as long as human beings are willing to listen to his message and believe it.

## To the Woman

*To the woman He said: "I will greatly multiply your sorrow and your conception; in pain you shall bring forth children; your desire shall be for your husband, and he shall rule over you"* (Genesis 3:16).

To get a full understanding of what God is saying here, we must recognize that He was not speaking curse or judgment. We have already discussed the *up-front* judgment of death. Now God is speaking effect. The cause was releasing sin in the earth by disobeying God and eating a fruit. Now God is speaking prophetically about the effect of that cause. As we saw in the example of the young son going with his dad to the airport, the *judgment* of being disobedient was not being permitted to go with his father again for a long time, and the *effect* of his disobedience was the great fear he experienced. Therefore, in these verses, God was not giving "law" that was to be adhered to for the rest of time. He was revealing the direction that Eve was about to take, which would *affect* the position of women generation after generation.

*"I will greatly multiply your sorrow and your conception; in pain you shall bring forth children."* According to Dr. Katharine Bushnell, a scholar of both the Hebrew and Greek languages who lived a century ago, the Septuagint translates the first part of this Scripture, *"A snare hath increased thy sorrow and thy sighing."*[1] The Septuagint is the first and oldest translation of the Hebrew Bible completed by Hebrew scribes. It is a Greek translation and the Bible that the apostles and evangelists of the first century used.[2]

I believe the Greek translation makes greater sense. First of all, *"I will greatly"* isn't even in the original Hebrew. Secondly, God had just pronounced to Eve the greatest promise ever given: Her seed was going to defeat satan. God was putting enmity between satan and the woman, separating her as one called out from the kingdom of this world; herein, she was a type of the Church (see 1 Pet. 2:9). Of course, the result would be sorrow and sighing, filling many days of her life.

I also believe this Scripture is speaking to multiple kinds of sorrow women would endure. In the Strong's Concordance, the word translated *sorrow* means, "worrisomeness: labor or pain." It comes from a root word that has been translated into words such as *displease, grieve, hurt,* and *be sorry.* It is the same word used in verse 17 when God is speaking to Adam. Women's lives would be afflicted with multiple sorrows. This is an effect, not a judgment. Nowhere, in any way, does God say to Eve, "Because you have done…"

The first sorrow to be addressed is that which results from the carnal gender mentality making sex the woman's obligation. There is nothing more grievous, more emotionally painful, and more burdensome than performing sex when it is no longer lovemaking. In my grandmothers' generation, sex was often referred to as "doing their duty." We'll speak more to this subject later.

Secondly—*"In pain you shall bring forth children."* Although they experience hard labor and pain to birth their babies, many women do not consider it sorrow. There is great joy when that small infant who has grown inside of her for nine months is finally placed into her arms. Next to this joy, the suffering becomes secondary. But this is not true for all women. To some, children have become more of a burden than a blessing. It is with sorrow they learn they are pregnant; it is with sorrow they bear their pregnancy; and it is with sorrow they birth their babies into their lives. Isn't that why abortion is now legal? Remember, these are the effects of sin and carnal mind thinking. We have lost something from the original state in which Adam and Eve were created, and it has turned what should be natural, joyous, and pleasurable into a burdensome sorrow.

There is a third sorrow that I believe to be the greatest of all. It is the sorrow and the grieving a mother endures when she sees the *effects* of sin in her children's lives. Sin can steal their innocence and sweetness and rob them of their health. It can break their hearts killing their zest for life, for their potential and productiveness. It can ultimately destroy their lives. And their mother grieves, sometimes over a grave. Eve came to know this sorrow well. One of her sons was murdered by another one of her own sons. That's just about as bad as it gets for a mother.

The fourth and last sorrow is what I call general sorrow. It is what has been suffered by women in general from all the oppression that satan has inflicted upon the female gender because of the enmity between him and them. He hates women because of their seed. The more satan can keep the female men oppressed from being all they were created to be, the more he can successfully oppress all of society. She is mother of all living. She is a life-giver. If she becomes unable to give life, it affects everyone around her.

*"Your desire shall be for your husband, and he shall rule over you."* In my search for identity as a woman, this has been one of the most baffling passages I have encountered. If her desire for her husband is an effect of sin being active in the earth, then something has to be wrong with it. But what is wrong with it?

Shouldn't she have a desire for her husband? Then on the other hand, I have known wives who have lost their desire for their husbands, and in our way of thinking, that is wrong. Something was missing from my understanding, but I didn't know what it was. I would think on it often, knowing somehow God would open my understanding. Sure enough, in a quiet time with Him, I heard the word "turn." Instantly, I saw it. Eve was going to *turn* her desire to her husband.

Months after this startling revelation, I was given a book in which I read that the word *teshuqa* that is translated "desire" in this text, was translated "turning" in six of the first eight translations written of Genesis, including the Septuagint.[3] "Desire" was not a part of the original Scriptures. Therefore, the Scripture would read, "*...and thy turning shall be to thy husband.*" Actually, the most literal interpretation would be, "*You are turning away to your husband, and he shall rule over you.*"

There are two other places in Scripture this word *teshuqa* is used—Genesis 4:7 and Song of Solomon 7:10. As we look at all three references, we recognize that this turning is more than a physical turning from one direction to another. This turning has a strong deep-hearted purpose in its motivation and reason for turning. The *Babylonian Talmud*, with its teaching of the "ten curses of Eve" is the first to render the word *teshuqa* as "desire" in this passage of Genesis 3:16; however, it renders the same word as "turning" in the passage of Genesis 4:7.[4] Does prejudice overrule consistency here? The *Talmud* is not a translation of the Scriptures, but a compilation of the traditions of the Jews. Among the first 12 translations of Old Testament Scripture, ten have translated *teshuqa* as "turning" in at least one of the three passages where it is found.[5] In Genesis 3:17, using the word "desire" can be and has been misleading.

As stated earlier, God is speaking words of effect in this verse. Eve's *turning* to her husband was one of the *effects* of sin and death being released in the earth. In other words, it was not

God's plan for Eve to turn to her husband. Why? When she turned to her husband, she turned away from whom? Who created and formed her very being? With whom did she walk in the cool of the day? Who was the source of all she needed? When she turned to her husband, she put him in the place that up to that time had been filled with God. It was God's rightful place—the place He had created for her that belonged to Him. And now she gave that place to her husband. She made her husband the source of all she needed and that, friends, is *idolatry.*

In Genesis 1:26 God defines for man what they are to rule over. "*...let them have dominion over the fish of the sea, over the birds of the air, and over the cattle, over all the earth and over every creeping thing that creeps on the earth.*" There is *no* mention here that man should rule over man, male or female. So why did God say, "*...and he shall rule over you*"?

I would like to quote Dr. Bushnell again:

> But what does all this mean if not that Adam, or man, is to be wonderfully rewarded for his part in that Garden fruit-eating? He is to be elevated to government over women; and to be allowed to dictate, by his own whims, how much or how little physical suffering she is to endure, as the price of his fleshly indulgence! And has God so honored man for all time as to give him this, which often amounts to the power of life and death over a fellow creature, forsooth because Adam accused God of unwisdom and sheltered Satan from blame?[6]

Jesus said, "*No man can serve two masters...*" (Matt. 6:24 KJV). Of course, this Scripture includes both the male men and the female men. How can a Christian woman be subject to two masters (or rulers)—Jesus and her husband? She is part of the Bride of Christ if Jesus is her Lord. Don't tell me submitting to Jesus and submitting to a husband are one and the same. I have lived over 60 years, and I have seen too much. They are *not* one and the same. Furthermore, men have never been required to submit to Jesus the same way women have been required to submit to husbands; therefore, the husbands' leadership or "headship" is many times motivated by the whims and comforts of their flesh.

Again, we need to remember that when God said, "...and he shall rule over you," He was speaking words of *effect*, not law. He was *not* saying, "I want the husband to rule over the wife. She cannot do anything or be anything other than what he allows her. *Her relationship with Me must yield to the commands of her husband.* She goes to church only if and when her husband allows. She can minister to or pray for someone only when her husband is by her side. She is never to function independently from the husband." Again, God was not laying down the law. He was saying that because she would put her husband in God's place, the result would be the husband ruling over her. The person whom you decide must meet your needs will be the one who rules over you. "*Do you not know that to whom you present yourselves slaves to obey, you are that one's slaves whom you obey...?*" (Rom. 6:16). However the husband responds or reacts to the wife's needs will *dictate* to her how she will react and respond to him. It will *dictate* to her who she is, her security, her acceptance, and her worth. It will rule her.

## TO THE MAN

*Then to Adam He said, "Because you have heeded the voice of your wife, and have eaten from the tree of which I commanded you, saying, 'You shall not eat of it': cursed is the ground for your sake; in toil you shall eat of it all the days of your life. Both thorns and thistles it shall bring forth for you, and you shall eat the herb of the field. In the sweat of your face you shall eat bread till you return to the ground, for out of it you were taken; for dust you are, and dust you shall return"* (Genesis 3:17-19).

*"Because you have heeded the voice of your wife...."* I can see this example in the back of my mind. Surely it didn't happen in my household...but maybe it did. As our children were growing up, we kept a large container that held all the many crayons that had accumulated over the years. I can see a mother walk into the family room and observe her son of about 10 years old sitting on the carpet peeling paper off the crayons. He is surrounded by small bits of different colored paper. She mildly or maybe more than mildly says to her son, "What are you doing?" Startled from his concentration and busyness, he suddenly becomes aware of his situation and the need for justification. He says, "I was bored. There is nothing to do around here." In that moment, a subtle form of passing the buck transpires, alluding to the determination, "It's your fault." The underlying message is, "If *you* had more interesting and fun things for me to do around here, I wouldn't have to peel paper off crayons." That subtle statement really means, "I refuse to take the blame so I pass it off to you." So Mom, in order to confront and take the punch out of his excuse, responds, "Since *you* are so bored, *you* can pick up every little piece of those papers. And then, since you are so bored, you can take the carpet cleaner and be very sure there is not a speck of crayon color left on that carpet."

I believe that in His first comment to Adam, God was confronting and deflating Adam's excuse or justification. We all have heard it, if not said it ourselves, "If Johnny jumps off the roof, are you going to jump off too?" I don't mean to make light of or to make fun of the seriousness of this situation. It is just that the simpler we can make the examples, the easier it will be to understand. God was not telling man to never listen to his wife. How can a marriage ever come into oneness and the multiplication dimension if the husband and wife do not listen to each other? Consider Genesis 21:12 where God told Abraham to listen to his wife, Sarah. The wrong part is not the act of listening to the other, but using the other's suggestion as justification to do the opposite of what you know God has said to do or not to do.

Adam *knew* he was *not* to eat from the tree. It was not subject to what his wife said or did.

*"Cursed is the ground for your sake; in toil you shall eat of it all the days of your life. Both thorns and thistles it shall bring forth for you, and you shall eat the herb of the field. In the sweat of your face you shall eat bread till you return to the ground, for out of it you were taken; for dust you are, and to dust you shall return."* In the beginning, God instructed Adam to keep the garden. He was to cultivate and work the ground so that it would produce. When God cursed the ground, it began to strive against man's efforts. It would take toil and the sweat of man's face or brow to make it yield so that he could eat.

I believe God's thoughts were something like this: *If you think you are going to rule this earth and make it productive and prosperous apart from Me, you have another thought coming. I am calling it out of order, and it will strive with you until you get back into order.* And how was Adam out of order? He not only lifted his thoughts above God's law and disobeyed God, causing himself to receive the nature of sin; he also hid, blamed, and refused to take responsibility for what he had done. I believe God calls it *"not repenting."* It would take the last Adam who would, unlike the first Adam, follow through in His purpose to make a way for man to come back into order. *"For we know that the whole creation groaneth and travaileth in pain together until now"* (Rom. 8:22 KJV). It has been waiting for the sons of God to manifest the life and authority of Jesus Christ, taking dominion and restoring God's order.

In the meantime, man has turned from God to the earth, and with his carnal mind full of pride, rebellion, and self-exaltation, has made himself god. He has lifted his own thoughts and opinions above the knowledge of God. He has dismissed God's laws and created his own. He sweats and toils, strives and stresses, and works and labors over the earth, and calls it success. He calls it life, even though he is being slowly beaten to death day after day.

When I have a project to do, whether large or small, I always mentally make plans and map out a course. I also mentally decide that the task should be *easy* enough if I simply stick to my course. Then between starting and finishing, I run into one problem, then another complication, and then something else does not work right. At some point of frustration I state, "*Nothing* is easy!" Isn't this an example of other kinds of thorns and thistles that cause man to toil and produce by the sweat of his brow? We know the apostle Paul dealt with "thorns" in his ministry. "*And lest I should be exalted above measure by the abundance of the revelations, a thorn in the flesh was given to me, a messenger of satan to buffet me, lest I be exalted above measure* (2 Cor. 12:7). Isn't it obvious that God will not facilitate man's self-serving nature which continues to exalt itself and thwarts the man's God-given purpose as a created being?

"*...for out of it you were taken; for dust you are, and to dust you shall return.*" This refers to physical death. It is the finishing of what was begun in the garden when man ate the forbidden fruit. Man's body was taken out of the ground, formed by the hands of God. It was designed to live forever. Now death from the moment of conception begins its relentless power against the human body. In youth it can begin subtly with soft poundings, like the gentle waves breaking on the seashores and then crescendo into torrent, earthshaking waves in old age. Sometimes it doesn't start so subtly, wasting no time with its vicious pounds on a young body. Then sometimes, as in abortion, suicide, or tragic accidents, it swoops in with one blow in full force. And the still or empty bodies, though professionally cared for and placed in a luxurious bed of satin and artistically carved and polished oak or pine, return to dust. Is this the end of life? Absolutely not!

## GOD COVERS

*Unto Adam also and to his wife did the Lord God make coats of skins, and clothed them* (Genesis 3:21 KJV).

God had a plan.

*"And according to the law almost all things are purified with blood, and without shedding of blood there is no remission"* (Heb. 9:22). According to Strong's Concordance, *remission* includes pardon, forgiveness, deliverance, and liberty. Since the fall or disobedience in the Garden of Eden, the price for pardon, forgiveness, deliverance, and liberty is shed blood. Why blood? *"Only be sure that you do not eat the blood, for the blood is the life; you may not eat the life with the meat"* (Deut. 12:23). The life of a person or animal is in its blood. The shedding of blood is the giving of life.

God not only gave the female man in Genesis 3:15 the promise of the Savior in her Seed, but now He affirms it on behalf of the male man and the female man by the shedding of blood. God killed an animal to provide a covering for Adam and Eve's nakedness. Once again, we are seeing type and shadow. There is no redemption in the blood of an animal. It was a type and shadow of the precious, priceless life blood of the Seed, the Son of Man and the Son of God, Jesus. Although it was a finished work because Jesus was slain before the foundation of the earth was laid, His blood would not be shed in the dimension of man's time until four thousand years later at the whipping post under Pontius Pilate's domain, on the grueling march down the stone streets, up the climb of Mt. Calvary, and on the vile rugged cross outside the walls of Jerusalem.

The animal skins were only a temporary covering. The redemption and salvation that was accomplished in the last Adam's obedience would be so powerfully complete and total that it would not just *cover* man's nakedness, it would *take away* or *eradicate* the shame and restore him to the place with God that the first Adam lost in his disobedience.

God didn't want robots. We don't *have* to love Him. We don't *have* to obey Him. By the work at the cross we GET to love Him and we GET to obey Him. When we really understand that, it truly becomes a privilege.

| SENT FROM
THE GARDEN

*Then the Lord God said, "Behold, the man has become like
one of Us, to know good and evil. And now, lest he put out his
hand and take also of the tree of life, and eat, and live forever"— therefore the Lord God sent him out of the garden of
Eden to till the ground from which he was taken. So He drove
out the man; and He placed cherubim at the east of the garden of Eden, and a flaming sword which turned every way, to
guard the way to the tree of life (Genesis 3:22-24).*

B efore Adam's disobedience, he was already like "Us." God
said in Genesis 1:26, *"Let Us make man in Our image,
according to Our likeness."* Now in Genesis 3:22 God is
saying, *"The man has become like one of Us."* So which one of Us
has the man become like? The One who knew both good and
evil. As we have stated before, Jesus, having been slain from the

foundation of the earth, is the only one of the Godhead who had experienced evil. He very intimately experienced evil when He bore the sins of all mankind as He hung nailed to the cross. The difference is that Jesus' obedience qualified Him to conquer sin. He was not overtaken by sin as the first Adam was. He overpowered sin, therefore breaking the power of sin on behalf of all mankind. Sin no longer has the power to send to hell the Christian who has been redeemed by the life blood Jesus shed.

The male man and the female man were created to eat from the tree of life and live forever. Dying came as judgment. If there had been no disobedience, there would have been no dying. However, it is still God's intent that man should eat from the Tree of Life and live forever. So why didn't Adam get a second chance? The second chance was given to the last Adam. The first Adam got his second chance when the last Adam succeeded where the first Adam had failed. Adam's salvation came through God's promise of Jesus' finished work which would be accomplished in the realm of time 4,000 years later.

Perhaps you have recognized by now that this Scripture in reference to being driven out of the garden is speaking about "the man." It doesn't say "man" as in mankind, and it doesn't say "them" as in the male man and the female man. Does this mean Eve was not driven out of the garden?

As a side note, it is essential when understanding the Scriptures, to stay consistent, and to stay consistent to the whole Word of God. If the Word is referring to the male man alone when stating "the man" in Genesis chapter 2, then we would have to stay consistent to that meaning in chapter 3.

So what about Eve? Did Adam alone have to take the fall? We do know for sure that it was Adam whom God held accountable for what happened in the Garden of Eden. *"Therefore, just as through **one man** sin entered the world, and death through sin, and thus death spread to all men, because all sinned"*

(Rom. 5:12, emphasis added). It was when the male man ate the forbidden fruit that sin became generational.

Maybe we could say that the "one man" here really means the male man and the female man together as one. But that wouldn't be true to the type and shadow. It was The One Man, Jesus, who alone took the responsibility of the second chance. His Bride had nothing to do with it, except for adding to her guilt in the brutal crucifixion.

So who did God hold totally responsible for mankind's salvation? It was Himself through His Son, the last Adam. The Church, His Bride, who is the "she" in this case, was totally helpless and could do *nothing* to bring about her salvation. *"But the free gift is not like that which came through the one who sinned; for on the one hand the judgment arose from one transgression resulting in condemnation, but on the other hand the free gift arose from many transgressions resulting in justification. For if by the transgression of the one, death reigned through the one, much more those who received the abundance of grace and of the gift of righteousness will reign in life through the One, Jesus Christ"* (Rom. 5:16-17 NAS). Salvation is a free gift. The receiver has nothing to do with the gift before it is received. In this case, even the receiving is made possible only by the power of God's Holy Spirit at work in the heart of the receiver. This Scripture says that *"by the transgression of the one, death reigned through the one,"* which means that it was through the male man, Adam, that the sin nature was passed on in his bloodline to all mankind.

I see no evidence in this Scripture that God sent Eve out of the garden. But if we back up to Genesis 3:16 again, God had already stated what she was going to do. She turned to her husband and followed him out. She loved him. If they were supposed to be one, shouldn't she have followed her husband out of the garden? That is certainly what the carnal gender mentality would say. Now I challenge you as the reader to keep an open mind until after you have read all I have to say about this and then make your judgment. *"Test all things; hold fast what is good"* (1 Thess. 5:21).

Does "becoming one" mean the woman has to sacrifice her own purpose? What was Eve's purpose? To help Adam, *or* to facilitate him? Hasn't carnal mind thinking added facilitating to submitting and helping? We could use some other words like humoring, placating, and agreeing when she doesn't really agree. What kind of a helpmate is that? In the context of these words it would be taking away her purpose and simply making her a servant. Her place would be to cook his meals, wash his clothes, clean his house, give him sex and maybe children, and keep her mouth shut. I know that sounds caddish. But it was exactly what we saw in the dream.

I believe Eve was admitting to her guilt or repenting when God questioned her, because *she received a Promise*. God's promises become ours through repentance. This Promise that Eve received was the greatest Promise ever given, the Promise of the Messiah, her Savior. Everyone who believes receives this Promise. We know she believed and received the Promise because, according to the original Hebrew of Genisis 4:1, when her first son was born she exclaimed, *"I have gotten a man—even The Coming One!"*[7] She thought her son was the promised Messiah. She was the first to receive a promise from God and then add her own expectation to it, only to be disappointed. However, it certainly didn't nullify the Promise.

The Promise was finally manifested in time through the woman, except this time her name was Mary. An angel from God told her that the power of the Holy Spirit would overshadow her Seed and she would conceive. She would bear and give birth to the Son of God (see Luke 1:26-38). Salvation was going to be birthed into the realm of time through the woman. Bringing salvation into the world was something that God and the woman did independently without the involvement of the man. Remember, it was when

Adam ate the forbidden fruit that sin became generational. He could no longer give pure seed.

It was Eve who handed the fruit to Adam. It was Mary who not only put salvation into the hands of her husband, Joseph, but also into the hands of all mankind who would reach out to take it. Mary's name is Greek for the name Miriam, and Miriam means "their rebellion." Mary's response to the angel sent to tell her that she had been chosen by God to give birth to Jesus was, *"Behold the maidservant of the Lord! Let it be to me according to your word"* (Luke 1:38a). It was not incidental that her name meant "their rebellion." She represented the rebellion that started in the Garden of Eden and then laid it down before God on behalf of all mankind when she said, *"Let it be to me according to your word."*

God gave vindication to Eve. He also gave to all women the open door to receive personally from Him, and then to give it to their children, their husbands, and even to all mankind. As a result of intimacy with God, what she gives will bear the saving nature of her God. Herein women can find their scriptural authority for ministry. The root word from which the word Eve comes means "to declare."

So what about Adam? *"For God so loved the world, that He gave His only begotten Son, that whosoever believeth in Him should not perish, but have everlasting life"* (John 3:16 KJV). Adam didn't verbally repent. Yet it appears that he didn't reject God in his heart. *"For He* [God] *knows the secrets of the heart"* (Ps. 44:21b). Adam hid his sin in his heart, allowing his pride to keep him from facing his blame. I believe Adam also believed the Promise. *"And Adam called his wife's name Eve; because she was the mother of all living"* (Gen. 3:20 KJV). It appears Adam knew and understood the Promise that Eve received. In the same moment when death had fallen on mankind and Adam experienced the burden of his guilt and shame, he named the woman Eve which means *"the mother of all living."* He knew she had already, through her confession and her faith in the Promise, recaptured life, and that through her all mankind could live. That didn't just mean breathing air; it also meant being retrieved from eternal death through her Seed.

Adam's Promise came to him through the woman Eve. The fulfillment of that Promise came through the woman named Mary. So why did Adam have to leave the garden? *"God resists the proud, but gives grace to the humble"* (1 Pet. 5:5b).

After His love and faithfulness to His Father, perhaps the next key attribute Jesus exhibited was humility. *"Who, being in the form of God, did not consider it robbery to be equal with God, but made Himself of no reputation, taking the form of a bondservant, and coming in the likeness of men. And being found in appearance as a man, He* **humbled** *Himself and became obedient to the point of death, even the death of the cross"* (Phil. 2:6-8, emphasis added).

*"Everyone proud in heart is an abomination to the Lord"* (Prov. 16:5a). Pride does not keep anyone who believes in Jesus as his Savior out of Heaven or from eternal life, but God does not bless or exalt the prideful. *"Therefore humble yourselves under the mighty hand of God, that He may exalt you in due time"* (1 Pet. 5:6).

In life here on earth, there are three dimensions in God or three levels of relationship a believer can have with God. God's plan is that these levels are progressive and that the believer moves from one level to the next until he is established in the third dimension or level. The first level we can call Egypt. Egypt represents the world with its bondages of slavery. A person can receive Jesus as his Savior yet never move out of his slave mentality, still living in the world's ways and never receiving what is rightfully his as a believer. Although he has eternal life, by not activating faith to grow in God, he receives little from God. *"But without faith it is impossible to please Him, for he who comes to God must believe that He is, and that He is a rewarder of those who diligently seek Him"* (Heb. 11:6). God never said we had to please Him to have eternal life—just believe in Jesus as

Savior. For those who understand the tabernacle of Moses, this level of relationship with God is settling into the outer court and going no further.

The second dimension or level of relationship with God can be called the wilderness. This level requires the faith and commitment to leave Egypt and come into the place of following God and allowing Him to take care of us. Just as He did for the Israelites in the wilderness, God provides all that is necessary for us to live. We find this dimension represented by the Holy Place in the tabernacle of Moses. It is the place of getting to know God, where our minds are renewed. It is a good place to be, but it is not the highest or best place.

There are several names we can give to the third dimension or level of relationship with God: Promised Land; Holy of Holies; the seventh day rest; returning to the garden; the Kingdom of God. All believers are in the Kingdom of God, but many believers never enter into Kingdom living. We come into Kingdom living only by exiting out of Egypt, journeying across the wilderness, and crossing the Jordan River. This Promised Land, however, does not refer to dying and going to Heaven. What is Kingdom living? *"For the kingdom of God is not eating and drinking, but righteousness and peace and joy in the Holy Spirit"* (Rom. 14:17). Kingdom living is where all the promises of God become manifest in our lives. It is where we rest from all our striving and laboring and Jesus lives His life through us. It is where we simply function with the mind of Christ and do great exploits. It is the place of the supernatural (see Rom. 14:17). We enter into Kingdom living only by dying to our self-life.

Adam did not choose to die to his self-life. He held on to it by refusing to admit his blame and hiding his sin in his heart. *"Blessed are those who wash their robes, that they may have the right to the tree of life and may go through the gates into the city"* (Rev. 22:14 NIV). He could not be allowed to stay in the garden, the place of Kingdom living. Did it nullify the Promise for him?

75

No. By his choice he lived the rest of his life below the level of relationship he once had with God. God never hated Adam, but He hated the pride, so He drove Adam out where pride belongs—among the thorns. The apostle Paul said, *"And lest I should be exalted above measure by the abundance of the revelations, a thorn in the flesh was given to me, a messenger of satan to buffet me, lest I be exalted above measure"* (2 Cor. 12:7).

In accordance to His nature, I believe God gave Eve the choice of staying or leaving the garden, already knowing what she would do. Adam had blamed her and she *felt* responsible. Women know this feeling well. It's the feeling that causes them to ignore purpose, become less than what they are, compromise what they think best, and become a facilitator. It's what lets the husband rule over them. Eve not only turned to Adam, making him her "need meeter," she also appointed herself to be his "need meeter," and Adam allowed her to be so. Religion has turned it into law.

After God had presented Eve to Adam, He said, *"Therefore shall a man leave his father and his mother, and shall cleave unto his wife: and they shall be one flesh"* (Gen. 2:24 KJV). Now it appears that it was the woman who left her Father Creator to cleave to her husband. By her choice she walked into the cave of the carnal gender mentality. It was quite a plunge downward from God being her "need meeter." Now the daughters of Eve are insecure regarding how to be a helpmate, and they live in confusion between what the carnal gender mentality dictates to them and what is crying out inside them from a dimension in their person that doesn't know it has a right to live.

It is this crying out, inside her, to be more than what she has believed religion and society has allowed her to be that is at the root of the feminist movement. It was and is a legitimate cry, but replacing one carnal mentality with another carnal mentality that wants to rob the male man of his identity and put him into a cave does not solve anything. It simply creates another set of problems.

It is not my purpose to blame Eve over Adam or to blame Adam over Eve. I believe both of them made choices that sent everything out of order. Surely it's time to stop playing the blame game and start focusing on how we can recapture God's order and end the deterioration of marriage. It's time to stop living each year just coping and enduring. It's time to look around and realize that if we would begin to live according to God's order, marriages would be working. I don't mean that we would only occasionally see or hear of a few who are making it work. I mean, the divorce rate in the church would not be close to matching the divorce rate in the world.

Adam and Eve leaving the garden did not mean purpose for mankind was lost. God's purpose remained in the woman's Seed and was brought forth in the earth again for all mankind through the birth of Jesus. And God continued to use the male man and the female man for the work of preparing the earth to receive its salvation.

"[God] *placed cherubim at the east of the garden of Eden, and a flaming sword which turned every way, to guard the way to the tree of life*" (Gen. 3:24b). Because sin is generational, we all have been born outside the garden. We were born outside the relationship, the purpose, and the destiny that Adam and Eve had in the beginning. Can we go back to it, or is it too late? It is God's will and intent that we go back. Jesus through His suffering, death, burial, and resurrection has become our Tree of Life and has made a way for us to return.

What does it mean to go back? It is going back to that place of purpose God had for mankind and the earth. It is returning to an innocent relationship between man and his God. It is going back to oneness between husband and wife. It is going back to multiplying, subduing the earth, and taking dominion. But it is *not* going back the way we came. God is eternal like a circle with no beginning and no end. When we hook up with the Circle, we go back by continuing to go forward. We can be finished with living life just day after day, month after month, and year after year without real purpose because we are now intentionally going some place. We can have purpose and know our lives count. We, both male and female, can know what it is to be loved and to love.

The big question is how badly do we want to go back? Badly enough to encounter the flaming sword? *"For the word of God is living and powerful, and sharper than any two-edged sword, piercing even to the division of soul and spirit, and of joints and marrow, and is a discerner of the thoughts and intents of the heart"* (Heb. 4:12). Are we willing to let the Sword circumcise our hearts cutting away the flesh of pride, rebellion, and self-exaltation that is being propagated generation after generation? Are we willing to let the Sword, when *turned every way*, pierce our carnal mind and change our beliefs and our thinking? Are we willing to let the Sword have free access to our lives cutting away everything that is a hindrance to our purpose and destiny and that doesn't bring glory to our God?

I believe there is a people within eyeshot of this book who want it badly enough. I believe there are people who want it so badly they are willing to see where they have erred and are willing to change their thinking. I believe there are enough people who want it so much that it will change the world.

| REPRODUCING
AFTER ITS
KIND

There is a law God put into effect when He created life: Everything that has life contains a seed, and the seed contains the same life enabling it to reproduce after its kind (see Gen. 1:12,21,24). In the seed of the apple is the life to reproduce more apples, not oranges. Lions reproduce more lions, not monkeys. People reproduce people who are like themselves. In the seed of the fruit from the tree of the knowledge of good and evil was the nature of the tree, the sin nature, the nature that pulls away from the righteousness of God to a self-gratifying, self-destructive way of life. Because a part of Adam was formed from the ground, the dust of the earth, he received the spiritual seed of a sin nature when he ate the fruit. In other words, the seed was planted into the ground, which was Adam, and began to reproduce itself through Adam. Sin became generational because it became part of man's nature that reproduced itself. It became part of the heritage that is passed on through the father's bloodline.

This is why it was imperative that Jesus be born from a virgin. If His father had been a human man, Jesus would have inherited the sin nature disqualifying Him as the spotless Lamb of God. Mary was impregnated supernaturally by God Himself. The life blood that pumped through Jesus' body was as pure as God is holy. Jesus was not born with a sin nature. He was like the first Adam in that He had the free will to choose to sin or not to sin, but He wasn't already a sinner by inheritance.

The point is that all people living today have a sin nature from our father Adam. All mankind is living under the same judgment of death and the same effects from the same cause. However, in our case, the effects have abounded, which means they have become greater in both quantity and intensity. *"But where sin abounded, grace abounded much more, so that as sin reigned in death, even so grace might reign through righteousness to eternal life through Jesus Christ our Lord"* (Rom. 5:20b-21). As we have been saying all along—God had a plan. His plan was entrusted to the last Adam, Jesus Christ our Lord.

Walking around on this earth are many male men and many female men, all of whom contain the life and nature that was in that seed from the tree of the knowledge of good and evil. We all were born in the likeness of Adam with the same sin nature received when eating the fruit. The effects that started in the Garden of Eden have continued like the ripples in the water from a dropped pebble, increasing larger and larger into today's world. These effects not only have *affected* our lives individually and corporately, but in many ways they have *overtaken* them. We are striving and struggling to survive wondering why so much seems to work against us. We put out so much and receive so little. There appear to be forces at work against us in the very atmosphere. The truth is we are fighting invisible forces that we do not understand, so how can we ever hope to defeat them?

Albert Einstein said that insanity is doing the same things over and over again but expecting different results. *Something* has got to change. Maybe it's time to reach out beyond old ways of thinking and old mind-sets to something different. The Bible says that every Christian in the Kingdom of God should be living in righteousness, peace, and joy (see Rom. 14:17). Are you? The Bible says that Jesus has made us free and given us liberty (see Gal. 5:1). Has He done this for you? *"Then Jesus said to those Jews who believed Him, 'If you abide in My word, you are My disciples indeed. And you shall know the truth, and the truth shall make you free' "* (John 8:31-32). Are you free? If truth brings about freedom, then lies must create bondage. If we are under any kind of bondage, then somewhere we have believed a lie. Personally I want freedom more than holding on to a lie, even if I have believed it as truth all my life.

We have entered the seventh millennium in time, the third day of grace in Jesus, and we are receiving from God great revelation. Revelation is seeing into the truth of God and understanding it the way He intended it to be understood, which often causes us to surrender what man has told us it should be. With each revelation we have to change our mentality and give up old ways of thinking. As we are seeing the truth, we are finding that the truth really does make us free. What wonderful liberty there is, walking in the Spirit, seeing and understanding God's Word. It is a liberty that is worth the struggle of giving up old sterile beliefs in which we have found false comfort for so long.

I am not saying that we are to compromise the truth of God. But truth is a journey of discovery. It doesn't end with our church doctrine. It can take us deeper and higher into the vastness of a God so far beyond our intellect that He could actually create our intellect. Why would we want to stay in a place that takes us around the same circles of doing the same things over and over with the same struggles, fears, disappointments, pain, sorrow, and few rewards? *"These things we also speak, not in words which man's wisdom teaches but which the Holy Spirit teaches, comparing spiritual things with spiritual. But the natural man does not receive the things of the Spirit of God, for they are foolishness to him; nor can he know them, because they are spiritually discerned. But he who is spiritual judges all things, yet he himself is rightly judged by no one. For 'who has known the mind of the Lord that he may instruct Him?' But we have the mind of Christ"* (1 Cor. 2:13-16). We could give up our safety of sameness, allow freedom and the mind of Christ within us, open our eyes to see something new about God, and embark on a great adventure.

As each bride and groom stands side by side on their wedding day making promises "till death do us part," they look forward to embarking on a great adventure. But oftentimes as years pass, the adventure turns into disappointment, pain, and heartache. It happens too often even among Christian couples in the church where marriage should be succeeding the most. Isn't it time we wake up to the fact that something is wrong? There are many Christian couples who are simply enduring their lives together because it is wrong to get a divorce. They went into their marriages with the honest intent that they were going to do it right. It was going to be at least as good as their parents' marriage, if not better. What happened? The carnal gender mentality is what happened. Ignorance of God's order is what happened, reproducing generation after generation with the same way of thinking, the same mentality, and the same behavior that leads us down the same dead-end road. We are not defeating the devil. We have created and furnished a well equipped playground for him to delight in destroying our marriages.

Yes, there does appear to be forces at work against us in the very atmosphere. Yes, we are fighting invisible forces that we do not understand, so how can we ever hope to defeat them? As we continue on from here, we will discover God's order and remedy our ignorance. We will identify these invisible forces that war against us through the carnal gender mentality. We are going to bring them into the light of Jesus' Word so we can see them, understand them, and become equipped to defeat them.

*chapter seven* | # WHO'S THE VICTIM?

W hen Adam blamed Eve and God for his blunder in the garden, he became a victim to them both. When Eve turned to the husband, she became his victim. They took on what I call the "victim mentality" in their relationship to each other, and it, too, has been passed on to the generations.

No one becomes a victim until they give assent to it mentally. Prisoners of war who have suffered great physical torture have given testimony to how they fought mentally to keep from becoming mental victims of the enemy. Two people can go through identical adverse circumstances where one accepts becoming the victim and becomes angry, resentful, and bitter; whereas, the other sees the situation as a challenge to grow in faith and spiritual strength and to become better having experienced it. Twelve spies were sent into the Promised Land. Ten saw themselves as victims and two saw themselves victorious (see

Num. 13:30-33). Once a person accepts and believes he is a victim, he will take it into every place and every relationship. He will feel he is being victimized even in situations where it doesn't exist. Once it is accepted mentally as truth, it becomes real to life resulting in the "victim mentality."

From observation I believe we all can agree that women in general have been pursuers of God more than men. Why? The reasoning involves the difference in the mental and emotional makeup of the male man and the female man. Men are more logical, and women are more emotional. It is true that men receive through their mental being first and then feel it, if they allow themselves to feel. If a man shuts away his emotions, then information never gets past his logic. On the other hand, women receive through their emotional being first and then process it mentally, if they allow themselves to think. A woman can be so insecure that she can be hindered in sound reasoning abilities. In any case, what difference does it make if it is received first mentally or emotionally? *God is God* and *Truth is Truth!* He comes up the same whether you think Him or feel Him. Surely the Spirit of God is at work equally in men's hearts and minds as well as women's hearts and minds.

Because of their emotional and intuitive nature, women may perceive God in ways men may not fully understand. Men, who are workers in the earth, should also be seeing Him in all they do. *"The wrath of God is being revealed from heaven against all the godlessness and wickedness of men who suppress the truth by their wickedness, since what may be known about God is plain to them, because God has made it plain to them. For since the creation of the world God's invisible qualities—His eternal power and divine nature—have been clearly seen, being understood from what has been made, so that men are without excuse"* (Rom. 1:18-20 NIV). The invisible attributes of God are clearly shown, seen, and understood by the things that are made or created so that there is no excuse to not know Him. I believe gender makeup has nothing to do with pursuing or resisting God. I believe it goes back to choices made in the Garden of Eden. Let's take a closer look and see what we find.

## THE MALE MAN

What is blame? Isn't it placing the responsibility and the fault of a consequence on someone or something? Blame can be placed justly or unjustly. If Adam had blamed himself or taken the responsibility and the fault for his own choice and actions, it would have been just blame. He was guilty. Regardless of the circumstances, He knew better. When he put the unjust blame on his wife, he was saying, "I became her victim. It's her fault and she's responsible." It was a lie. He always had the power and opportunity to say, "No." He knew what he was not supposed to do.

I don't believe it was because of his overwhelming love for her that he chose to eat. If he loved her in that way, why didn't he stop her from eating, or why didn't he intercede or intervene before God on her behalf? Why wasn't he consistent to the type and shadow after which he was created? What happened to his overwhelming love when he blamed her? I do believe Adam greatly loved Eve, but it was not this love that motivated him to disobey God.

Adam, by hiding his iniquity and blame, and placing the responsibility and the fault on his wife, gave her the power to make him her victim, and it has become a significant point in the carnal gender mentality. The men in the dream were content keeping their wives in the prison cave. And so are husbands today. Of course, they are very quick to defend that they are no one's victim. So why do wives hear comments like, "You always want everything your way." "You just want to take over." "If you wouldn't be so ___, then I wouldn't have to be so ___." You can fill in the blanks with lots of different descriptions. Many husbands are afraid that if they allow their wives total access into their lives, the wives will take over and they will be left less than a man. That, people, is a *victim mentality*. Therefore, it is safer to keep wives in the cave.

In addition, Adam, by hiding his own iniquity and blame, blamed God for giving him this woman. He had already been hiding from God's presence, causing God to look for him and ask where he was. Doesn't that sound like a victim? Men are still hiding, instead of pursuing God as women often do. They are still in aloneness which is that mental and emotional private place to which men retreat. It is where they hide their inadequacies and keep secrets. Even though he may be saved and going to Heaven, until a man accepts his responsibility and his fault and faces his blame and his shame, he will always be hiding from God. He will keep himself on the outside fringes of a real spiritual life, never becoming totally sold out to the One *"who is able to do exceedingly abundantly above all that we ask or think, according to the power that works in us"* (Eph. 3:20).

## THE FEMALE MAN

When Eve accepted Adam's blame and became guilty, she also became his victim. She turned to him with the attitude and mentality of, "Please, please make me feel good about myself again. Please, please take away my guilt and make me feel loved and worthy to be part of your life. I need you. I need your approval and acceptance so I can be a real woman." This is a victim mentality and is what keeps women locked in the cave of carnal gender mentality.

I have seen many women who have put their lives on hold waiting for the husband to finally be and do what they *think* they need their husband to be and do so they can finally be happy. Their value and identity as a person and a woman is wrapped up in their man, which we have already identified as idolatry—and it wears a man out. He gets tired of always having to try to figure out what he is supposed to do. He gets tired of not doing things good enough and not being good enough for his wife. No wonder men get sick of it and want to get away to their games and activities. He will eventually lose respect for her. A woman who has put her life on hold waiting for a man is wasting what God has given her to be and to do. I know women who have waited their whole lives.

In the 60s there were women who began to express their resentment of this need for a man. But rather than pursuing God for identity, they took a giant leap out from the cave into what we call the feminist movement. They were expecting liberty, but all they did was exchange one form of bondage for another. Perhaps all they succeeded in doing was changing places. While they now may have moved outside the cave, they have thrown their men into one. They are free to express all they are any way they want to express it. They can even take over the man's place and do it as good as he can. Rebelling against the carnal gender mentality has succeeded in only creating another carnal mentality. God's order is still ignored, so life and marriage are in no better shape.

A wife who is a victim is like a child needing a daddy to rescue her. A real husband wants a real, mature woman who will increase him, not be a leach who wants to suck the life out of him.

## Victims in a Marriage

So what happens when two victims get married? It becomes a competition, not a marriage. Competition and marriage shouldn't even be in the same sentence much less in the same house. They are opposites. By God's definition of marriage and oneness as described earlier in this book, competition is an enemy. Competition will *never* let oneness develop and will eventually destroy a marriage.

But it is inevitable that two victims living in the same house *will* compete, unless one has become so resolved to becoming a victim that he or she has ceased striving. Otherwise, they compete over who gets to be the most tired, who worked the hardest today, so who has to go tend to the children. They compete over who's spending the money and how much, keeping score so one doesn't come up having more. They compete over who's right and who's wrong and who gets to have their way. They compete over who should have to do the chores this time. That could include such things as taking out the trash, bathing the toddlers, feeding the dog, cleaning out the car, or taking the children to piano lessons.

Victims will even compete over things they do not have nor ever had control over, such as who was born in the "right" state, who went to the best schools as children, and whose parents spoiled them. I have witnessed spouses speak negatively about the state where their mate came from. This communicates that the mate is devalued simply because they were born in a certain state. What a waste of life! What a waste of relationship when the multiplication dimension is possible. Any spouse who is secure in who they are and where they came from will always be able to honor the place God chose to birth the one they should love the most.

Victims always see themselves as the disadvantaged. Remember, this is a mentality. A victim, at some point in his or her life, at least subconsciously, agreed to become a victim. It has become part of who they are. They feel victim, they think victim, and they act victim. It is perceived that everyone, even those who love them, are really out to get them or use them. They just know that they are going to come up as being less, having less, being left behind, and without what is rightfully theirs. Oneness doesn't fit in this equation. It's all about "me taking care of me."

A victim actually sabotages his or her own life. Every victim by the very nature of what a victim is must designate a "bad guy" or a "bully." In a marriage, guess who the bad guy gets to be? It is impossible for a person with a victim mentality not to see their spouse at times as being the bad guy. So much for a healthy marriage!

The victim walks in and doesn't get the attention they feel they should have from the spouse. There could be five legitimate reasons why the spouse didn't give the expected attention, but the victim refuses to see or believe it. The victim labels the spouse as the bad guy by judging them and saying, "You really don't care about me." If we could get a picture of what is happening in their emotional beings, we would see the victim taking the spouse's love for them and belittling it. Then they throw it on the floor and stomp on it communicating the attitude that the spouse's love is not good enough for them.

The victim has just sabotaged their own life and actually cuts off from themselves what they really want. Marriage cannot happen nor can any relationship grow in this atmosphere. Remember, we reproduce after our kind, so our children are also learning to be victims. Children can consider their parents as the bad guys. It is a sad, troublesome place when parents allow themselves to become the children's victims.

*"Every city or house divided against itself will not stand"* (Matt. 12:25b). What is *competition*? The Encarta Dictionary defines it as the activity of doing something with the goal of out-performing others or winning something.[8] In marriage, that means taking sides one against the other. We have been trying to set a goal of and motivate others to see and desire the greater dimension of marriage we have identified as the multiplication dimension. What we are seeing here is that competition divides, not multiplies, and Jesus said a *"house divided against itself will not stand."* Competition in marriage tears down and destroys.

Isn't it time we learn how to support each other? I challenge anyone who struggles with the thoughts and feelings of being a victim to declare war against that mentality. You must choose to believe in the love of your mate over how you are feeling. If you continue to believe your mate really doesn't love you when they don't do this or when they do that, then you will stay defeated. Actively make decisions and follow through on choices to prefer your mate first instead of competing with him or her. Take full responsibility for your victim mentality and ask your heavenly Father to show you how to lay hold of your total victory.

*God, deliver us from this leach-like victim mentality that continually seeks a certain reaction from others—this mentality which determines that other's love is never enough. We are literally sucking the life out of each other leaving us sick, weak, and impoverished in our relationships when we should be increasing each other. Set us free from this self-destructive mind-set. Establish in us the mind-set that You are for us and not against us, that You go before us and make a way for us, that greater is He (the Almighty God) that is in us than he (satan, the enemy of our souls) that is in the world.*

When we are in Christ, it is impossible to be a victim.

| # THE GENDER MENTALITY— WOMEN

Like their mother Eve, most women today have turned to their husband and set him in a place where God belongs. Therefore, that which God could so richly and bountifully give is now required from the husband. These requirements usually include and are determined by what the wife feels she needs at the given moment to feel good about herself. We are talking more than the physical needs of food, clothing, and shelter. Women who have sufficient food, clothing, and shelter can still not feel good about themselves and continue to wonder why their needs are not being met. These needs are often so deep in her emotional being that she doesn't even know what they are. She just knows she feels needy. Something very important is missing from her life.

Therefore, we must discover and define what these important emotional needs are. Simply put, they are *feeling secure, feeling accepted* (unconditional love), and *feeling worth* or *value*. A woman, because of her emotional makeup, *must* feel good about herself. Contrary to religious condemnation, it is not righteous for a woman to neglect herself. If she is not full of security, acceptance, and worth, how can she possibly give these things to others?

These emotional needs are foundational to her identity. She defines her identity as a person, as a woman, as a wife, and as a mother by her feelings of security, acceptance, and value as she functions in these areas of her life. When she turns to her husband for these needs, it becomes his responsibility to give her this security, acceptance, and value so she can feel good about herself and function as a whole person. When a husband fails to "be God" by failing to make her feel good about herself, the wife feels abandoned, neglected, and cheated.

The wife's behavioral response to the husband's apparent failure usually falls somewhere between two extremes. At one end of the spectrum is the woman who has become a nothing. She doesn't think, can't make decisions, makes petty conversation, and keeps her true feelings concealed, even from herself. She is a performer and a conformer, saying and doing only what she believes her husband expects of her. What she says and wants changes according to what she believes is expected at the time. She doesn't speak out of her own convictions. She's too busy pleasing to get what she needs to even know what her convictions are. She always says what her husband wants to hear whether it is the truth or not. Truth to her is what he says and what he wants. Apart from her husband she can't function.

At the other end of the spectrum is the woman who resents the fact that her security, acceptance, worth, and identity are dependent upon this man. He began failing her from day one (oftentimes just like her father). Now she is bound to someone who is preventing her from having all she needs to finally *feel* her life is worth something. This is a lie. But the concept has been so communicated and universally accepted as "right" that it is believed to be true. So she rebels. By all appearances she is rebelling against her husband, but in reality she is rebelling against a lie. She can become mean and demeaning. She can belittle and debase. She will take over and become very controlling and downright wicked. Some women are out to prove they don't need a man, which merely proves they still believe they do.

Most women function somewhere in between these two extremes or travel back and forth to some degree learning how to use kindness, manipulation, and guilt. Many women will do almost anything to get a morsel of what they *feel* they need, even prostitution in all the forms that can take. Wives will "sell" themselves, even to their own husbands, by performing acts of lying, stealing, and sex (all in the name of submission) to get what they perceive they need from him. They have literally placed themselves under the man's rule, which is the result of sin, eating the forbidden fruit. It is how, what, when, where, and why he responds to her that is ruling her.

I am not saying wives are not to consider their husband's preferences. That is something a typical loving wife does. But when she gives up her likes and dislikes, her interests and hobbies, and her personality in how she dresses, wears her hair, and socializes, then she has placed herself under his rule. When she gives up her individuality and totally neglects her inner person, making her life all about him, he is ruling over her. Remember the lifelessness of the cave women in the dream. Their lives merely existed for the husband. And they thought it was the right way.

Eventually, after doing all she can do, yet still failing to get her husband to be what she needs, she will despair and become despondent, like the women Patsy saw in the dream, who accepted that this is the way it is. Or she will become desperate, realizing she has only one opportunity to live life, thinking her situation is robbing her of that life and feeling trapped in it.

The women who despair and become despondent resign themselves to a life where they are committed to the needs of the husband and the children, while sending their own needs into an emotional mausoleum. They give up any potential for purpose beyond husband and children. Their destiny becomes to die before they grow too old and decrepit, and hopefully see their children happy and becoming more than they were. And what is keeping them in this place? The carnal gender mentality. If she ever considers "getting out" in some way, she will soon dismiss the thought because of guilt, shame, or lack of courage. For Christian women, religion forbids it, calling it sin and disobedience to God.

Eve was the recipient of Adam's blame; now, over 6,000 years later, not much has changed. A friend of mine said that there should be a T-shirt made for women that reads, "Husband's Scapegoat." Women who don't have a healthy relationship with their heavenly Father which in turn causes them to be whole as an individual, most often accept the burden of this blame. They won't leave the cave or stand up to their own husbands because in some way it's their fault. The carnal gender mentality tells women they don't have the right to do either of these.

*I am NOT advocating that women leave their husbands. I am NOT saying that being a wife and mother is not important. I believe them to be the MOST important roles of a woman, just as a husband and father should be the MOST important roles of a man.* However, if men are allowed the full expression of their individuality in a career and hobbies, then why should women not be allowed the same? God commanded the woman also to subdue the earth and take dominion, and today's world is opening more doors for her to do so. Did God create her with individual abilities, talents, interests, and potentials and then require her never to come into the full expressions of those things to be a wife and mother? *Perhaps if we were not bound to the carnal gender mentality, God would show us ways in which this could be done, effectively and in balance, and with no one—wife, husband, or children—being neglected, but everyone being increased.*

While desperate women are still fewer in number than those who have become resigned, their population is ever increasing. For some, settling into and enduring the empty, meaningless life they feel they are living becomes unbearable. Desperation can reach a point that even a "good Christian" woman can do far-out uncharacteristic things, such as take a job out of town, have an affair, immerse herself in a cause, turn to her children causing unhealthy "apron strings," run away and desert the entire family, divorce the husband, or commit suicide.

We know about abused wives who are trapped in the carnal gender mentality. Many of them come to believe they deserve the verbal tongue lashings, the slaps, the death grips, and the all-out beatings. They think that if they could just become a better wife, then he would be a better husband. That's what they are often told, and the carnal mentality accepts it. But a woman can become desperate enough to be willing to get out of her situation and endure the aloneness along with the guilt, shame, criticism, and disapproval of her failure that she believes will be her fate. The ones who become this desperate yet can't face these consequences are the ones who run away or commit suicide. We could blame this behavior on how women are made, but God didn't make women to live in these circumstances. I believe it is carnal mentality that has taken the way women were made and twisted it just enough to keep them in the gender mentality cave.

I have a friend in our Bible study who had a best friend in school. Her friend married a man who became a pastor of a spirit-filled denominational church, and they had two children. Secretly, he abused and beat her. Unfortunately, she felt there was no way out. She certainly couldn't criticize or expose her husband—he was a pastor. It could ruin his life and his career. So, in desperation, she committed suicide. She did what she thought was the only alternative. She removed from his life what he blamed was failing him—herself. That, friends, is the result of the carnal gender mentality.

chapter nine | THE GENDER
MENTALITY—
MEN

"*Therefore shall a man leave his father and his mother, and shall cleave unto his wife: and they shall be one flesh*" (Gen. 2:24 KJV, emphasis added). Webster defines *cleave* as "to adhere; cling to; to be faithful." *Cleave* is another word I have spent much time considering. Not even the Amplified Version of the Bible gives much attention to the word. The definition is simple, but how does it play out in our everyday lives and in the relationship of marriage? How does a husband *cleave* to his wife? What does it look like?

One day I was thinking about the lack of or fear of commitment I was seeing in men. I was seeking God for an understanding so I could address it with God's solutions that always come with grace and life. I found that Webster defines *commit* as "to bind by a promise, pledge." Immediately the word *cleave* popped into my mind. The word *bind* goes right along with the words *adhere, cling to,* and *cleave.* When a man marries, he is to leave his father and mother and commit himself to his wife, and they shall be one flesh. Now I thought I was seeing something.

Christ emptied Himself of everything that was rightfully His as a part of the Godhead for the sake of God's purpose for His Bride. Knowing that He was making for Himself a Bride worthy to present to Himself, He gave up Himself. He gave up all control and trusted totally in His Father's instructions and provisions.

> *Husbands, love your wives, just as Christ also loved the church and gave Himself for her, that He might sanctify and cleanse her with the washing of water by the word, that He might present her to Himself a glorious church, not having spot or wrinkle or any such thing, but that she should be holy and without blemish. So husbands ought to love their own wives as their own bodies; he who loves his wife loves himself. For no one ever hated his own flesh, but nourishes and cherishes it, just as the Lord does the church* (Ephesians 5:25-29).

Christ is the example husbands are to follow, but He is not who men are following. I believe we can blame the carnal gender mentality. We recognize that the lies of this mentality have also put men in bondage. As a result, they are being robbed of the best God created for them. They are being robbed of the kind of helpmate who can bring to them the potential of entering into the multiplication dimension and the greatness that they are searching for in the earth.

Just as Jesus made for Himself a Bride worthy to present to Himself, each husband, by cleaving to his bride, by loving and *being committed,* can make her into the wife who is worthy of himself. Perhaps one of the problems is that the husband doesn't feel worth in himself; therefore, he can't make her more worthy than he personally feels. Some husbands may subconsciously think that they need to bring their wives down to their level of value. What a pitiful place to be for both the husband and his wife. Then he blames her, when it is himself he sees as unworthy.

There is a part of the uncommitted husband that has never married. He has kept a part of himself single with one foot outside the circle or bond of marriage. He has not yet given up all of his aloneness that God said was not good. What is *aloneness*? It is that mental and emotional private place to which men retreat. It is the place where they *hide* their disappointments, pains, and fears. It is the place where they hide hopes and dreams. It is the place where they keep secrets. As a result, they will even separate themselves physically and go off to be alone. But God said, "It is not good." We could also define *aloneness* as independence. Commitment and independence do not make good partners.

In most cases, when a woman speaks her vows on her wedding day and gives herself to her husband on her wedding night, she believes he is committing himself to her as she is to him and that with him she has found a safe place. She believes he means what he says on that wedding day and that it is his desire to become one with her. The uncommitted husband, perhaps unintentionally, is a deceiver, withholding from the wife something that rightfully belongs to her by God's definition of marriage. Ultimately, the behavior of an uncommitted husband can push the wife away, causing him to cut off from himself what rightfully belongs to him.

The lack of commitment results in a "pick and choose" mentality. He gets to pick and choose when he wants to be there for her and when he doesn't. He gets to "pick and choose" what he will do for her and what he won't. He gets to "pick and choose" when and how she is welcome into his life. Surely we can recognize this is not how Christ loved the Church and gave Himself for her.

This mentality keeps the husband in control based upon his likes and dislikes, his time and convenience, his mood, what it will cost him, and his inadequacies, insecurities, and fears. This is not losing his life for her sake. It is holding on to it very tightly and securely above the life of his wife. He is cleaving to his life, not to his wife.

The uncommitted husband makes his own rules, usually without much consideration of the wife's needs and desires. Since he has never fully committed himself to the wife, there is little awareness of her needs and desires; and if he is aware of any needs, he certainly does not consider himself as responsible for them. The result will be living a life of double standards: His independence is okay, but her independence is failure in being submissive; he can do what he wants, but she is supposed to be there for him; if she "requires" anything from him, it means she always wants her way; she is to commit to a specific time, but he will be there when she sees him coming. Does the wife have the same option of "pick and choose"?

And, of course, most uncommitted husbands must always, at all times, avoid any appearance of being henpecked. If he should act committed to the wife, he will appear less than a man. If he bares his heart to her, he will appear weak. He can't publicly defend her because everyone will think he answers to her. And how does he speak about her in casual conversation with the guys? Does he speak highly of her, or does he tell all the ways he is critical of her calling her "the old lady" or something perhaps more demeaning. In most situations he will yield to his "unhenpecked code of ethics."

There is one more element that can be present in this kind of mentality. In our "absent father" society that we find ourselves today, there are men who as little boys didn't get all their emotional needs met for security, acceptance, and value. At some point in their lives while growing up, some young boys may begin to experience something, usually in their sports involvement but not limited to sports involvement only, where their achievement begins to get attention. This attention along with a sense of doing well begins to feed these starved emotional needs. At this point, the tendency is to mentally and emotionally move in and set up camp. Life goes on and they get older, but they are still tied to the place where, because of their achievement, they received at least some morsels of security, acceptance, and value. Now, years later, their identity and value are still wrapped up in what was cool, fun, and successful for them as a boy. Therefore, a part of them has never grown up. They are still bound to the boy.

This mentality will rule them even when making decisions in their homes and marriages. They may sacrifice time and money that should be spent on their families to keep this involvement alive and justify it with, "I work hard and I need my time to relax and unwind. I bring home the money so I deserve it." Simple examples could be sports, working, hunting, motorcycling, rebuilding cars, playing war games, playing the computer, being tough, or just hanging out with the boys. Commitment does not mean that a man should not have time to relax and unwind or participate in extracurricular activities, but it does require the man to grow up so he can come into right relationship with the needs of the whole family.

We should also mention the young boy who feels the only time he gets attention is when he does something wrong or bad. If this is the only identity he can find for himself, he could start down a path of behavior that will destroy him and bring much grief to those who love him.

Then there are those males who have come to identify themselves by their sexual prowess. There is certainly no lack of attention for them in this oversexed society within our world today. However, with this identity, commitment to one wife in the way we are describing may be next to impossible. Wives value their husbands' loving abilities over their sexual abilities.

The husband's lack of commitment creates an unhealthy emotional environment for his family. Not knowing what they can count on him doing or when he will be there for them creates insecurity. Choosing or "saving" his life (likes, dislikes, time, convenience, expense, mood, inadequacies, insecurities, and fears) instead of giving his life causes his wife and family to feel devalued. A family cannot be strong living in a world of "maybe's." They need a constant, steadfast, consistent, faithful husband and father. They need a man, not someone hiding in his aloneness. Sooner or later the husband's lack of commitment will result in the loss of his wife's and children's trust and respect.

So if men are commanded by God to love, to cling to, and to commit themselves to their wives, then why do they fear these things? To better understand the fear, we will break it down into three separate categories. The first fear is the fear of destruction (see Heb. 2:14-15). For a man to be committed to another person, it means coming out of aloneness and giving up absolute control of his life. But his Adamic victim mentality way of thinking tells him that to give up control could mean being ravaged, ruined, consumed, overthrown, sabotaged, and victimized; and not many men are willing to take such a risk. These are lies that dominate victim thinking and cause men to hold on to control.

To choose control over commitment reveals a lack of trust in God. It is a lack of the man knowing his place in Christ. "*The name of the Lord is a strong tower; the righteous run to it and are safe*" (Prov. 18:10). Until a man is free from his victim mentality, he will never really know his place in Christ. The dominating lie of control tells the man that if he gives up control of his life, he will become less of a man. However, when a man gives up control to Jesus, allowing Jesus to live His life through him, how can that possibly make him less than a man? Once again, it is how the carnal gender mentality has taught us to think. It's a lie, but it feels like the truth through and through. Each man ultimately has to choose how he is going to live his life—in the lie or in the truth. A life of commitment will have its moments of pain, but he who loses his life for Christ's sake will find it. *"Then Jesus said to His disciples, "If anyone desires to come after Me, let him deny himself, and take up his cross, and follow Me. For whoever desires to save his life will lose it, but whoever loses his life for My sake will find it"* (Matt. 16:24-25).

The second fear is the fear of being exposed or the fear of being naked. *"I heard Your voice in the garden, and I was afraid because I was naked; and I hid myself"* (Gen. 3:10). Marriage is more than physical nakedness. It also requires nakedness of the soul. Women are not sexually aroused seeing the naked body of the man as much as they are seeing his naked heart. However, it is difficult for a man to expose his heart because that is where he hides his inadequacies (see Job 31:33). By staying uncommitted he keeps himself in control so he will never be put into a position of exposing his inadequacies. He is afraid that commitment may require something of him he doesn't measure up to, which would result in him showing himself as less of a man than he is trying to present to the world and to his wife.

When a man chooses to hide his feelings of inadequacy over commitment, he is again revealing his lack of confidence in his God. He has not come face-to-face with God or himself, being honest about himself. All men have inadequacies of some kind, but to believe inadequacies make him less of a man is a lie from the pit of hell. Trusting God enough to reveal his true feelings and thoughts and expose the hidden things in his heart can result in a healthy marriage. The wife calls it intimacy.

How do men protect their aloneness and how do they hide their feelings of inadequacy? Men protect their aloneness by keeping silent and telling the woman to "keep silent" or "be quiet" or "shut up." Or perhaps it is simply expressed, "I don't want to talk about it." They refuse to get involved in games, projects, activities, etc. where they feel inadequate, saying they don't have time or they don't want to, rather than admitting they feel insecure. Some men out-and-out lie to cover up their mistakes, their failures, and their inabilities. So much for healthy relationships.

The third fear is the fear of losing his battle for his identity. It is the fight for survival, for security, acceptance, and value. This mentality says, "I am responsible for my own survival. I must be tough and in control. If I commit my life to God and to my wife, I will lose it and become a nothing."

> Then He said to them all, "If anyone desires to come after Me, let him deny himself, and take up his cross daily, and follow Me. For whoever desires to save his life will lose it, but whoever loses his life for My sake will save it. For what profit is it to a man if he gains the whole world, and is himself destroyed or lost?" (Luke 9:23-25).

Jesus was saying, "Men (and women), deny yourselves, deny letting your fears and your inadequacies rule you, deny or give up your fight for identity and even your own survival. Be willing to lose it all and cast (commit) your survival over onto Me. I want to give you life, real life, My life, life abundant. This is a real man."

Adam, when confronted by God, found himself facing exposure. He tried to take the focus off himself and put it onto his wife. He directed the blame to Eve and also tried to implicate God. "If I have covered my transgressions as Adam, by hiding my iniquity in my bosom" (Job 31:33). It is amazing how quickly Adam could expose and blame the one he was so in love with for the sake of hiding his own wrongdoing. He exposed her to keep himself covered. Whereas, *Jesus exposed Himself in flesh and blood on the cross of a criminal to cover His Bride.*

Considering Adam's reaction, we see this same tendency among men today. When things don't go right for them, when they feel the weight of life, and when in the heat of anger or frustration, it can be easy for them to, in some way, blame the wife. It is at these times they are most aware of their inadequacies. They would rather blame the wife, the one they love the most, than to allow their inadequacies to be exposed.

If a man has identified himself by his standard of performance, then to reveal less than that performance, is, in his way of thinking, showing himself to be less of a man. Overshadowing this lie is the lie that his wife is in love with the identity he is trying to protect. Wow, guys! That's a tough, burdensome place to live. The man who chooses commitment to his wife and to his marriage will have to face and destroy these lies.

Eve did not grab Adam, force his mouth open, and shove the fruit down his throat. He, by an act of his own free will, chose to eat. He should have been enough of a man before God to own up to and admit to his disobedience. Likewise today, a godly man should be enough of a man to take responsibility before God for his own behavior, be accountable for his own choices, and admit to his own sin. To do so would render his fears powerless.

My husband recently asked me, "What is 'man enough' "? Without thinking or even hesitating I answered, "Doing the right thing." After we discussed it and I took some time to think about it, I wondered if there really was such a thing as "man enough" or "woman enough" for that matter. Shouldn't it be "person enough"? Every day we are confronted with situations, decisions, and choices. It has little to do with gender. A person, any person, should have enough self-respect and integrity to want to do what is right. It is called character. The quality of character is measured by the choices a person makes.

The problem is that gender mentality has perverted how the character of a man is measured. The strength of a man has been perverted into being tough and macho. His tenderness has been perverted into being weak or sissy. If he cries, he is a wimp. Doing what's right has been lowered on the list of priorities when measuring if he is man enough. It is a tough time for men. With all that the carnal gender mentality and the feminists' mentality has piled on them along with a society that has gone sexually wild, it is a wonder a man can actually know what is right to do. Again, it is coming back to God's definitions and His order that will put a man on solid ground. That is where he will discover who he really is and find the motivation, the strength, and the character to do what's right.

> *And He Himself gave some to be apostles, some prophets, some evangelists, and some pastors and teachers, for the equipping of the saints for the work of ministry, for the edifying of the body of Christ, till we all come to the unity of the faith and of the knowledge of the Son of God, to a perfect man, to the measure of the stature of the fullness of Christ; that we should no longer be children, tossed to and fro and carried about with every wind of doctrine, by the trickery of men, in the cunning craftiness of deceitful plotting, but, speaking the truth in love, may grow up in all things into Him who is the head—Christ* (Ephesians 4:11-15).

After I came to this understanding of commitment or the lack of, I thought perhaps I also now understood "clinging." Then I received a call from my daughter-in-law who had been praying for some friends and had decided to do a word study on the word "cling." She said that in all her searching she never came across the word "commit" in association with "cling." So I continued my searching and discovered that a marriage relationship starts with commitment but is to move on and grow into a greater and different dimension that God calls, "cling." I also recognized that until a husband becomes committed, he will never see or understand "cling." As we begin to discuss the godly gender mentality, hopefully I will be able to, with the help of His Spirit, describe "cling" with all its meaning.

chapter ten | PRIDE AND
REBELLION

Before going on, we must address the topics of pride and rebellion. We need to have a clear understanding of pride and rebellion and how they can keep us from our God-given inheritance and destiny. Pride and rebellion do not have to be learned; they come by inheritance from our father, Adam. They come with the sin nature that is passed down from generation to generation.

Pride says, "*I will!*" It is putting your wants, thoughts, opinions, and beliefs above what God says. It is living your life your way regardless of what God and His Word says. It is making you, the created, and your way of thinking override God, the Creator, and His truth. Pride is a form of idolatry.

Rebellion says, "*I won't!*" It is defiance of authority. It is defiance of God as the highest authority and defiance of the authorities He has placed on the earth. God looks past our behavior and judges our rebellion by what He sees in our heart. It is not enough to behave in compliance with authority; true submission is a matter of the heart. Most have heard the illustration of the little boy who was instructed by his teacher to sit down. He sat down but said, "I am sitting down on the outside, but on the inside I am still standing up." A person who complies with authority while complaining and whining still has rebellion in his heart because *"out of the abundance of the heart the mouth speaks"* (Matt. 12:34b).

Rebellious children, rebellious husbands, and rebellious wives are deceived into thinking they are protecting themselves from parents, teachers, and spouses who want to control them and destroy their value and identity. So pride comes into the picture and says, "I have to take care of *me* first. I have to be sure I get what's mine first." Pride sees humility as simply letting others run over them.

Both men and women have many ways to defend and justify their pride and rebellion. They don't realize that what they believe to be protecting them is actually keeping them separated from God, from God's blessings and provisions, and from real love relationships with others. Until God gives them the eyes to see, they are blinded to the death and destruction that is at work in their lives because of their own pride and rebellion. They are deceived into believing that to admit to having pride and rebellion and giving them up would make them too vulnerable to people and life's circumstances; their end result, however, is the very thing they are fighting against, which is destruction. *"And he who does not take his cross and follow after Me is not worthy of Me. He who finds his life will lose it, and he who loses his life for My sake will find it"* (Matt. 10:38-39). The truth is that until pride and rebellion are broken, they will never move on into maturity receiving their God-given inheritance of righteousness, peace, and joy in the Holy Spirit.

The truths that have been presented on the pages of this book should cause not only women but also men to live in a liberty that allows them to pursue the fullness of who they are and their destinies. I encourage the reader to *"stand fast therefore in the liberty by which Christ has made us free, and do not be entangled again with a yoke of bondage"* (Gal. 5:1). I also encourage you with this Scripture: *"For you, brethren, have been called to liberty; only do not use liberty as an opportunity for the flesh, but through love serve one another. For all the law is fulfilled in one word, even in this: 'You shall love your neighbor as yourself' "* (Gal. 5:13-14). We certainly cannot walk in this kind of liberty with love if we also have pride and rebellion.

One of the truths that have been discussed is that God did not create Eve to cook meals, wash clothes, and clean house. Does this mean women can now say, "I don't have to do these things"? Certainly not! To make it our choice as to what our individual responsibilities should be would mean rebellion is still not broken. In Titus 2:5, the Word instructs the older women to teach the younger women how to be keepers of the home. Those who are in submission to God and who have a yielded heart desire God to tell them what their responsibilities are and are willing to do the things God says to do.

It is rebellion that says, "I want to be married and have children, but I am not going to clean house and cook meals too." It is rebellion that says, "If you don't do what I think you should do, then I am not going to do my part." It is pride that says, "I don't feel like doing it. It is my turn to be served." It is pride and rebellion that believe they have the right to decide what "my responsibilities" are and what they aren't. Ladies, God has not freed us just to do our own thing when we want to do it. Our freedom does not give us the right to abdicate our rightful "place" as God leads us in the home. It frees us from having to conform to the identity that religion and society puts on us. Our freedom does not give us the right to be free from "the requirements" and then turn and cast those requirements on to our husbands or someone else. It is a yielded heart to God that says, "I will do whatever You say do, Lord. My part is what You say my part is. My part and my doing my part is *not* determined by what my spouse or anyone else does or does not do. I want to be like You, Lord. You came to serve; therefore, I choose to serve, not to be served."

Only when pride and rebellion are broken and our heart becomes the heart of a servant can we faithfully walk in our liberty without using it to satisfy the flesh. When God says, "This is the way—walk in it," we willingly choose to do so. Even when God tells us to do some things that we really don't want to do, we willingly choose to do them. We are in love with Him, and it is that love that compels us—not law, not legalism, and not religion.

*chapter eleven* | # WHAT IS MARRIAGE?

Marriage is when a man and a woman come together in covenant with God and each other to become one flesh (see Gen. 2:24). We talk oneness, but perhaps we don't have a clue what it really means from God's perspective. It appears that we spend our entire married lives together just trying to figure out how to become whole and find some happiness, yet never develop oneness. Perhaps we need to take a better look and see if we need to change our thinking on the subject of marriage.

Remember, in the beginning, Adam and Eve were not needy. They were not on a journey to find wholeness and happiness. That was their starting place. God said to them, "Be fruitful and multiply." This was their journey. Although it meant having babies, it also meant they were to be fruitful, first individually, and then multiply together in *every aspect of their beings and capabilities.* In so doing they would replenish the earth, subdue it, and take dominion.

What we are seeing in marriage today is two separate people trying to gain wholeness and well-being by demanding it from the other. Or, she demands it from him as he turns to get it from his work, occupation, or career. Home to him is simply where he goes to eat and rest so he can get back to the job; and marriage is where he gets sex. Husbands and wives are competing to see who can become the greatest victim, wasting their married lives, and greatly limiting their individual lives. Forget about life abundant; they are just trying to survive living with this other person.

I know this because I lived it. By my mid-30s I had tried and used everything in my power to get my husband into the place where I didn't feel needy anymore. At times, I would use kindness, and when that didn't work, I would turn to manipulation and guilt. I agreed with him even when I didn't. I tried to get involved in his interests, taking up golf and hating it. Because he participated in every sport available, I went to his football games, his basketball games, his softball games, and was his biggest fan. When it came to going to plays or concerts, I took a grumbling husband, or I went alone, or I didn't go. I actually believed I had no security, acceptance, worth, or identity unless my husband provided it. Of course, he failed because he wasn't God. I would be and do what I was "supposed" to be or do. And when he failed to give what I needed, I felt abandoned, neglected, and cheated, because this was the only life I was ever going to have, and I was stuck with it. I literally felt my youth was being wasted away day by day.

Nowadays divorce is an easy option, but for me it was no option. So I began to search the Word of God to find out what was wrong with me in hopes I could discover something that would bring some fulfillment and contentment to my life. Without realizing it at the time, I was really putting God in His rightful place, and I have not been disappointed with the results. I found what I was looking for, and it was not dependent on any man other than the Man, Jesus. I found my security, my acceptance, and my worth in Him. I found my wholeness and my identity in Him. And finally, I was ready to learn how to be a wife.

We cannot bypass relationship with our God and then expect to find all we are longing for in marriage or in life. We might think we are fighting and striving against people and circumstances that are working against us. "If this person would do right, or if that person would get off my back, or if these circumstances would change, then I could be happy, then I could have some peace and make my life count." I'm sorry, but this thinking is deception. If we can't let God raise us up to His place of security, acceptance, and value in the midst of people and circumstances, it will never happen. So, how does God raise us up? By renewing our minds, giving us the mind of Christ, or just plain and simple—changing our thinking.

*And do not be conformed to this world, but be transformed by the renewing of your mind, that you may prove what is that good and acceptable and perfect will of God* (Romans 12:2).

If we insist on holding on to our carnal gender mentality thinking, even though it is not reaping fruits of righteousness, peace, and joy (which is the Kingdom of God), then we will remain in our rut of mundane, coping, and enduring life. Women will remain in the cave, and men will be content having them stay there. We can pray and hope for something better, but never quite get there. However, that's just not good enough for me. I believe what the Bible tells me that I can have, *I can have.* Since there is no being or power on earth or in Heaven that can keep it from me, then I am the only one who can stand in my way. How do I stand in my way when I really want something better? By refusing to give up my "stinking thinking."

Let me describe a scenario with which many should identify: The wife comes to the husband and says, "We have to talk." Then she begins to say things like, "I need more of a relationship with you. I feel like I really don't matter that much to you. The only time you give me attention is when you want sex. I need more quality time with you. I feel so alone." Now the husband's reaction will depend on how many times she has previously had this discussion with him. The first few times he will probably get offended and defensive, deny her accusations, and justify himself. They will end up walking away from the encounter with her believing he won't listen to her and that he really doesn't care, and him believing she wants everything her way and that's her problem. Nothing is solved or resolved, just made worse. It appears they have taken one giant step backward from oneness.

If the wife is persistent in pursuing the relationship she believes she needs, then the husband will find himself in this conversation regularly. Pretty soon he figures he needs to change his reaction. His first reaction has accomplished nothing, so he needs to find what he has to do to get her off his back. Now he says, "I will try to do better." And he does try to do better—for a week or two or three. Then everything gravitates back to how it was before.

Can't we agree that this relationship is just going around in circles, which will eventually spiral down to a dead end? What is wrong with this scenario? Here are two people who are supposed to be growing into oneness, who come into an encounter or confrontation, each thinking their own way and walk out of the encounter still thinking their own way. The result is *nothing changes*. The husband may really mean it when he says he is going to try to do better, but if nothing changes in his thinking, nothing is going to permanently change in his behavior. He will always revert back to previous behavior.

So how do we stop the cycle? Both wife and husband need to be willing to do something differently and honestly ask God first and then ask themselves and each other several questions: "Where am I thinking wrong? What are my wrong perceptions? How am I supposed to be seeing this? What is the truth about my marriage relationship? Have I placed judgment on my spouse and my marriage? Am I being self-centered?" Then we have to be willing to see and own up to the truth. Remember, it is the truth that we come to know personally that makes us free. If we retain the lies and continue to justify them, we retain the bondage. Somewhere, thinking has to change.

Getting honest in marriage is horrifically difficult to do. It is why we say marriage is "hard work." At the root of our wrong thinking or wrong perceptions can be rejection, resentment, jealousy, insignificance, etc. and probably a whole lot of fear, anger, and pain. In fact, we have established mind-sets to protect ourselves: "Nobody's going to hurt me like that again." "It's my way or the highway." "If they really see the truth about me, they will abandon me." These are not just roadblocks to oneness, they are iron walls; and to bring them down means facing hard, painful issues. The question is: Do we have the guts to do it? If we want a good, healthy, godly marriage, then our heavenly Father will faithfully empower and grace us to face our fear, anger, and pain, and defeat them.

At this point, pride shows itself to be a powerful enemy. We have insisted on being right for so long that we would rather die or at least stay in bondage than to admit to being wrong. We may try to get away with secretly owning up to being wrong, but God's Word says, "*Confess your faults one to another, and pray one for another, that ye may be healed. The effectual fervent prayer of a righteous man availeth much*" (Jas. 5:16 KJV). I know this Scripture is usually used in reference to physical healing, but we cannot separate physical healing from soul healing. Remember, the Bible says in Third John 2, "*Beloved, I wish above all things that thou mayest prosper and be in health, even as thy soul prospereth*" (KJV). Healing comes from confessing faults and praying, not hiding them in secret.

117

To whom do we confess? The person or persons to whom God sends us. He may send us to a "safe" person who will listen to us, speak forgiveness to us, and encourage us. Ultimately He will send us to those we have failed and wounded. It is impossible to have carnal thinking in a relationship without causing wounds. The question is: Do you want God's greatness for you, or not? Do you want God's greatness for your marriage, or not? If you do, then kill your pride and do what may be the hardest thing you have ever done in your life. Admit to your wrong.

This is what marriage is. It is a place where we can lose our life so we can find it. *"If anyone desires to come after Me, let him deny himself, and take up his cross, and follow Me. For whoever desires to save his life will lose it, but whoever loses his life for My sake will find it"* (Matt. 16:24b-25). It is the process of becoming one, bearing fruit, and entering into the dimension of multiplication. There is a greatness beyond what we are experiencing that is worth all we need to lose in order to gain it. Are you willing to take the risk?

Becoming one does not mean giving up individuality. Jesus said, *"Have you not read that He who made them at the beginning 'made them male and female,' and said, 'For this reason a man shall leave his father and mother and be joined to his wife, and the two shall become one flesh?' So then, they are no longer two but one flesh. Therefore what God has joined together, let not man separate"* (Matt. 19:4-6). Notice that this Scripture says that husband and wife are to become *"one flesh,"* not one soul or one spirit. Flesh is the body. Two are joined together as one body, and contained in that body are all the individual talents, gifts, and abilities that make up each soul and each spirit. When they become one, they do not lose who they are individually in their soul or spirit. The person of the man is not to overtake the person of the woman. They each remain who they are, but yield it to the multiplication process to increase each other.

Let's look again at multiplication. For multiplication to have a product or a result that is more than zero, the smallest multiplication equation, except for fractions, is one times one. Zero times one will always result in zero. For a woman or a man to abandon any part of who they are as an individual in their soul, would be to offer zero to that part in the marriage equation. Wouldn't this make increase in the marriage impossible?

Multiplying fractions results in an answer that is smaller than one times one, and look at the results: One times one-half produces only one-half. One-half times one-half equals one-fourth. The result is diminishing, not increasing. And diminishing is what happens when either spouse withholds any part of themselves from the other. Again, we see that marriage should be two *whole* people joining together in the fullness of all they are individually to become one flesh. Marriage isn't 50/50, is it? It must be 100/100.

When one spouse is not coming through with their 100 percent, the other spouse may try to compensate. But when someone is already giving 100 percent, how can they possibly give more? It results in pushing and striving, which can eventually lead to resentment for having to carry too much of the responsibility. However, when the two work together in balance, they increase without losing their individuality.

My husband is a county judge and a community leader. Most days when he leaves for work, I know little or nothing about his schedule or his specific duties for the day. Of course, he never discusses an impending court case with me. Occasionally, if he is presented with an unusual or difficult case, he will discuss it with me after the fact. He shares his life with me in hopes I can give life back to him in the form of affirmation and assurance, not from my knowledge of the law, but from my knowledge of him. In addition, as county judge, he oversees certain county business. Occasionally, there are issues that he discusses with me wanting the dimension of vision and understanding that comes from our two perspectives at work together. This is where multiplication happens. He continues to function individually at his job, but he is increased because of the multiplication that happens in our marriage.

My husband's first step into politics was to be elected to the city commission. After that, he served as mayor for several years. While serving as mayor and county judge, there were, among others, three major projects he was instrumental in accomplishing. As a result, three monument plaques have been erected, two of which include the name of "Mayor Richard Peet," and the third says, "Judge Richard Peet." They don't include "Mayor Richard and Carol Peet." I had nothing to do with those projects. I have had a lot to do with Richard Peet, but I had nothing to do with the projects. It was Richard functioning in his individuality as God made him to function. I receive personal honor through his accomplishments and it is sufficient for me to just silently stand by my husband's side.

This example of my husband is probably typical of many marriages and would receive no complaint. Now let's look at the other side of the coin.

I have a ministry called Carol Peet Ministries. My husband knew the call of God on my life when he married me, and he knew my relationship with God was the most important thing to me. He has totally accepted it and never in all the years we have been married has expected that to change. In fact, he hasn't just accepted it; he has gotten behind it and encouraged it. But he was not the one who spent hours on his face before God seeking answers. He didn't spend hours upon hours in the Word trying to understand. He didn't spend the days and weeks in prayer and fasting that birthed Carol Peet Ministries. It was Carol functioning in her individuality as God made her to function. But in no way does it diminish Richard Peet. He may sit in silence as I minister, but what cannot be seen is the honor and enlargement he is personally experiencing.

It must be emphasized here again that competition cannot have a part in marriage. Competition does not allow freedom of expression to both individuals. It seeks to diminish or causes one's value to lessen for the sake of the other.

Yes, I know what it says in John 3:30—*"He must increase, but I must decrease."* We are supposed to decrease, but it is in our self-life, which includes self-motivation, self-gratification, self-promotion, and self-exaltation, in which we are to decrease. Actually, our self-life is to die. Even though the act of baptism is an act of death to the self-life, it is realized experientially little by little as we go through the process of dying daily. As our self-life decreases, Jesus' life in us increases. Let me share some Scripture with you:

> *Then God blessed them, and God said to them, "Be fruitful and multiply; fill the earth and subdue it; have dominion over the fish of the sea, over the birds of the air, and over every living thing that moves on the earth"* (Genesis 1:28).

> *Enlarge the place of your tent, and let them stretch out the curtains of your dwellings; do not spare; lengthen your cords, and strengthen your stakes. For you shall expand to the right and to the left, and your descendants will inherit the nations, and make the desolate cities inhabited* (Isaiah 54:2-3).

> *He shall be like a tree planted by the rivers of water, that brings forth its fruit in its season, whose leaf also shall not wither; and whatever he does shall prosper* (Psalm 1:3).

All these Scriptures speak increase. The best yet is Colossians 2:18-19:

> *Let no one cheat you of your reward, taking delight in false humility and worship of angels, intruding into those things which he has not seen, vainly puffed up by his fleshly mind, and not holding fast to the Head, from whom all the body,*

*nourished and knit together by joints and ligaments, grows with the increase that is from God.*

When we speak of greatness, again, we are not talking about the greatness of the self-life. We mean obtaining the greatness for which we were created. "Not that I have already attained, or am already perfected; but I press on, that I may lay hold of that for which Christ Jesus has also laid hold of me" (Phil. 3:12). It could mean being known by the masses as a person functions in his destiny. It could also mean living in obscurity as Anna who prayed daily in the temple at Jerusalem. Her greatness allowed her to see and recognize her Messiah who was yet a baby being held in Mary's arms (see Luke 2:36-38).

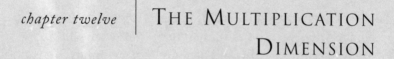

chapter twelve | THE MULTIPLICATION
DIMENSION

### REAL INTIMACY OR BARRENNESS

We may not fully grasp the depth, but surely we can recognize the grief-stricken sorrow in the heart of a barren woman. Women were created with a womb and the God-given desire to be fruitful. They were created to receive seed, to bear it and nurture it, and then to birth it into the natural realm. Some, for various reasons, may choose not to have children. But for those who yield to their desire but find, for no apparent reason or reasons beyond their control, that their womb is denied, there is great lamenting. Hannah was so grieved as she sought God for a child, that the priest, Eli, thought she was drunk (see 1 Sam. 1:13). Likewise, Sarah's sorrow drove her to desperate means when she sent her husband to her servant's bed (see Gen. 16:1-4). What we see here is a woman's barrenness in the first dimension.

There are other kinds of barrenness women can experience. When God put Adam and his wife, Eve, into the Garden of Eden, He instructed them to "be fruitful and multiply." Of course, we know they were intended to have children and bring forth another generation that in turn was to bring forth another generation. This is how they, and now we, are to multiply in the physical, which is the first dimension. But physical is only one aspect of the total human person. We are also mental, emotional, social, and spiritual beings, and in these areas we are also to "be fruitful and multiply."

The second dimension of barrenness that women can experience involves the dimension of the soul where we function mentally, emotionally, and socially. Yes, a woman can function well mentally, emotionally, and socially as a person and do great exploits independent of a man. But in her marriage she was designed by God to be a receiver and a helper. Her nature and purpose in the second dimension of her marriage is no different than that of the first dimension. She is a receiver and a helper. When no seed is being offered to her, when no seed is being imparted into the womb of her heart, she begins to feel void of purpose and impotent as a helper in the second dimension. The result is barrenness. She may call it loneliness, having no meaning or purpose, or living an empty life, but it is barrenness. Barrenness in the second dimension is the lack of intimacy in the marriage and can kill her passion to receive seed in the first dimension.

Remember it takes two to enter into the dimension of multiplication. One times zero is zero, whereas one times one is *one*. Through marriage, God gave the multiplied potential for greatness to the two becoming one. We have learned that this also applies to their potential mentally, emotionally, and socially, as well as physically. This power of multiplication happens only when seed is being given and received. How is seed given and received in the second dimension? In the parables of the sower (see Matt. 13:3-30), seed is given by speaking a truth about the nature of God. It is received when it is taken into the heart, pondered, believed, embraced, and allowed to become one with the receiver. Therefore, seed in the second dimension is given and received through *communication!* It is heart-to-heart, soul-to-soul communication. *This is intimacy!*

When the man reveals the nature of his inner person to his wife, when he shares with her who and what he is mentally and emotionally, he is giving her seed. Giving seed is talking about hopes and dreams, goals in life, and plans for the future. It is talking about insecurities, failures, and fears, letdowns and disappointments, and rejections and pain. It is discussing decisions and choices that have to be made. It is talking about memories of the past (good and bad), likes and dislikes, and what really bugs you. It is discussing and talking about the issues of both lives. *"Keep thy heart with all diligence; for out of it are the issues of life"* (Prov. 4:23 KJV). It is listening to, finding out, discovering, and learning the other person. A man "knowing" his wife is not just sex. He should know her heart as well as he knows her body. *"Likewise, ye husbands, dwell with them according to knowledge, giving honor unto the wife, as unto the weaker vessel, and as being heirs together of the grace of life; that your prayers be not hindered"* (1 Pet. 3:7 KJV). *This is intimacy!*

Seed is also given and received socially when there is interaction such as working and playing together. Working together on jobs or projects and sharing fun times in life are essential in the dimension of multiplication. Couples who believe they can't work together are couples who really don't "know" each other. Pressing through and communicating about those things that hinder couples in working together can take them through a process of learning to "know" each other. Is it easy? *No!* But the results of multiplication can be well worth it. Although there can be room for separate interests, a couple who does not regularly have fun together will have a large void in the multiplication dimension.

As the wife receives the seed of the revelation of her husband's inner nature into the womb of her soul, she will ponder it in her heart and nurture it, which will give her power to birth life to it. In other words, she hears his dream. She receives his dream, holding it in the womb of her heart, and she finds that it connects with and penetrates the potential that is deep within her. She ponders it and nurtures it. She embraces it as her dream, becoming one with it. Then she gives life to it in the form of words, speaking hope, encouragement, strength, and possibilities. This is her function as his helpmate in the second dimension. It is the function of intimacy, and it can take marriage to greater heights. Isn't it also how the Bride of Christ is to function in the earth?

The wife can also receive the seed of revelation of her husband's inner fears, failures, and pain into the womb of her heart, finding that it touches and penetrates potential deep within her. As she ponders and nurtures it, life will be birthed that can speak love, encouragement, and healing to his fears, failures, and pain. It is this intimacy that allows her to function as his helpmate in the second dimension, and it can create greater potential for the marriage.

If the husband does not become intimate with his wife and communicate with her, if he does not share his heart or his nature with her, the womb of her soul in the marriage is barren. She is not given what she needs to grow life to give to him. She feels discontent, dissatisfied, and a failure as a helpmate. Barrenness in the second dimension can also cause an unhappy, lamenting wife.

Now we can understand how a wife can begin to lose her desire for sex and even come to hate it. The barrenness that she feels can rob her of the security, acceptance, and value she needs to function as a wife. If she is not accepted and considered important enough to be offered seed to the womb of her soul, then she can begin to feel like she is simply her husband's personal prostitute in the physical dimension. Love to the woman is the intimacy that happens in the second dimension; therefore, when that intimacy is absent, she no longer considers sex as love-making—it is an obligation.

We have defined barrenness in the physical and in the soul, which is mental, emotional, and social. Now let's look at the spiritual. All seed in the spiritual must come from God. Remember, when God reveals Himself to us, it comes in the form of seed that we, both male and female, receive. As we believe it and embrace it, we become one with it. We become the vessels in which and through which He reproduces His life. This is what we call having an intimate relationship with God. Because the male is part of the Bride of Christ, he must function in the spirit realm as the female functions in being the receiver of the seed. To his head, Christ, he is the receiver, and then he turns to the wife and is the giver of the seed he has received. It goes without saying that if the husband is not being intimate with Christ, he is not receiving spiritual seed from Him, so he has no spiritual seed to give. He must realize that he has to present himself to Christ with the same willingness, openness, and passion that he desires his wife to present herself to him.

Because in Christ there is no male or female, the woman can also receive seed from Him and become fruitful and productive in reproducing His life (just like Mary did in the first dimension). But in the marriage where there should be the power of multiplication, the husband must be receiving and giving spiritual seed. He can't just be receiving it. He must also give it to multiply. Spiritual seed is given in the same way seed is given to the womb of the soul—through communication, which is how intimacy happens.

Spiritual barrenness in the spiritual dimension is different from the barrenness in the second dimension of the marriage. In the second dimension of marriage, Jesus will not trespass into the place He has given to the husband. Jesus will not give seed He has ordered and supplied the husband to give. Barrenness in the marriage will remain barren until the husband gives seed. Also, Jesus will not trespass into the place He has given to the wife. He will not receive seed the husband wants to give, when the wife is not willing to receive it. Barrenness in the marriage will remain barren until the wife receives the seed.

An individual person in intimacy with Jesus is never left barren spiritually. His seed is plentiful, and He is always ready and willing to give it to those who come to Him in intimacy. Spiritually, as an individual, we need never feel barren. A husband or a wife can feel complete, secure, accepted, unconditionally loved, valued, and fruitful in their relationship with God, yet they can still feel empty or barren in the relationship with their spouse. It was to a married couple whom God gave the commission to be fruitful, multiply, subdue the earth, and have dominion. With this in mind, can we be content having only a relationship with God, while ignoring and bypassing our marriage, and still plan to take dominion?

*"And God blessed them, and God said unto them, Be fruitful, and multiply, and replenish the earth, and subdue it: and have dominion over the fish of the sea, and over the fowl of the air, and over every living thing that moveth upon the earth"* (Gen. 1:28 KJV). I believe that to subdue the earth and have dominion over it, it is going to require the greatness that only comes through the process of multiplication. We will not be able to enter into the third dimension of the Kingdom of God until we bring marriage back into God's order and follow the plan in the way God has ordered it to be done.

Surely we can see that at the core of a successful marriage is intimacy, the ability to give and receive seed in all dimensions. Giving and receiving seed is the marriage relationship functioning in order. If we don't get this right, then we will not get any of it right. We will simply be going through the motions of marriage without the real substance. Oneness will be out of the question. We can just forget about multiplication and greatness.

So, how can those who don't marry enter into the dimension of multiplication? When there is no spouse, then Jesus, without trespassing, can enter into that place of completing the multiplication equation of "one times one is one." Paul is our scriptural example.

## FAILURE IN GIVING AND RECEIVING SEED

Just as there are barren women who don't want or cannot have children, there are barren women who won't or can't receive second-dimension seed from their husband. Also, there are impotent men who can't or won't give seed in the second dimension. There appears to be various reasons for this, but it all goes back to their lack of security, acceptance, and value along with a perverted identity. By a perverted identity, I mean anything we believe about ourselves that is not what and who God created us to be—everything we believe about ourselves that is *not* the truth. It usually happens long before the person is married.

We have discussed how everything reproduces after its kind, and that parents reproduce in their children who and what they have been. If they lack security, acceptance, and value, or if they have a perverted identity, these life patterns will be passed along to the children. Parents who never knew intimacy are unable to give intimacy to their children. Mothers who are filled with resentment and negative attitudes toward men can communicate attitudes that cause their sons to be insecure in their ability to give seed, and cause their daughters to close up the womb of their souls rejecting intimacy with a man. Fathers who are not involved in their children's lives or fathers who are harsh and abusive can likewise have negative influences.

There are other people such as siblings, extended family members, teachers, coaches, neighbors, and even church leaders who are in positions to negatively affect how children learn to see themselves.

It is not so uncommon for children, boys as well as girls, to find themselves, through no fault of their own, in victimizing circumstances, such as sexual abuse, which feed them lies about who and what they are.

Let's face it, we all have had to go through "stuff" when growing up, and all of it has had an effect on us. Experiences, good and bad, have their part in telling us who we are and what we can and cannot do. Chances are most of us have had to deal with or are dealing with a perverted identity. Although it is important to come to an understanding and a reconciliation of all these negative influences, it is of extreme importance that we do not allow them to continue to identify us. It is of extreme importance that we no longer allow them to dictate to us our security, our acceptance, and our value; otherwise, we can never afford to become vulnerable enough to come into intimacy. We must keep ourselves protected.

We have identified five aspects or parts of the human being: physical, mental, emotional, social, and spiritual. We can also call them five avenues through which we relate to God, ourselves, and each other. If over time we receive repeated rejection in one of these parts, we will withdraw that part and shut it down. Consequently, it cannot give or receive seed.

For example, a young child functioning in a normal young child mentality does something awkward—has an accident or spills something—and the parent says something like, "You should know better than that. You are so stupid. Don't you have any brains in that head?" Once the child believes these statements as truth, he or she begins to withdraw mentally, and ceases to function in the mental abilities he or she does have. Soon the child will be living up to the accusations. This is a picture of how a person becomes rejected.

As you can see, we are not rejected until we accept a lie as the truth. It doesn't matter what others say to us, and it doesn't matter how ugly and mean they are to us; these things cannot cause us to be rejected until we accept them as rejection. We can accept rejection in one, two, and even all five aspects of the human being; and when it happens, we cease to function in those areas. It doesn't mean we can't function or we don't have the ability to function; it means we have shut those areas down, refusing to allow them to function. We don't want to experience more rejection. Consequently, in the areas we shut down, we cannot give or receive seed.

It would be wonderful if we could provide a list of do's and don'ts that would bring everyone into the whole and healthy place they need to be so that they are able to give and receive seed, but it just doesn't work that way. Each individual has to come into his own personal, intimate relationship with his Creator, where he finds everything that is missing from his life, and where he can untwist everything that has been made crooked about his identity. I have written a course study entitled "Living Resurrection Life" that can help guide individuals and groups toward discovering their full God-given identity.

The truth is no one has to stay barren or impotent. There is healing for the soul, and it comes by truth. *"Then said Jesus to those Jews which believed on Him, If ye continue in My word, then are ye My disciples indeed; and ye shall know the truth, and the truth shall make you free "* (John 8:31-32 KJV). Free from what? Free from everything that has us bound or imprisoned. It is the truth that we *know* that makes us free. We can know the truth only by seeking it.

*Ask, and it shall be given you; seek, and ye shall find; knock, and it shall be opened unto you: for every one that asketh receiveth; and he that seeketh findeth; and to him that knocketh it shall be opened. Or what man is there of you, whom if his son ask bread, will he give him a stone? Or if he ask a fish, will he give him a serpent? If ye then, being evil, know how to give good gifts unto your children, how much more shall your Father which is in heaven give good things to them that ask Him?* (Matthew 7:7-11 KJV)

If you really want to know the truth, then you will take the time and effort to seek the truth. That means, read the Word, listen to the Word, and meditate or think on the Word. You will not be disappointed. It is likely that nothing you think is significant will happen the first day you begin to seek, and maybe not the first week. But I assure you that with consistent persistence, God will show up and words from His Word will begin to pop out to you. That is God speaking to you. Listen to them, think on them, and fit them into your life. The truth will make you free.

## SEED GIVEN AND RECEIVED ILLEGALLY

A relationship with another person is the greatest gift God has given to mankind next to relationship with Him. We could visit all the Seven Wonders of the World and be awed with their magnificence, but they could never give to us the companionship, the encouragement, and the sense of belonging that happens in our daily relationships. Our homes could be furnished with all the most modern inventions and furnishings available and enhanced with the most artistic décor created, but would only be sterile buildings of loneliness without the interactions of relationships.

All our relationships are valuable and have their part in adding dimension, purpose, joy, fulfillment, interest, and help to our lives. There is the parent-child relationship, the sibling relationship, the teacher-student relationship, the business relationship, and best friend relationship. Of course, the most unique relationship is the relationship between a husband and his wife. It is the only relationship where the two are to become one.

In the first dimension of the natural or physical, we understand that seed can be given and received illegally.

*The wrath of God is being revealed from heaven against all the godlessness and wickedness of men who suppress the truth by their wickedness, since what may be known about God is plain to them, because God has made it plain to them. For since the creation of the world God's invisible qualities—His eternal power and divine nature—have been clearly seen, being understood from what has been made, so that men are without excuse. For although they knew God, they neither glorified Him as God nor gave thanks to Him, **but their thinking became futile and their foolish hearts were darkened.** Although they clamed to be wise, they became fools and exchanged the glory of the immortal God for images made to look like mortal man and birds and animals and reptiles. Therefore God gave them over in the sinful desires of their hearts to sexual impurity for the degrading of their bodies with one another. **They exchanged the truth of God for a lie,** and worshiped and served created things rather than the Creator—who is forever praised. Amen Because of this, God gave them over to shameful lusts. Even their women exchanged natural relations for unnatural ones. In the same way the men also abandoned natural relations with women and were inflamed with lust for one another. Men committed indecent acts with other men, and received in themselves the due penalty for their perversion. Furthermore, since they did not think it worthwhile to retain the knowledge of God, He gave them over to a depraved mind, to do what ought not to be done* (Romans 1:18-28 NIV, emphasis added).

Notice in verse 21 that because man didn't glorify and praise God, their thinking became futile and their hearts were darkened. *Darkness* means lack of *knowledge.* In other words, they ignored God. How do you ignore God? How do you ignore anyone? You don't listen to them. When one of our sons was a junior in college, he took off for California with some of his friends over spring break without telling us. I am the mother of three sons, and from the time they were born I have prayed, "Lord, when they ever try to step outside the legal bounds You have set for them, please let them get caught." They knew I prayed that way, and from their own experiences, they knew it worked. The second day our son was gone, we found out about it. When he returned he said, "I decided I would rather have to apologize when I got back than to take a chance on telling you before and having you say I shouldn't go." He didn't ask us to help him *know* what was best for him. This is the way Christians ignore God. We would rather do things our way than to take a chance of seeking God and discovering that He doesn't agree with us. No place is this any truer than with our sexual desires and pleasures.

In the physical, giving and receiving seed illegally (or according to this Scripture, unnaturally) includes incest, homosexuality, masturbation, fornication, and adultery. When there are illegalities in the physical, we will always find corresponding illegalities in the second dimension of the soul. In fact, illegalities start in the soul as we entertain illegal thoughts before they are ever carried out in the physical. Jesus said, "*You have heard that it was said to those of old, 'You shall not commit adultery.' But I say to you that whoever looks at a woman to lust for her has already committed adultery with her in his heart*" (Matt. 5:27-28).

An individual may allow illegal scenarios to be played out in his or her mind, thinking he or she would never really do it. Society calls it "fantasizing." But once something is conceived in the mind, it can very likely become a physical activity. Isn't it a law of nature that everything that is conceived wants to be birthed?

As we have identified giving and receiving seed illegally in the physical, let us now identify the corresponding illegalities that can be active in giving and receiving seed in the dimension of the soul. Again, let me say that all our relationships are important and have their place in our lives. It is only when we allow another relationship to fill a place or function of intimacy that belongs only to the spouse that we begin to cross the illegal line.

We can call it incest when a spouse still goes to mom or dad to get what should now come from the intimate relationship with the mate, when mom or dad is being chosen over the mate. Does the parent hear the "news" before the mate? Is anything discussed with the parent first? Is the parent's opinion always favored and trusted over the mate's? Are there "apron strings" that need to be cut?

Moms and Dads, have you put your children into the place that belongs to the mate? Do you choose your children over your mate? Moms have the greater tendency toward this. The husband, because he has problems or just doesn't have it right, may be leaving his wife barren in her soul, but that does not justify her turning to her children to fill the void or seeking intimacy from her children. A parent may even confide to his or her children while hiding it from the spouse. To do so creates unhealthy "apron strings," giving the children a false responsibility and a perverted loyalty to their parent. This is second-dimension incest.

A best-friend relationship is a special one with its own kind of intimacy. Many of us doubt that we could have ever gotten through some hard times if it hadn't have been for the faithfulness of a best friend. And best friends usually know us the best. Actually, the husband and the wife should be each other's best friend and know each other best, but we haven't understood intimacy, the giving and receiving of seed in the second dimension. I think we are beginning to see the point here and recognize that there is a line that even best friends cannot legally cross. Please do not hear that I am calling best-friend relationships illegal. They are valuable and have their place. They become wrong only when we turn to the best friend for the intimacy that belongs to the mate. How do we know when this has happened? We know by honestly asking ourselves before the Lord, "Is there any place where I have chosen my friend over my mate?"

There can be those spouses who have never turned from their friends to come into intimacy with their mate. Their interaction with their friends is as important if not more important than what is going on in their marriage. We can call it second-dimension homosexuality. Seed that is supposed to be given to the wife is being given to the guys on the golf course, in the locker room, at the coffee shop, at the pool hall, or on the job. His friends know more about what is going on in his private life and what he is thinking than his wife does. How much does the wife hear secondhand from someone else or never hears at all?

Can we call it second-dimension lesbianism when barren women open their wombs to seedless relations with friends over lunch, in the fellowship hall kitchen, at the beauty shop, at the mall, or on the job? It can be called gossip or a "pity party." Do they get to hear all the "ugly" things about the husband? And how many secrets are being kept from the husband that only the ladies know?

I dare say that every adulterous affair started with giving and receiving illegal seed in the second dimension first. Even if they are not being sexually active physically, can't we still call it adultery when a man and woman, who are not married to each other, function in the intimacy of giving and receiving seed in the soul, which belongs only to the husband and wife? How do you know that it is illegal seed? It is illegal seed when you justify it with your spouse's failures: "My wife does not understand me." "I just can't talk to my spouse." "My husband doesn't listen to me." "He is never there for me."

*And Judah said unto Onan, Go in unto thy brother's wife, and marry her, and raise up seed to thy brother. And Onan knew that the seed should not be his; and it came to pass, when he went in unto his brother's wife, that he spilled it on the ground, lest that he should give seed to his brother. And the thing which he did displeased the Lord: wherefore he slew him also* (Genesis 38:8-10 KJV).

It was the Jewish custom that if a man died leaving his wife widowed, his brother would take the widow for his own wife, giving her children who would help take care of her in her old age. It displeased God that Onan spilled his seed on the ground.

Let's talk about married individuals who want to stay in their aloneness. We can call them loners. It is usually abandonment and pain that causes aloneness. Loner husbands still have seed to give in the second dimension, and they have wives who are still waiting to receive their seed. But it appears safer to remain alone in the dimension of the soul. So he functions alone and makes independent plans and decisions, keeping them to himself, which is no different from masturbation. Man is made of the dust from the *ground,* and to keep his seed just for himself is simply spilling it out on the ground. However, God gave him seed for the purpose of becoming fruitful. Seed spilt on the ground dies without ever coming into fruition, and his wife remains barren in the second dimension.

Wives who are loners are sterile. Like the man, it is abandonment and pain that makes a woman a loner. Their hearts become so callused that seed cannot penetrate. They can fill their role faithfully and efficiently, oftentimes waiting on the husband hand and foot, but they cannot relate with their husband to the depth of receiving his seed. They cannot hear his heart, embrace his dreams, or connect with his pain, so barrenness remains.

I call this chapter on giving and receiving seed the real core of the marriage relationship. This is where real relationship happens. This is the foundation of marriage and is the beginning of entering into the multiplication dimension. This is intimacy, and sex hasn't even been mentioned. So what about sex?

chapter thirteen | SO WHAT ABOUT SEX?

First of all, sex is *not* intimacy! If a man can walk off the street into the bed of a prostitute, who is a perfect stranger, then sex is not intimacy. If a husband can come home from a day on the job and get into bed with his wife, to whom he has hardly spoken and given no attention, and expect her to perform sex, then sex is not intimacy. *Sex, if done right, should be the result of intimacy.* In fact, becoming sexually active before intimacy develops, can make sex the greatest hindrance to intimacy. A man who is getting his sexual desires satisfied cannot understand what the woman is talking about when she says she needs relationship and intimacy. He walks away believing she has a problem. Sex is not intimacy.

Secondly, the Bible never calls sex a need. It is a desire (see Deut. 5:21; 21:11; 2 Chron. 11:23; Dan. 11:37). Society calls sex a need. What is a *need*? Webster's Dictionary defines it as "a necessity or something required." Air is a necessity. Food and water are necessities. Shelter and clothing are necessities. A necessity is something a person can't live without. To a diabetic, insulin is a necessity. To someone whose kidneys have shut down, dialysis is a necessity. Sex is not a necessity. Identifying it as a need has taken it out of its proper place in the balance of life. Sex has become more and more important, making other things such as relationship and intimacy in the second dimension less important. It has become out of order as God ordered it in marriage.

If sex were a necessity, then why would God limit it to the marriage relationship only? He makes it plain in His Word that fornication or sex before marriage is not in His order. Abstinence for single people who never marry or for some reason find themselves no longer married is His order. When society defined sex as a need, it justified ignoring God's order for the sake of sexual pleasure at will, which is really lust. Now, having sex whenever and with whomever has become accepted as being comfortable with one's sexuality and being able to express one's self freely. But the fact is, it's still out of God's order, diminishing its real purpose in marriage; and when we operate out of God's order, there are consequences.

We all are aware of these consequences—sexually transmitted diseases, unwanted pregnancies, abortion, and children being raised by single parents. But the consequence I would like to discuss is what it has done to the marriage relationship. Sex being given and taken so freely outside the marriage has diminished the value of marriage in the minds of society. It has not diminished marriage nor can it diminish marriage. Marriage is what God calls it. Anything we add to it or take away from it and still call marriage is not marriage. Marriage is what God calls it, and I have tried to describe His definition throughout this writing. It is when the value of marriage has been diminished that we begin to question why we should be committed to something that is going to take lots of effort, hard work, and trusting God to establish?

When people realize that it will require more of them than perhaps they will receive in return, it becomes too easy to get out.

Once marriage has been diminished in the minds of society, then individuals begin to settle for less. Relationships are no longer based on love, intimacy, and the giving and receiving of seed in the second dimension, but on selfish desire which turns into lust. What is called love is only an illusion of love. It is what each has created in their carnal mind that they think to be love. If one partner doesn't live up to the other partner's expectation of love, then it justifies the right to terminate the relationship. That isn't love. Potential of greatness is lost. Ruling and taking dominion turns into controlling and manipulating to be sure "I get what I want. It's my life and I'll do it my way." Thus, the multiplication dimension is never discovered.

Thirdly, sex is not an obligation. The husband comes home from a day on the job having little or nothing to say to his wife. He gets the newspaper and parks himself in front of the television, or maybe he changes clothes and goes out to the garage or his workshop to do whatever he does. When dinner is ready, he comes to the table. Again conversation is sparse, and he responds only when it is absolutely necessary. Or maybe he does talk during dinner about what is wrong at home or wrong on the job. After dinner, he returns to where he came from before dinner. Granted this could be an occasional, typical evening in any household, but what about day after day after day? The husband has given his wife no attention and in no way has communicated her value to him. It's bedtime and they get into bed. Sometimes he stills smells like his job or whatever he has been doing in the garage. Then his hand comes to her breast. He has not held her or kissed her or told her he loves her. He hasn't even communicated with her. What is she supposed to do? He has given her no attention much less quality time of intimacy. So what is she supposed to do? She may know he loves her, but she is feeling no love. He has said nothing to move her emotionally. He has given nothing to touch the heart of her sexuality which rests in her emotions. She is not feeling like a woman in love. She is feeling like an object or a piece of meat to be handled. So what does she do? Does he want to make love or get sex?

Of course, he does go to work every day and brings home a good paycheck. He provides her a nice home, food for the table, clothes on her back, and a car to drive. He comes home tired. What more should she expect? And if she doesn't take care of his "needs," then she just might drive him into the arms of another woman who is very willing to do so. Now, sex becomes an obligation. She owes it to him. If he didn't love her, he wouldn't have married her. So what is she supposed to do? Give him sex? Or does she have the right to hold out for intimacy and real love-making? There may not be a difference to him, but there is a great difference to her and she is one whole part of the equation. She is one whole part of the relationship, one whole part of the marriage, and her part is just as important.

Most likely from the husband's perspective, he really wants to "make love," but he does not understand the way she needs to be loved to be able to respond to him. *"Husbands, likewise, dwell with them with understanding..."* (1 Pet. 3:7). So does the husband get angry, blame his wife for being a "cold fish," and walk out on her, or does he take the time and effort to learn and understand her? God has made it the husband's responsibility to learn and understand his wife. Just like Jesus has the ability to draw us unto Him in a way that ignites in us the passionate desire to know and love Him, each husband has the ability to ignite passionate desire in his wife. He discovers that ability when he learns and understands her.

There is one point I would like to make very clear. Even if the wife is not meeting the husband's physical, sexual "needs" what right does he have getting those "needs" met illegally? It could be that he is not meeting her emotional needs. Is one more important than the other? Does the wife have the same right to get her needs met illegally?

God did not make the wife like the husband, and it is *not* her fault that she is different. She is what she is. And she doesn't have to apologize for it. She doesn't have to excuse it, justify it, or accept ridicule for it. She is not a man and cannot be expected to act or respond like a man. She does not get "turned on" so much by what she sees, but more so by how she is made to feel. She is not frigid or a "cold fish" if she can't "jump into bed as easily and quickly as the husband can. God made her that way. Anyone who thinks that the wife should be able to give sex to her husband whether she feels like it or not, does not know or understand the basic makeup of a woman. Vulgar jokes at the work place, billboards along the route home showing almost naked women or men, and sex-infiltrated television commercials do not make her horney. And she is not obligated to "take care" of her horney husband who has been turned on by anything else other than their love relationship. It can make a woman feel ugly and dirty when she has to perform sex in this environment. She can eventually come to the place where she begins to cringe when she is touched, which ultimately leads to hating sex altogether.

There is also the husband who, all of a sudden, becomes really helpful when he wants sex. He'll clean up the table, run the vacuum cleaner, or do deeds that are normally out of character for him. Is this not making sex an obligation? If he truly wants to help her, he will be consistent in his help, not just when he wants something from her.

*Let the husband render unto the wife due benevolence: and likewise also the wife unto the husband. The wife hath not power of her own body, but the husband: and likewise also the husband hath not power of his own body, but the wife. Defraud ye not one the other, except it be with consent for a time, that ye may give yourselves to fasting and prayer; and come together again, that satan tempt you not for your incontinency. But I speak this by permission, and not of commandment (1 Corinthians 7:3-6 KJV).*

Before we delve into this Scripture, I would like to point out that when statements like this are made in the Bible, they are not intended to become another "law" to live by, nor are they intended to beat us up with condemnation. God is communicating His ways and His standards. To us they are to become goals. We don't come into our Christian walk already whole and complete, ready to live in perfection. We must allow ourselves and God time to reveal His truth to us His way, and allow that truth to free us and grow us up. Our prayer is, "Father, I don't really understand this, but whatever it means, I want it working in my life. I want my life to conform to Your ways. Please teach me, show me, and mold me into what pleases You."

Now, let's look at the Scripture. Taking it at face value, it does appear to be laying down the law. But when we look at it in light of our example of Christ and His Bride, we begin to see it differently. Jesus willingly chose to give His body to His Bride. He made a point of that in the Garden of Gethsemane. When the crowd came to arrest Him, and after He identified Himself, those who were after Him fell backward to the ground, which proved they couldn't touch Him unless He allowed it. And when Peter cut off the ear of the priest's servant, Jesus said to him, "*Or do you think that I cannot now pray to My Father, and He will provide Me with more than twelve legions of angels?*" (Matt. 26:53). Jesus had a choice. He had the power to end the whole mess right then and there. Even though His body would be beaten, lashed, and brutalized, He endured it willingly, not out of obligation, and not for what He would obligate His Bride to give in return. With a pure love motive, He gave His body as a sacrifice for His Bride. Does that mean His Bride now owns it and has authority over it? I believe it simply means she has free access to it. She has access to everything Jesus' body is and all that it provided through its crucifixion and resurrection. Not only that, His Bride is the only one who has the right to His body. He will not give it illegally to another.

In response to what Jesus gave, each person has an option to take that sacrifice and make it his own. There is no obligation other than to believe. But when each believer encounters His all-consuming love, that love ignites the desire and willingness to make a life-giving choice. *"I beseech you therefore, brethren, by the mercies of God, that you present your bodies a living sacrifice..."* (Rom. 12:1). That means that we don't just keep Him tucked away in our hearts, but we allow Him full access to live His life through our bodies. It is not an obligation. It is our free love choice. We give Him the full right to our lives, and what now legally belongs to Him we give to no other. We love Him because He first loved us.

Does this mean Jesus owns the Bride's body? He certainly could, but that is not how He chooses to relate with her. He never takes away her free will. She is always allowed her free will of choice. She just falls so deeply in love with Him that all she wants is what He wants. It is in this light that First Corinthians chapter 7 should be read and understood. When the husband matures in Christ to come to love his wife sacrificially, his wife will fall so deeply in love with him that her will always wants to please him. Sacrificially means giving up his life for her just like Christ gave up His life for the Church. The wife is the only one who has a right to the husband's body, and he is the only one who has a right to her body, but access is by love and through love, not obligation.

If the wife is requiring certain things from her husband before she will yield to him, then she is just as guilty of obligation. She has no right to make him "pay" to get sex. My good friend says that there was a time in her marriage that she thought if her husband would "wine and dine" her and occasionally give her gifts, she would feel more loved and could be more responsive to him. Then God showed her it would and could never be done with physical things, and to require such would be prostitution. These kinds of physical things are nice and can bring pleasure to a woman's heart, but should be given and received as true love expressions, not to give in order to get something in return. These things cannot replace intimacy, the giving and receiving of seed in the second dimension. The only thing a wife has a right to require from her husband is true lovemaking, which brings us to the next and fourth point.

Sex is not to be used as a woman's power to control or manipulate the husband. To do so would not only be selfish but also mean, vicious, and disobedient to God. Even though I do believe a woman has the right to hold out for real lovemaking, I also believe she needs to know from God that she has that right and not from some author who has written a book. Of course, with regard to any problem, talking about it should be the first course of action. Lots of things can be resolved, and intimacy can happen when two people married to each other talk about problems with open minds. Closed minds are another problem in themselves, even if they are caused only by a lack of understanding. Sometimes it takes more than talking to open a closed mind.

So far, I have been talking about the healthy male and female who have not gotten involved in perversions. Perversions turn what is healthy into unhealthy and what should be natural into abnormal and unnatural for both the female and male. Over my years of ministry I have had women come to me confused about having to submit to their husbands' sexual perversions. These are church women with husbands involved in the church who expect perverse acts from their wives. Ladies, let me tell you, "You *do not* have to do it!" Participating in sex perversions is no different than robbing a bank or using drugs because your husband told you to do so. It is your body, and you do not have to defile it in the name of submission.

Also, over the years, I have had Christian women reveal to me that they have become personally trapped in sexual perversion. As we look around our world today, we cannot help but see sexual images everywhere. It can be confusing to young men and women who are trying to understand their sexuality.

It is probably more difficult for men. Their visual sense is more connected to their sexual sense, making it a major battle to protect themselves from illegal stimuli. For women, it is hearing that is more connected with their sexual sense, which can be more easily protected.

I fully recognize the reality of both men and women becoming sexually addicted in some form. I do not condemn you. Please believe me when I say that the addiction does not identify you. *You are not your behavior.* There is no place that any of us can find ourselves that is so horrible that God cannot give help, healing, and restoration. The tragedy is not that we find ourselves in addiction; the tragedy is to allow ourselves to stay there. I am sure if you have an addiction and have taken an interest to read this book, you have also tried with all the power and strength you could muster to stop what you are doing. After failing over and over again, there may not be much hope of possibility left in you. The truth is *you can't do it alone.* God has a way for you. Perhaps you have allowed your addiction to keep you separated from God, thinking you must clean yourself up first before God will accept you or have anything to do with you. *That is a lie!* Only God can clean you up. He wants to. Stop putting your energy into stopping your addiction and put it into seeking and finding God.

There are viable Christian ministries who know how to help those with sexual addictions. They know how to help because they have been there. Because of our strong human pride, it is extremely difficult to show up at such a ministry and reveal an addiction. But it may be your only opportunity to being set free.

Any healthy man who is married to a healthy woman and who takes the time and effort to learn how to give seed in the second dimension will have no problem with his sexual relationship. He will find her as "turned on" to him as he is "turned on" to her. Who is it that causes us to fall in love with Jesus? It is Jesus who woos us with His Spirit. We love Him because He first loved us (see 1 Jn. 4:19). Who is it that makes us into that Bride who is worthy to be presented to Jesus? *"That He might sanctify and cleanse it with the washing of water by the word, that He might present it to Himself a glorious church, not having spot, or wrinkle, or any such thing; but that it should be holy and without blemish"* (Eph. 5:26-27 KJV). It is Jesus Himself who makes His Bride what is worthy and pleasing to Him. I believe every husband has within himself the God-given ability to cause his wife not only to love him, but also to desire him. However, he will have to pursue his relationship with Jesus to discover how to pursue his wife.

Sex is a beautiful happening that starts with the deepest feeling of love and grows into intense longing, yearning, and desire, and then becomes a passionate, dynamic, pleasurable experience that can actually create life. It is a gift from God that He intended for pleasure and to enable mankind to procreate. It is the ultimate expression of love and oneness. The male and female were first formed in one body, then God separated them, and then He told them to become one.

Why would God create an expression for mankind that is so powerful, intense, and pleasurable? Because it is a type, an example in the physical of the expression of love He desires to happen between Himself and His Bride. How do we learn to understand things in the spiritual? By observing and experiencing things He has created in the physical. God created mankind to be physical and placed them in a physical environment and more or less said, "Look around at all I created and learn about Me." *"For since the creation of the world His invisible attributes are clearly seen, being understood by the things that are made, even His eternal power and Godhead, so that they are without excuse"* (Rom. 1:20).

Let's go back to the marriage that was established first—Christ and the Church. Remember, Jesus was slain before the foundation of the earth was laid. It was already a finished work when His death was manifested in our realm of time and when He became the Bridegroom with whom the Bride, the Church, is to become one. The God-given expression of love and oneness with Jesus, the Bridegroom, is worshiping Him in spirit and truth. Please realize the intense longing He has for us to come near to Him, to come into His presence with hearts open and ready for Him to passionately engulf us and fill us with His love. The result is He deposits His life in us so that we may birth it into the world.

In the intimacy with and in the worship of God, He procreates His life in and through His believers. This is a spiritual experience. To be sure that no one adds to what I am saying, I must include that there is nothing physically sexual about it. That would be perversion. If the body gets involved, it is only in such ways as bowing on its knees or raising its hands. Relationship and intimacy with God is in the spirit.

I believe God wants us to come back into His order, having His mind and attitude toward the sexual relationship in marriage. We have debased it, making it not much more than animalistic behavior by our smutty language, our vulgar sense of humor, and our perverse pleasure. If God made it to be a type in the physical of something He desires with His Bride in the spiritual, then it should be held in the same high regard, honor, respect, and reverence as worship.

*chapter fourteen* | GODLY GENDER
MENTALITY

*Then the word of the Lord came to him [Elijah], saying,*
*"Get away from here and turn eastward, and hide by the*
*Brook Cherith, which flows into the Jordan. And it will be*
*that you shall drink from the brook, and I have commanded*
*the ravens to feed you there." So he went and did according*
*to the word of the Lord, for he went and stayed by the Brook*
*Cherith, which flows into the Jordan. The ravens brought*
*him bread and meat in the morning, and bread and meat in*
*the evening; and he drank from the brook. And it happened*
*after a while that the brook dried up, because there had been*
*no rain in the land. Then the word of the Lord came to him,*
*saying, "Arise, go to Zarephath, which belongs to Sidon, and*
*dwell there"* (1 Kings 17:2-9a).

God had sent Elijah to the Brook Cherith as a safe place for him to dwell and provided even food and water for Elijah. I like to mentally put myself in the same circumstances I read about in the Bible and try to imagine what it would feel like to be there, what I would be thinking, and what I would say and do. In this situation, if I were a renowned prophet of God and He gave me a safe place with food and water in the midst of all the evil circumstances under King Ahab's rule with Jezebel as queen, I would want to settle in for the duration. I would not be ready nor would I want to hear God say, "It's time to go." He would probably have to dry up the brook to get me going. I truly appreciate God's patient and faithful understanding of us.

Perhaps Elijah was not much different than I would be in this situation in that he needed help in hearing what God wanted him to do. The brook would eventually dry up because it stopped raining, but if ravens were bringing Elijah food every day, then there would have been water in that brook for as long as God provided, rain or no rain. Go on and read the verses that follow in First Kings chapter 17, and you will find a widow whose oil bottle and flour barrel never emptied for about three years until it rained again. She took and used from them every day. I believe by drying up the brook, God put a problem in Elijah's life to move him in a new direction.

The point I want to make is that most often before God can show us something new or something different, He has to create a need in us to find or discover it. If we don't need something, we most likely stay in the safety zone and the comfort of what we know. Until we need something from God, we usually do not seek it. But only when we are seeking it, will we know it when we find it.

Peace is intangible. We cannot see it. So how do we know what it is? We don't know what it is until we do not have it. It is when we become aware that something is missing from our life;

it is the sense that life is not okay that makes us motivated to begin seeking what is missing. We may not know peace is what we are looking for, but when we find it, we know it. We know it because it fits the place of what was missing and makes life okay.

Hypothetically, let's take a Christian married couple in their early 30s. Individually they love and are committed to the Lord, and together they attend church regularly. However, they are having problems in their marriage. Any attempts they make toward resolution end in anger and more pain. The marriage appears to be in stalemate. Both husband and wife are discouraged and losing hope. Does this mean they have irreconcilable differences? *Or* could it possibly mean they are trying to make the old carnal gender mentality work and God is trying to set them up to show them something different, something new and even better—something we call the godly gender mentality.

Thirty years ago, I was in that place of being very aware that there were "things" missing from my life. I had no idea what was missing. I just knew that my life was not okay. I was desperate for God to show me what was wrong with me. I know now that it wasn't so much what was wrong with me as God wanted to show me something new, something different, and something better. He wanted to show me truth from His perspective so that truth could make me free. To do so He had to put me in the place to be able to see it in an understanding way. He created such a need in me that I began to seek Him with my whole heart.

What is seeking God with your whole heart? It is when desperation to know the truth is so strong and determined that it will break through mind-sets, traditions, and prejudices. It will face fears, anger, and pain. It is being in the place where God can show you a valley of dry bones and ask you if they can live; and instead of saying, "Of course not!" you say, "Well, maybe so. Only You know, Lord."

Throughout this writing I have used terms such as "most people," "many will," "most of the time," etc. I am not basing these terms on studies or statistics. I am basing them on what I have seen and experienced from the vantage points God has placed me for over 60 years. If you fit in as one of "most people," then I have something to say to you that can help you. If you do not fit in, then I congratulate you on your success in finding your place of happiness and fulfillment as a person and in your marriage. The truths God has shown me are very unique to me and to what I have known. But I am not unique in that I have the only corner on them. Ecclesiastes states many times that there is nothing new under the sun. What I have seen has been seen by others.

Yet, I believe we are about to see it in a much bigger way. Now is God's time to bring down throughout the earth this carnal gender mentality the devil has been using to destroy women and their potential. Where there is destruction of women's potential, there will also be men not functioning in their potential. Look at the countries around the world. The more the women are oppressed, the more backward the country. Which comes first: the chicken or the egg? God is now on the move through Eve's Seed which is beginning to rise up in the manifestation of the sons of God to show forth His Kingdom of which there will be no end. His Kingdom is the place where all His people, the male man and the female man, can function freely in all that they are, because in Christ there is no male or female.

There are those who seem content in the carnal gender mentality that religion has promoted in past generations and into this generation. They believe that this gender mentality is working and allows both men and women to function freely in all that they are with all their abilities and gifts. They probably believe this mentality is successful in creating healthy and fulfilled marriages. But if you are one who is desperately seeking because it is not happening for you, then you will know the truth when you see it. It is going to fit, filling what has been empty, making what has been crooked straight, and making life okay.

It is difficult to put into a few words the desperate need I was experiencing so long ago that drove me into seeking. I know that I felt a total failure as a daughter, a wife, a mother, and a woman. I was an obedient child and a submissive wife. I did, and didn't do everything, just as religion instructed, and I still felt a failure. My parents were good to me, and my husband gave me all the freedom to be who I was, and I still felt a failure.

I was a small child when I came to know the Lord and never rebelled or rejected my faith. I learned the religious Christian life well. During the time in my 30s it appeared that every time I tried to function in my spirituality, I received disapproval because I was a woman doing what I shouldn't be doing. Therefore, I felt a failure as a Christian woman. I was in confusion as to what my legal place was in the Body of Christ.

As I said, God was setting me up to show me something new, different, and better. All of it didn't come quickly. It came little by little, precept upon precept, over many years. And little by little, I began making wonderful discoveries about God and myself, and they would fit into where I felt something missing. My life began to get okay. This book is a culmination of things He showed me.

I know that this carnal gender mentality has been very prevalent in the earth and has been promoted by both the world and the church. Therefore, we have heard many times that husbands and wives are supposed to meet each other's needs, which is the cave mentality depicted in the dream. Let us go back again to the human example God Himself gave us when He first established marriage, Adam and Eve. When God formed Eve and presented her to Adam, we find two individuals healthy, strong, and capable in spirit, soul, and body. They were *not* needy. Everything they needed had been provided for by God.

So, are husbands and wives supposed to meet each other's needs? The answer is *"No."* They are not *supposed* to. God has freed us from law, even in the marriage. As long as she has to do this and he has to do that, they are still functioning under law. The law kills. The marriage can become an existence of dead works. No wonder we are not happy. There is no giving and receiving of second dimension seed, no exchange of life, and certainly no moving into purpose activating the multiplication dimension.

Yes, there will be needs we meet in each other, but not because we are "supposed" to. *It will be the natural result of husband and wife coming into right order with God.* It will be the natural result of loving God and loving each other. It will be the natural result of intimacy, the giving and receiving of seed in the second dimension. When all obligations are gone, we will be free to simply respond to each other in love.

What we see from the example of Adam and Eve is a dimension beyond meeting each other's needs. It's the dimension of "oneness." *"Therefore a man shall leave his father and mother and be joined to his wife, and they shall become one flesh"* (Gen. 2:24).

When husbands and wives are so totally free from the demands and obligations of the other's needs, they can become open, unplugged channels through which God can flow, meeting certain needs of the other. There are needs God may and will take care of this way. Certainly we can be channels through which God can consistently encourage the other in their emotional needs of security, acceptance, and value. The point is, *all* needs are to be turned to God. He chooses how, when, and where these needs are met. Many needs will be met solely by God through each individual's personal relationship with Him. Then, what occurs between God and the husband will naturally overflow and meet needs of the wife, and what happens between God and the wife will naturally overflow and meet needs of the husband. This goes along with giving and receiving seed in the second dimension.

It is important to recognize that no other human being, including spouse, can limit or keep us from all God has for us. *"For the Lord God is a sun and shield; the Lord will give grace and glory; no good thing will He withhold from those who walk uprightly. O Lord of hosts, blessed is the man who trusts in you!"* (Ps. 84:11-12). Any limitation in our lives, beyond our power in Christ to eliminate, should be viewed as a temporary boundary God has given to us for our good. We cannot blame our spouse when God does not do something in our lives that we desire. When His times and purposes have been accomplished, the boundary will be lifted. Therefore, no spouse can be accused or blamed for lack of blessing and prosperity in the other's life. As the Scripture says, *"Blessed is the man* [and woman] *who trusts in You!"*

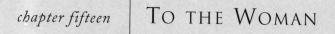

*chapter fifteen* | TO THE WOMAN

### TURN BACK TO GOD

So, Ladies, how did women get into the cave of the carnal gender mentality? They focused the goal and purpose of their lives on their marriage relationship instead of on their relationship with God. They allowed the relationship with their man to measure and determine the value and quality of their lives instead of their relationship with their God. It is what women have done since the time of Eve, which has put them in the cave. It is the woman's fault that she is in the cave, and as long as she blames the man for keeping her there, she is in deception. The ego of men have only allowed it and willingly agreed to it, but women must bear the weight of the blame. Remember, this is a mentality, a belief structure that rules the behavior. No one forces us to believe anything, not even God. God can show us the truth, but it is our choice to accept that truth into our belief structure. It is our choice to change our mind once we have seen the truth. And now that we have seen the truth, where do we go from here?

The first step is for women to choose to come back into order as God created it and intended it to be in the beginning. Each woman is to turn back to God what Eve turned away from God when she followed Adam out of the Garden of Eden. She is to allow God His rightfully created place as her "need meeter." This means she removes from her husband all the responsibilities, requirements, obligations, expectations, and demands she has placed on him since day one, freeing him and trusting him into God's capable hands to form him into the husband God (not the wife) wants him to be. The husband is no longer to be her "need meeter."

I know this is not what some of you want to hear. You have waited for years for your husband to finally "see the light" and become the husband you have been dreaming about. And you have dreamed it over and over, day and night. You have created a concept in your mind of what is going to happen and how wonderful it will be. You have confessed it over and over, and you have asked many to agree with you that God is going to do it. Let's look at this Scripture:

> But as it is written: "Eye has not seen, nor ear heard, nor have entered into the heart of man the things which God has prepared for those who love Him" (1 Corinthians 2:9).

According to this Scripture, whatever we are capable of dreaming up is not God. Yes, God is faithful to us. Yes, God wants to do a good work in your husband's life. He also wants to improve your life. But He is *not* going to do it your way. It will not look anything like you think it should. If you have put your faith in your dream, then you are being distracted, and you are going to be disappointed. We are to put our faith in God and then leave it alone. God will do what you have not seen nor heard nor what you can figure out in your heart. What God is going to do will be greater and better than what you have conceived in your imagination. Trusting God and obeying Him with your heart attitude toward your husband is where you are to be spending your energy. God will be faithful to your faith in Him.

I know some of you are saying, "But God has told me..." I would never discredit what God has told anyone. I understand it, because that is how I live my life. I am always listening for that inner voice. But I also am aware that in learning to know and discern that inner voice, we can get it wrong. I also know that what we hear from God we can misinterpret within the boundaries of our limited understanding. Being right is not more important than knowing the truth. It is truth that makes us free, not the changes that take place in a husband. The strongest indicator that you may have it wrong is how much anger you feel stirring inside you right now as you read these words. Women who really want to know the truth have eliminated their need for truth to be a certain way; therefore, there is nothing to be angry about.

A woman is to free her husband of all the responsibilities, requirements, obligations, and demands she has placed on him and love him just like he is, even with all his failures. Now I can hear some of you saying, "I don't know that I even love him anymore." I understand that. The carnal gender mentality ravages the emotions of women. A woman can spend time and effort in trying to do everything right, and then get so little in return to replenish her worth. Then she condemns herself for being so selfish and failing to live up to the standard she believes she is to live by. True feelings of love become lost.

I remember the day I came face-to-face with this reality, knowing I had to make a decision. What I really wanted was *feeling* like a woman in love, being loved by a man. But that wasn't one of my options. I either had to choose to be faithful to the commitment of love I made on my wedding day or walk out. I didn't like either option. I was beginning to feel despair and hopelessness. Then God gave me a vision.

I was high up, looking down into a brick-walled room square in shape. It had no ceiling, so I could see into it clearly. It looked like a cell. Using directions as we do when reading a map, on the south wall were double doors made of solid iron. These doors were locked from the inside. Inside the room was my husband sitting on the floor crunched up into the northeast corner. Outside the west wall was sitting an earthen pot, which I knew represented me. We all have seen a shattered windshield that is still intact without a piece missing. That is what the earthen pot looked like. I realized that in attempts to get inside to my husband, the pot had thrown itself against that brick wall time and time again only making things worse. He had pulled away from my position as far as he could, and one more blow to the wall would destroy the pot.

For the first time, I saw that I did not possess the power to make or keep my marriage, and for the first time I saw that it was not my responsibility to make or keep my marriage. I had stepped into a place that belonged to God, and I had also put my husband into a place that belonged to God. The more I tried to get what I needed from him, the more he pulled away because he didn't know or understand what he was supposed to do. I had to face the fact that I was in a place of emptiness (second-dimension barrenness), and there was absolutely *nothing* I could do to fix it.

Now I was confronted with a decision, and my options were to be faithful to the commitment of love I had made on my wedding day or walk out. Thank God for His grace to make the right choice. I chose to remain in a commitment of love whether I felt it or not. I made God my "need meeter," and I know God can give any other woman the same grace and courage to make such a choice.

When women choose to make God their "need meter," it is revealed in their lives in various ways. Some need to get off their husbands' backs, quit complaining and pointing out everything he appears to be doing wrong, and stop telling him what to do and how to do it. Others have to refrain from performing and conforming to his likes and dislikes, and back off from doing everything for him. That means, start being honest with him even if it does provoke his disapproval.

Performing and conforming involves dishonesty. It is the wife not being who she is. By moving in, telling him only what he wants to hear, and "taking care of things," she facilitates the stunting of his growth in becoming the man God intends him to be. She helps dwarf him in his God-given place. Consequently, he will never realize the potential in his God-given authority to solve problems. He will never realize the potential of his strength and support as a husband and a father because she has taken care of all the problems. Sometimes, she even hides the problems from him.

Some women may have to make choices in all the areas mentioned above. The Holy Spirit will be your guide and your teacher. He will help you to know how He wants you to handle your circumstances. It is still supposed to be a work of grace, not legalism with all its rules. Flow with God's grace and peace. When we are functioning in God's will, we can know the empowerment of His grace and the wonderful comfort of His peace in the midst and upheaval of the worst storms. That's what happens when God is your "need meeter." No one, neither woman or man, will need to do what God's grace does not empower them to do.

There is one more thing a woman may have to face when choosing to turn back to God. Will the husband stay if she starts acting differently? This can create a mountain of fear that can keep a woman locked into the place of second-dimension barrenness. What you do, my friend, is between you and God. You certainly have that freedom. It is not my place or anyone else's place to tell you what to do. The truth is he could walk out, which means he has not really taken his place as a husband in the first place. Only you can choose whether to allow your life to be diminished in order to keep your man or take the risk knowing that God has the power to make what is right and just happen for you.

I personally came to the realization that I was performing the role of helpmate instead of being a helpmate. I saw that I was shortchanging my husband. He wasn't getting the helpmate in me that was rightfully his and that he deserved by God's standard. I had seen very vividly that I couldn't keep my marriage, so I came to the conclusion that if I thought God couldn't keep it, I was foolish to keep trying. I then threw the whole thing, lock, stock, and barrel, into His hands putting my faith *in Him*—not in what He was going to do. It was both one of the most fearful and one of the best decisions I ever made.

How does the husband respond or react when the wife turns her needs to God? Some husbands will actually experience immediate relief when the burdens of their wives' needs are lifted. In fact, eventually all husbands will know the relief. It may take time, but God will be faithful to teach them and lead them into this new dimension of marriage where there will be a renewed, restored, and happy wife.

In the meantime, there will be husbands whose first reaction will be to feel rejected and abandoned. He is used to his wife catering to his flesh, taking care of his responsibilities, and pretty much being his servant, all under the guise of being submissive. From the beginning of the marriage she has presented to her husband a false person, a façade, and a pretense instead of who she really is. Her real person has gotten lost in the pursuit of getting her needs met. Now, all of a sudden, to the husband, she is acting "out of character." He doesn't understand what is happening, and even worse, he doesn't know what to do. This can be very threatening to him, but *it is the best thing that could ever happen to him in his marriage.* He is on the road to getting the helpmate who will multiply great dimensions to his life.

## Take Your Life Off Hold

I have heard several sermons over my many years that instructed women not to get spiritually ahead of their husbands. They were encouraged to wait on him to move into spiritual things first. It sounds very religious, but I would always wonder what the scriptural basis was for such instruction. The Word admonishes all believers to seek God with all their hearts, to study the Word, and grow into maturity. Where does it say that any believer is to hold off waiting for another to do it first? The Shunammite woman didn't wait for her husband when she went after the prophet on behalf of her dead son (see 2 Kings 4:12-37). Abigail didn't wait for her husband when she intervened to save his life by pursuing King David (see 1 Sam. 25:2-37). Jael didn't wait for her husband to come home when she lured Sisera into her tent to hide and rest and then drove a tent peg through his brain (see Judges 4:17-22).

I do believe that God, and only God, can ask a believer, any believer, to put ministry on hold for a temporary time, and He may confirm it by speaking it through a husband or a pastor. True ministry belongs to God and should function in obedience to Him. There was a time in the early 80s that God called me apart unto Him. I knew I was to lay aside ministry for a while to allow my Father God to bring me into a greater intimacy with Him. The decade of the 80s was my time to concentrate on getting to *know* my Father. But I never put my spirituality or my spiritual growth on hold. I never put my life, or the living of my full life as I knew it then, or the adding to my life on hold. Ladies, this is the only chance at this life we are ever going to have. We not only have the right, we have the obligation of good stewardship to live it to the fullest.

Any woman who has put her life "on hold" waiting for her husband to change, to finally see what he should be, or to finally love her how she needs to be loved, has got to give it up. I am not saying give up your faith in God and His working in your husband's life. I am saying give up being a victim and get your life moving again. Pull down and eradicate the expectations you have created in your mind of how it should be. Stop wallowing in whining, self-pity, and discouragement. Get some life into you and start finding out what God's purpose is for you today and what He wants you to do to make this day productive instead of wasted away. Girl, this is the only time you have—today. How many more todays are you going to waste away?

It is God's place in the woman's life to establish her security. *"The Lord is my rock, and my fortress, and my deliverer; my God, my strength, in whom I will trust; my buckler, and the horn of my salvation, and my high tower"* (Ps. 18:2 KJV). *"The name of the Lord is a strong tower: the righteous runneth into it, and is safe"* (Prov. 18:10 KJV). Women cannot put their lives on hold waiting for the environment of their senses (what they see, what they ear, etc.) to become safe. They cannot wait for people in their lives, mainly their husbands, to start acting "right" and talking "right" so they can feel safe. These things may never happen, and women will have spent their whole lives waiting in vain. Give up the waiting and turn to God; press in to find total and complete security in Him and Him alone. The decision has to be made. Does He take care of you in *all* things and in *all* ways, or does He not? Is He or is He not responsible for your survival? If He is, then take the responsibility off everyone else. Set them free. Your destiny is dependent on this decision because you will never mature or know true happiness without it.

It is God's place in a woman's life to establish her as one accepted, loved unconditionally, and valued.

*Blessed be the God and Father of our Lord Jesus Christ, who has blessed us with every spiritual blessing in the heavenly places in Christ, just as He chose us in Him before the foundation of the world, that we should be holy and without blame before Him in love, having predestined us to adoption as sons by Jesus Christ to Himself, according to the good pleasure of His will, to the praise of the glory of His grace, by which He has made us accepted in the Beloved. In Him we have redemption through His blood, the forgiveness of sins, according to the riches of His grace which He made to abound toward us in all wisdom and prudence, having made known to us the mystery of His will, according to His good pleasure which He purposed in Himself, that in the dispensation of the fullness of the times He might gather together in one all things in Christ, both which are in heaven and which are on earth—in Him. In Him also we have obtained an inheritance, being predestined according to the purpose of Him who works all things according to the counsel of His will, that we who first trusted in Christ should be to the praise of His glory. In Him you also trusted, after you heard the word of truth, the gospel of your salvation; in whom also, having believed, you were sealed with the Holy Spirit of promise, who is the guarantee of our inheritance until the redemption of the purchased possession, to the praise of His glory* (Ephesians 1:3-14).

*But God, who is rich in mercy, because of His great love with which He loved us, even when we were dead in trespasses, made us alive together with Christ (by grace you have been saved), and raised us up together, and made us sit together in the heavenly places in Christ Jesus, that in the ages to come He might show the exceeding riches of His grace in His kindness toward us in Christ Jesus. For by grace you have been saved through faith, and that not of yourselves; it is the gift of God, not of works, lest anyone should boast* (Ephesians 2:4-9).

Women put their lives on hold waiting for someone to finally love them. The problem is *not* that they have no one to love them; the problem is in believing they *are* loved. Ladies, until you know God loves you, you don't even know you *are* lovable. It is time to stop putting people, particularly husbands, in the position of always having to prove their love to you and your value to them. It is a terrible thing to accuse a loved one of not loving you. It pushes them away causing them to either strive in their relationship with you or to give up and quit. Neither is conducive to a healthy relationship.

Therefore, the next decisions to be made are: Does God love me? Has He chosen me? Am I accepted in the Beloved? Do I have value as an independent person because He lives in me? Has He predestined that I should receive His inheritance? Has He sealed me with the Holy Spirit of promise? Woman, turn to and seek God until you *know* that you know the answer is "yes" to every question beyond any doubt. It is essential to wholeness, healthy relationships, and destiny.

It is God's place to give the woman her identity. *"He that hath an ear, let him hear what the Spirit saith unto the churches; to him that overcometh will I give to eat of the hidden manna, **and will give him a white stone, and in the stone a new name written, which no man knoweth saving he that receiveth it"*** (Rev. 2:17 KJV, emphasis added). When the woman turns to God allowing Him to establish her in His security, His unconditional love, and His worth, she begins to see herself as a different person. The work that God does inside her is like Him giving her the white stone spoken of in Revelation, which is a type of Jesus and the purity of His righteousness. He will give her a new name, a new identity that will erase the old identity that sin and the world has placed upon her. She will become whom He says she is, not what she thinks she should be, not what her husband thinks she should be, and certainly not what religion and the carnal gender mentality says she should be. This is something that happens deep inside her where God's Spirit lives with her spirit. It is something that happens in her relationship with her Father God and is such an intimate thing that no other person can see it or really know it. She will know it because she has longed for it as far back as her memory can go. It is the only real thing she will ever find that truly satisfies. Even her husband cannot see it. The only thing that others will see is the fruit from it. (This is not just a woman thing. God does the same in the heart of a man.)

We are seeing that only God can bring wholeness to a woman. Only He can give her what her heart has been longing for since she first became aware of herself. Only He can give her what she has tried to demand from her husband. A husband is a man, and a man does not have the ability to establish a woman in her God-given identity.

Husbands do not have the power to establish security, acceptance, and worth in their wives, but they can be instruments to encourage those things and help create a fertile environment for them to be established. Or they can be instruments of adversity that create a polluted environment. In any case, each individual woman is responsible to God to let Him meet her needs and grow her into the mature godly person He originally designed her to be regardless of the environment her spouse is creating.

When you have taken your life off hold, it is then time to find out some things about yourself. What does God want to do with your life? What is your purpose beyond wife, mother, and homemaker in the commission to take dominion? Have you developed your talents? Are you going to live your whole life without painting those pictures or writing that book, poems, or songs, or making that idea a reality, or whatever else it is God has put in you? Are you going to start that business? If nothing else, it is good stewardship. Do you think God deposited abilities in you that He never intended for you to put to use? I don't think so. Whatever you have, whatever you can do, God knew you were a woman when He put those abilities in you. You have a right to their full expression.

## ARE YOU EMOTIONALLY BALANCED?

Wives, you can be a great asset or a heavy liability to your husbands' lives depending upon how you function as an emotional being. You are an emotional being. God made you that way and said it was good. You receive information into your emotional being first and then process it mentally. What do you suppose was God's purpose for making you this way?

Men are physical and live in the "real" world of logic and reasoning. They see it; they figure it out; and they do it. Women perceive that there can be more to it than that. They can see or sense things happening that cannot be seen by the physical eye.

Let's put it in picture form. The man is about doing what it is he does, functioning in the physical realm. He may deal with fact and figures, costs and ratios, or formulas and equations. He may deal with tools, machinery, equipment, or merchandise. He may deal with cause and effect. He uses great reasoning ability to make this world function efficiently, progressively, healthily, safely, and economically for the best of all mankind. So as man is busy with what he can see, there can be an invisible "smog" that can move in to pollute his work. This invisible smog can be made up of seductive, self-seeking motives of greed, power, lust, and fame. It can work against a man from the inside or outside and has the power to pollute and destroy his productiveness and even his purpose. This smog is not so invisible to the emotional being of a woman, especially if it is encroaching toward her man. The emotional being of a wife can be a warning beacon to alert her husband of the destructive smog that is beginning to intrude into his realm of influence and dominion.

More specific examples can include a coworker who should not be trusted; a prospective business partner who may have ulterior motives; a helpless, single, female neighbor who is after more than the moving of something heavy; the timing on a decision such as buying a new home or car; or bringing sensitive balance in raising the children.

Why must a woman be emotionally balanced? If her emotional being is not in balance with her total being or if her emotional being is not in God's order, she will be caught up with the imaginary enemies of all the "what if's," "could be's," and "may be's." She loses discernment of what is real and what isn't. All the fears of what *could* happen keep her mentally occupied. Her fear of rejection keeps her emotionally on edge, at times doubting even her husband's love for her. Her fear of failure keeps her stunted as a person, as a wife, and a mother. In this place she is not a beacon for her husband. She is not a helper. She is a liability on which he has to spend time and energy to calm down and then pump up and encourage today, and then has to do it again tomorrow. Instead of her emotional being increasing him, it takes and drains life from him.

A Christian woman who is not emotionally balanced has not come to trust God nor has put her confidence in Him to take care of her emotional needs. She may say she trusts Him, but it is only lip service. How can any woman say she trusts God and believes He is for her and still be caught up in the "what if's," "could be's," and "may be's"? *It is impossible.* This woman needs to take a real look at her faith. Yes, I understand this happened to you and that happened to you in your past. But if you are a wife and mother, it is time for you to finally cast those things onto your God, forgive your offenders, accept God's forgiveness, healing, and grace, and get over it. Sweetheart, you have got to grow up in your emotions and your faith. As long as your emotions are imbalanced, they will be destructive.

The wife whose emotions are not in balance is not healthy enough to receive seed from her husband. There is some seed he cannot even consider giving to her because she will go into an emotional frenzy that could mess her up for days. It is really no different than taking his seed and throwing it back into his face. Now he feels he has to keep secrets to protect her. If there is no seed, there is no oneness, no multiplication, no increase, and no greatness.

How does a woman come into emotional balance? By coming into God's order and allowing Him to heal her emotional needs of security, acceptance or unconditional love and value. It is getting real about her trust in God. It is getting tough and fighting the battle of trusting God rather than allow vain imaginations to occupy and dominate her thought life. The battle (for men also) is in the mind and will be won or lost by what the will chooses to believe when faced with the enemies of "what if," "could be," and "may be." Face the fact that it is not "what if"; it is *when* you walk through the valley of the shadow of death. But also face the fact that it is not "maybe"; it is He *is* with you (see Ps. 23:4). The emotionally imbalanced will focus on "the valley of the shadow of death." The emotionally balanced will focus on "He is with me."

## SUBMISSION

*Submitting yourselves one to another in the fear of God. Wives, **submit yourselves** unto your own husbands, as unto the Lord. For the husband is the head of the wife, even as Christ is the head of the church: and He is the savior of the body. Therefore as the church is subject unto Christ, so let the wives be to their own husbands in every thing* (Ephesians 5:21-24 KJV, emphasis added).

The word "*submit*" in Ephesians 5:22 and Colossians 3:18 is taken from two Greek words meaning to place under and to arrange in an orderly manner. There is something very unique that happens in a wife who has come into God's order and gone through the process of turning her needs back to the Lord, allowing Him to be her "need meeter" and her source of security, acceptance, and value. She becomes submissive. It is the *natural* result of coming into God's order. She becomes submissive to God and to her husband. Her heart, her attitude, and her character will reflect submissiveness.

A wife whose security, acceptance, and value are in the Lord, is a whole woman. A whole woman has nothing to be afraid of, has nothing to lose, has nothing to protect or defend, has nothing to prove, etc. Submission for a whole woman is relief. It is a cozy nest in which to snuggle up. She sees it as a place where she functions best. It removes from her life the stress and striving that is so hard on her emotional being. It is the environment that brings the best out of her and makes her happy.

Because she has also removed herself from the place of her husband's "rule," she has eliminated from her life the need to rebel. By "rule" I mean the place Eve put herself when she followed Adam out of the garden. By "rule" I mean making her husband her "need meeter." By "rule" I mean she is no longer performing for, or requiring from her husband, simply so that her needs will be met. He is free, leaving nothing for her to rebel against. Rebellion is not an issue when there is nothing to rebel against.

Please see that it has been the lie that women have believed about their marriage relationship that they have rebelled against. It was what she believed was the truth that bound her, restricted her, and limited her. The marriage relationship in God's order gives her the liberty and the limitless potential to be all she is. When the lie is gone and she sees the truth, it doesn't matter what her husband is like. He can be the most self-centered, male chauvinistic, heathenish, crude, and rude man. She can still be free to love him with a beautiful attitude of submission. She knows who she is. She is confident and secure in who she is. She is safe in her relationship with God. It is no longer belittling, debasing, intimidating, or diminishing to love her husband.

How is a wife to submit? Let me give you an example. You have purchased a different home. Even though it is an older home that in many ways is outdated, you can see its potential and want to bring it into all this potential that you can see. The problem is that you really don't know how to go about it. You recognize that you need someone else who can also see the same potential and has certain abilities that can help you accomplish your vision. So you begin to search for just the right person. When you find a possible helper, you ask them to submit to you what they can do for you and how much it will cost you.

God says to the man, "It is not good that you be alone. I have made a 'help' for you." The man begins to look around for that "help" God has made for him. How does he know when he has found her? How does he know this is the one God has made for him? She sees, understands, and identifies with his vision. She appears to have all the right "stuff" he wants added to his life. She makes him feel more than he is alone.

If everything is functioning in God's order, when the man asks the "help" whom he has found, to marry him, what he is really saying is, "I see in you potential beyond me that can make me more than I can be alone. Will you submit to me all that you are and all that you have to help me reach my goals, accomplish my vision, and fulfill the purposes of my life? If you are willing, I promise to always be there for you (commitment). I will leave my father and my mother, and I will cleave to you taking you with me into my future of hopes and dreams fulfilled, of possibilities of greatness, and of a destiny that God alone has set before us. I will learn to know and understand you. I will learn what is in your heart and cherish it as a precious gem. (The Bible compares it to a ruby.) I will make you more than you can be alone. What is it going to cost me?"

If everything is functioning in God's order, when the "help" responds to his proposal, she is really saying, "I submit, offer, and yield to you all that I am and all that I have to increase you. I will hold nothing back from you. It will cost you your life." This is how a wife is to submit.

Marriage is joint-leadership, joint-taking dominion, and joint-fruitfulness. This is *one* times *one* equals *one* (1 x 1 = 1); both ones are equal, or it is not 1 x 1. They must be equal in substance, in value, and in strength or authority. If not totally equal, the equation would be one times some fraction, making the product less than one. Therefore, marriage is not the husband being the boss and the wife obeying. Let me prove it with the Scripture that I used at the beginning of this section—Ephesians 5:21-24.

Please look at this Scripture again and notice the two words that are typed in bold and italics—*submit yourselves*. These two words are not in the original Greek texts. They have been added by the translators. Therefore, the Scripture would read, "*Submitting yourselves one to another in the fear of God. Wives, unto your own husbands, as unto the Lord.*" When we read the phrase, "*Wives, unto your own husbands,*" the only way we can know what wives are to do to their own husbands is to go back to the previous sentence, "*Submitting yourselves one to another....*" So the "*submitting*" in the phrase "*submitting yourselves one to another*" is the same "*submitting*" for wives to submit unto their own husbands. Do we agree that the "*submitting*" in the phrase "*submitting yourselves one to another*" has the same meaning as the "*submitting*" for wives to "*submit unto their own husbands*"? Obviously, if it is the same word for both phrases, then it has the same meaning. Therefore, all Christians are to *submit* to each other, just like wives are to *submit* to their husbands.

So does *submitting* to one another in the fear of the Lord mean every believer has to fit into everyone else's plans, doing what they say, and obeying? If so, then we are in trouble, and chaos would result.

If it really means *submitting* to each other what you are, your giftedness, your abilities, your encouragement, your help to increase each other, then it makes more sense.

Looking at the Scripture again, we read, *"Therefore as the church is subject unto Christ, so let the wives be to their own husbands in every thing."* The word translated *"subject"* in this sentence is the identical Greek word as *"submitting"* in *"Submitting yourselves one to another in the fear of God."* Perhaps the Church still doesn't have a clear picture of its relationship with its God. Even though we rightfully call Jesus the King of kings, it does not mean He is our dictator. God wants to relate to us, the Church, as a Father and a Husband. He wants a family He can love and take care of, not subjects or slaves He can rule.

In this permissive, almost fatherless generation that we live in today, it is difficult to really bring into balance the right relationship we should be pursuing with God. The true understanding of and the respect for fathers and husbands is virtually lost. Oftentimes, religion communicates God as a stern, demanding, untouchable power who is just waiting and watching for us to do something wrong, and then He will let us have it! This is a lie. Years ago, I heard a preacher say, "If we should speak out a curse word, we have no doubt God hears us, but when we cry for help, we doubt it reaches His ears." He is a loving Father and a loving Husband who woos us to come and willingly submit to Him our lives with all they include, so He can make us into more than what we thought we could be. As a result, His Bride will increase Him in the earth.

Yes, I know the definitions the concordances give for *submission*, but I also know that Bible translators and definition writers can pen only what they have come to believe. We have shown how the real truth was even misconstrued way back in the Garden of Eden. And now that I have placed this information before you, whose report are you going to believe? Remember, God backs up and supports what He says is truth.

The wife not only brings with her all the talents and abilities God has given to her but also a heritage that has come to her through her father's bloodline. I am not talking just about wealth and possessions; I am talking about calling, purpose, and destiny. Those things do not change nor diminish because she has married a man with a different name. Instead they are to be joined with all the husband is and with his heritage to increase them both in the multiplication dimension. When her heart attitude is right, it becomes an honor to submit everything to him and allow those things to be called by his name. It is God's plan. It is His way.

For every organization, every committee, and every business there has to be a leader, a chairman. It takes leadership for that institution to function efficiently and get the job done. The same goes for a marriage and a family. God chose the husband to be the "chairman" of the family, and the husband and wife are in joint-leadership. As "chairman" there are decisions he should make. Let him make those decisions. This doesn't mean he makes all the decisions, nor does he make decisions independently without the wife's input. It does mean he has the ultimate authority to see that the decisions are made. He has the ultimate responsibility to find out what God's order is for his home and then, he has the ultimate authority to see that his home functions in God's order. Because the wife is a coleader in the home, a coleader in taking dominion, and a joint heir, the husband should consider it essential to listen to her and receive her input. She is one whole part in the equation that makes things happen.

Submission would be wonderful and easy to do if the husband was a terrific and perfect guy, and was taking his place as head and leader the way God intended. But if he is not perfect, if he is a "wimp" in his place of authority as a leader in the home, or if he is a bossy dictator, then it is not so wonderful and easy. If he is a negative complainer who is afraid to make decisions, or an absentee father who never makes decisions, then how does she submit to his chairmanship? It isn't easy and can be very confusing to the submitted wife who is trying to do it right. Once again, she must depend on the God who lives in her, trusting His guidance and resting in His grace and comfort. The encouragement and reassurance from a mature spiritual woman who has successfully gone through her own "stuff" can be extremely beneficial. Please know God is not going to neglect you. Let Him work in you. He will be faithful to you in your marriage. We have already discussed that wives do not have to stay in abusive marriages.

It has always amazed me how religion can come down so hard on the submission of wives and go so easy on the submission of husbands. If the carnal gender mentality was as strict and demanding of husbands submitting to Christ as wives submitting to husbands, it would be a different world. After all, when the Word says that the husband is the head of his wife, it also says that Christ is the head of the husband (see 1 Cor. 11:3). If wives are to dress to please their husbands, then husbands should dress to please Jesus. But have they even bothered to find out what pleases Jesus? If wives are not to spend money without their husband's permission, then husbands should not spend money without Jesus' permission. Have they even bothered to ask for His permission? If wives are to always please their husbands and fit into his plans, then husbands are to always please Jesus and fit into His plans. I have been around the church all my life, which includes many years, and I have seen few husbands, or few men for that matter, who have sought to *always* please Jesus and fit into His plans. It's a double standard created by the carnal gender mentality.

Therefore, Ladies, it is imperative to have a clear understanding of God's definition and order for marriage. If God is so definite that you are no longer to yield to your carnal flesh and that you are to die to your old carnal nature, then why would He demand that you submit or obey, as religion can require, to your husband's carnal flesh? When you understand God's definition of marriage and come into His order, you will know when to be like Sarah who was silent in Abraham's deception of presenting her as his sister, or be like Abigail who took matters into her own hands.

## You Are not a Sexual Victim

There is a percentage of women, how many I have no way of knowing, who have been so robbed of their personal identity that they do not have the ability to say "no" to men. They want to say "no," and they try to say "no," but they have no power to follow through with their "no." It has been judged that even when they say "no," they don't really mean it. Because I have battled with this lack of identity myself, I know that it is a real problem for many women. I protected myself from getting into trouble by avoiding intimacy with males. Rather than just saying "no," I would manipulate and maneuver to get out of compromising situations. In these situations, the woman may feel no sexual desire whatsoever, and in fact, she may hate being touched, yet she still can't say "no."

I have actually counseled a very young wife who married a young man who had essentially date raped her. As a result, she found herself pregnant. She was in extreme darkness as to her rights as a person much less a woman. The darkness of the carnal gender mentality cave blinded her from the truth, and she was ignorant of her right and ability to say "no" and then to enforce her "no." She hated the life she found herself living but felt that somehow what happened was her fault, and she was miserable.

The carnal gender mentality communicates to women that their identity and their worth is in their body, and that their body was created for the man. Instead of thinking and feeling, *I am a person of value. No man is going to take advantage of me and use me. I am more valuable than this*; these women are feeling, *I was created for the man. This is my only real value. If I say "no," then I am nothing. I will walk out of this situation being nothing in my purpose on this earth. I do not have a right to deny my purpose.* This is what these women are *feeling,* but they are actually *thinking* very little. If they could really think it through, they might *feel* differently. But the carnal gender mentality has robbed them of the basic primacy of their rights so that they have no thoughts or established beliefs with which to reason. They have no foundational truth of personal value and identity outside the definition that this carnal mentality has given them. They are left vulnerable with no power to fight for their integrity. Why else would a woman allow herself to be used and abused.

Recently, Tammy Wilbon, a member of our ministry who is presently attending law school, called me to relate an event that had just happened in one of her classes. As she was speaking, I knew it was significant and asked her to write it down. I would like to share it with you.

In my Criminal Law class in law school, we were studying the crime of forcible rape, and in all the rape cases we studied, the women had not physically resisted the rape. Consequently, the cases were hard to decide because in order to prove that the forcible element of rape occurred, the victims needed to have put up some form of resistance. One woman was actually walked to the house by her former boyfriend where he raped her. He verbally abducted her from her college campus and forced her to walk with him to his home. Though he had no gun and did not drag her, it was clear that she felt threatened and that her only choice was to go. However, before arriving to the house where she was raped, she walked by many from whom she could've asked for help. She didn't. And upon arrival to the house, instead of running, even waited in a room when the rapist left her alone. She did not phone police until she arrived at her home some time later. She obviously lost her case, but had you read the case, I believe you would have no doubt that this woman had been raped. However, there was no way for the courts to prove it.[9]

At the time I was attending this class, the law had decided to eliminate the requirement of resistance by the victim, and the professor had proposed the question whether or not we agreed with this change. In our book, a feminist made the following statement on this issue: *"In a very real sense, the 'reasonable' woman under the view of the ...judges ...is not a woman at all. Their version of a reasonable person is one who does not scare easily, one who does not feel vulnerability, one who is not passive, one who fights back, not cries. The reasonable woman, it seems, is not a schoolboy 'sissy.' She is a real man."* Susan Estrich[10] (emphasis added).

This passage made me angry when I read it, but I wasn't sure why. However, I knew that I had decided that women did need to resist and that the law could do little to help them if they didn't. However, since in the past the laws had functioned to use resistance as a test for credibility, it began to be this taboo requirement that presupposed victims of rape to be liars and required women to do the impossible—fight off a man intent upon raping her. So the question was asked, and I who had made a decision not to participate in the class sat there feeling something rise inside me and my heart start to race. At one point, a classmate sitting beside me asked if I was okay. I went into the hall hoping that my mouth would not have to open, but it didn't help. After returning to the classroom, I grudgingly raised my hand feeling like Jeremiah who had fire shut up in his bones. The professor called on me and I said the following things: "Resistance has to stay. If the woman does not resist, there is no way that the law can prove that she has been raped due to the nature of the crime of rape. We need to tell women—

much like we tell children not to get into cars with strangers—*that they must not allow their minds to shut down in these situations*—they must will their minds to work and think of two objectives. One is, How can I get out of this situation? If they determine that they can't escape the situation, then number two is, How can I prove he did this so that he gets punished and never does this again? This is not the time for the woman to blame herself for what is happening to her because even if she were selling herself on the street, she doesn't deserve to be raped. There will come a time to evaluate her mistakes; now is not that time. If he leaves her alone, she has to run. If he takes her keys, then she must walk. What that woman was describing [quote above] is not a woman who cries and gets scared and doesn't fight; she is describing a victim, and as long as women see themselves that way, they will continue to be victimized. If we continue to be like women of the world who say, 'Here you go, take what you want; I can't do anything about it,' then the law can't help us and we can't help ourselves."

The silence in the classroom was supernatural—that's the only way I can describe it. I had a shaky voice, and though I believe I have accurately reproduced what I said, all I really remember are the first words. It was not I speaking, but God, and others could tell it was so. One lady looked back at me and replied that we, in the classroom, were all strong and educated women, but to expect this of other women...well, she just thought I was trying to blame the women. I said to her that I believed that all women felt in some way that they were subjugated to men and thus potential victims, and the idea that they didn't have to become victims could be communicated. I said, "I don't mean to suggest that I know what I would do in the situation. But we must think and not fall into the victim role so easily. I am not trying to blame these women; I am trying to *empower* them."

Later in the class, I was able to say that even though lots of women felt they couldn't claim rape, they had given in to having sex when they didn't want to; and that it was this same mentality that took over when these women allowed themselves to be raped out of helplessness. About a class or two later, I read an account in my law book from a woman who had taken a trip to the mountains with a coworker, and because he had pestered her all night, had sex with him. At the end of her essay she said the following: "Now wiser and less polite, I would not whimper but shout! Not for help, but for my own integrity—to let him know how I felt about his boorish assumptions. I would surrender only if he held me down and forced me. And then I could call it rape."[11] This is what I, and I believe God, meant.

Women, we want to empower you. The carnal gender mentality has caused women to believe that they are subjugated not just to their husbands but also to men in general. It is one of the strongest, yet silent beliefs in the carnal gender mentality that makes women feel that men have carte blanche access to them. If you are one who identifies in any way with what I am describing here, it is time for you to start shouting for your own integrity. *You are no man's victim or property!* You have the right and the authority of God to set your own boundaries. You can say, "No!" Any man who refuses to take your "No" for his answer is a rapist, and *it is not your fault*.

It doesn't matter now about the choices any woman has made in her past. It doesn't matter how many times she has said, "Yes," instead of "No." She *can* say, "*No*," now. *You* can say, "*No*," now. Truth has empowered you. You can and should fight for your right to *not* be a "victim."

## DON'T DUMB DOWN

We have a young African-American woman in our ministry. As I have made an effort to know her, to learn and understand her as one coming from a different ethnic environment, I have come to realize that most days of her life she has been made aware of the fact that she is black. Her skin color is a conscious influence in many of the daily decisions and choices she makes: where to eat or shop; where to go for entertainment; where to live; and where to go to church. In contrast, I never think about my skin color in the course of my day. I have known the freedom of traveling through my day without this weighty influence dragging me down and limiting me in what I "should" do and what I "should not" do.

While I have never known this burden because of skin color, I have known it because I was born a woman. Ladies, you know what I mean. We all have learned how to play the games that keep the man feeling "macho" so that our day functions well. We have learned how to approach the male, not just the husband but also the boss, the businessman, and even the pastor, so that they don't feel "threatened" and we can keep our lives gliding on smooth waters. If we don't, then we may come across as a woman who knows more or better than they do, and many "they's" can't handle that. When a man is not secure in his own manhood, he can't have a woman coming across as smarter or knowing something he doesn't. So, women have learned how to play around it.

One method women use is to "dumb down." They present themselves as not knowing what they know. They maneuver and manipulate conversation to make it appear the man knows more and that he is causing her to understand and bringing them to a place of common agreement. I have done this many times knowing that if I presented myself as the knowing and intelligent woman that I am, I would get shut off and shut down immediately.

This is especially true in the church. Even though they say submission does not make a woman less of a person, less is what they really believe because of the carnal gender mentality. When a Christian woman actually reveals her confident, intelligent, and knowing person, she is instead perceived as dominating and unsubmissive. Then they start coming down on her husband because he does not have her "under control." *It is pure prejudice!*

Many times in the course of my life when making decisions, I didn't just consider "Do I know or do I not know? Am I able to do it or am I not able to do it?" but I also had to consider "Even if I do know, and even if I am able to do it, should I or shouldn't I because I was born a woman?" Whether I should speak or not speak was not based on if I had something to say and contribute, but on the fact that I was born a woman.

To play it safe, women "dumb down," but what they are really doing is facilitating man's weakness. If he is insecure in his manhood, if he still does not know who he is in Christ, then that is his problem. It has even been said from pulpits that wives should make their husbands think decisions were "his idea." Ladies, it is time to stop playing your games to maneuver around *his* problem. It is time for him to face his problem before God and get over it.

Actually, "dumbing down" or using any other method of maneuvering around the man's problem is witchcraft and needs to be recognized for what it is. All forms of control and manipulation fall into the category of witchcraft.

Women can and have used their sexuality to maneuver around men. Isn't this just another form of "dumbing down"? My mind immediately goes back to the 70s variety show, "Hee Haw." It was one of the most blatantly disgusting and demeaning displays of feminine sexuality and dumbness. Feminine sexuality has become a commodity used to sell anything from cat litter to sneakers. A high school teacher recently told me about a phenomenon taking place today in America's high schools. Girls are purposely making poor grades to appear unintelligent because it is more sexually attractive. Remember, we said that the carnal gender mentality abounds or increases with each generation. Can it get worse than this?

Intelligence rightfully belongs to women also. God gave women their minds, not to figure out how to play games to get what they want, but to learn of Him and His righteousness. He gave each woman a mind that is to be renewed into the mind of Christ for her to use to take dominion and function in His Kingdom. Don't diminish it by "dumbing down." Give it its rightful place of intelligence and respect.

## YOUR MINISTRY TO YOUR HUSBAND

*And the Lord God said, It is not good that the man should be alone; I will make him an help meet for him. And out of the ground the Lord God formed every beast of the field, and every fowl of the air; and brought them unto Adam to see what he would call them: and whatsoever Adam called every living creature, that was the name thereof. And Adam gave names to all cattle, and to the fowl of the air, and to every beast of the field; but for Adam there was not found an help meet for him (Genesis 2:18-20).*

"It is not good for man to be alone." Ladies, that is God's judgment of the situation. It is not good for your husband to be alone. God created and formed you to fill his aloneness and gave you the authority and the ability to do so. It also appears from this text that there is no other creature on the earth that can do it.

What is aloneness? It is that mental and emotional private place to which men retreat. It is the place where they hide their disappointments, pains, and fears. It is the place where they hide hopes and dreams. It is the place where they keep secrets. As a result, some will even separate themselves physically and go off to be alone. But God said, "It is not good."

We have stated that men protect their aloneness by keeping silent and telling the woman to "keep silent" or "be quiet" or "shut up." Or perhaps it is simply expressed, "I don't want to talk about it."

So God has given to the woman the authority and ability to minister to the man's aloneness, *except*, He will *not* release her to that ministry *until* she has turned back to God. Otherwise, her heart motive will be selfish. She will be using her God-given authority to manipulate and control to get what she feels she needs from the man. Only when her heart motives are pure, can she be a godly minister to her husband.

There are many wives who have been wounded by the reactions from their husbands when they have confronted them prematurely. The wife needs to be healthy in her emotions, healthy in her security, acceptance, and value to keep from being devastated from painful reactions. Any animal including humans, male and female, husbands and wives, strike out when feeling cornered. Are you ready to handle any reaction from your husband? Only healthy and mature wives can follow the leading of the Holy Spirit and operate in His order and His timing and then not feel sideswiped by their husbands' reactions.

It seems it would be good if we could make a list of all that women could do to accomplish this assignment. But then we would just end up with law, and women know how the law kills. The best way to do it is to be natural and walk in the Spirit. After all, each wife was chosen to be *the* wife to that husband, so the best thing to be is naturally herself. She doesn't have to perform something she is not, and she doesn't have to be like her mother or his mother. She can speak the truth in love instead of saying what he wants to hear. She can be honest about her likes and dislikes. She can tell him what she appreciates about him and what she does not appreciate about him. She can even disagree with him. Then there will be times God will send her to confront him about something God says is significant in his life.

(Special note: It doesn't matter the circumstances surrounding the cause of a marriage. Once that marriage has been committed to God and His purpose, it then becomes a God thing with all the promises applying. *"And we know that all things work together for good to those who love God, to those who are the called according to His purpose"* (Rom. 8:28). Any marriage that came about for the "wrong reasons" cannot be legally abandoned with the excuse that God didn't join them together. To make a marriage a "right" marriage, simply commit it to the Lord.)

Once a woman has turned her needs back to God and has come to rest in who she is as a person, then she can trust the Spirit of God who lives in her, to teach her, lead her, and guide her in being the wife and fulfilling her ministry as the wife to her husband. There will be times the Spirit will say to keep silent and do nothing. Therefore, to say something and/or do something can and probably will drive the husband further into his aloneness. However, there will also be times when the Spirit will instruct the wife to say something or do something. To not say it or do it would be facilitating and to a degree encouraging his aloneness.

As the woman comes into the place where she is functioning with pure motives, God will give her a vision of the man He created her husband to be. He will give her insight into the husband's life, enabling her to minister to him in a very powerful, constructive, and life-giving way. It will not always be an easy thing to do. In fact, at times it will be very difficult. When a man's aloneness is being threatened, he can react in some very intimidating, aggressive, and painful ways to cause his wife to cower and back off. The wife whose security, acceptance, and value are established in God will be able to stand firm in who she is and remain consistent in her place as helpmate and not walk away wounded.

Remember, *God said* it was not good for the man to be alone. It was not the woman's judgment or decision. As we move into a new dimension with God, it is essential for women to turn their needs back to God so they can be released into their first and most important ministry—being a helpmate.

## RESPECT YOUR HUSBAND

Usually much earlier before a husband comes on the scene, women have already had dominant male relationships and influences in their lives. Their father, grandfathers, brothers, cousins, teachers, and boyfriends are the most common ones. Women already have certain beliefs and attitudes about men built into their mentality or belief structure before they meet the man with whom they want to spend the rest of their lives. Each woman brings her belief structure into her marriage and begins to "fit" it into her relationship with her husband. Of course, this belief structure is based on the types of men that surrounded her and how they treated her. It could have been good; it could have been bad; and it's all part of her belief structure.

The point is that the wife will then look at her husband through her belief structure, which could cause her to add to or take away something from what he really is. For example, if the men in her life before marriage were honest, trustworthy, caring, and wonderful men, then she will probably always think the best of her husband, having no suspicions and believing him even if he is lying to her face. If she was lied to and deserted by men while growing up, she will probably be suspicious and have difficulty believing her husband even if he is always truthful.

So, Ladies, do you have any wrong attitudes or beliefs about men? Isn't it obvious that wrong beliefs and attitudes will affect your marriage relationship and definitely hinder your ministry to your husband? It is like trying to do a job with broken and defective tools. How do you know if you have wrong beliefs and attitudes? Jesus said, *"For out of the abundance of the heart the mouth speaks"* (Matt. 12:34b). Listen to the things you say. "Typical man!" "Just like a man." *"Men!"* "Men don't care about you." In this Scripture, Jesus says that if it is in your belief structure, it will come out of your mouth. If it is not in your belief structure, you won't even think to say it. Excuses like, "I was just joking" are justifications and avoidance of seeing the truth.

There is another extremely important part to wives' ministry to their husbands, but until their belief structure is healthy and until their attitudes are positive, they will never be able to successfully give this very important ingredient. Scripture indicates that husbands need *respect* like wives need love. Did that statement cause a minor explosion inside? If so, that's another clue that women must get honest before God about their perspective of men. I understand the great pain some women have experienced from the treatment by men, but please don't stay in the place where that pain influences your mentality. God wants you free, but you may have to do some real repenting and forgiving to receive the deep healing you need. Ask God to give you a mature spiritual woman who can lead you out of your pain into total healing and freedom in Jesus.

*"Nevertheless let each one of you in particular so love his own wife as himself,* **and let the wife see that she respects her husband"** (Eph. 5:33, emphasis added). This sounds like a command to me. Webster defines respect as "to feel or show honor or esteem for, to show consideration for." Now I hear some of you saying, "I don't see much to respect. He has destroyed any respect I ever had for him." The Scripture doesn't say, "Let the wife see that she respects her husband, only if he is respectable and deserves it." Does this mean women have to put on an act and say things they don't mean? Heaven forbid, no! Respect does not mean placate.

The husband is commanded to love his wife. Nowhere is the wife commanded to love her husband. Ladies, women don't have to be commanded to do something that is part of their nature to do. Loving the husband is the easy thing for her to do. Women can love a husband for whom they have no respect. It is respect that is God's command for women. When a husband has been selfish, taking so much and giving so little, and when he has avoided relationship leaving all the responsibilities of children and home to the wife, respect can look next to impossible. However, because God has commanded it, women who obey God have no choice.

So, how do you respect a husband when you feel no respect? First, you ask God to let you see into the heart of your husband's life, and then begin looking. Start looking at where and to whom he was born. That is the place *God chose* to bring him into the earth realm. Respect God's wise choice. Whoever they are and whatever they are, these are the parents God chose to give life to your husband. Respect God's wise choice. Somewhere in his bloodline, although it may be obscure and hidden beneath mounds of destruction, is a God-given heritage to be discovered and retrieved for God's purpose. Respect his God-given heritage. With God's vision you can see that his starting place, whether it included wealth or poverty, love or rejection, surrounded by security or destruction, was the launching pad from which God chose to send your husband into his destiny, his heritage, and his greatness. Respect God's wise choice.

With God's vision, look at the events that God chose to allow into your husband's life as he grew into manhood. See the good ones that brought positive influences and affirmation. See the bad ones that brought negative influences causing wounds to his identity and value. Respect God's wise choice. With God's vision you can see that where he came from and what he has gone through in his informative years was the "nest" God chose to place him; and if you are really seeing with God's vision, you will see that it was in that particular "nest" God authorized and empowered him for a future in God's plan.

With God's vision, the vision of the Spirit, look past what you see in the flesh and see the potential of the great man of God that he is. Respect the great man of God that he is. With God's vision, you can see that even what you haven't respected about him has played a part in God making him into that great man that he is. See your husband as the living stone God has placed into his spiritual slingshot and is preparing to, or perhaps already has, catapulted into purpose, destiny, and promise. See everything you haven't respected about your husband as the negative pull that stretches the expandable strings of that slingshot giving it the force that is needed to send him into his God-given future of greatness and accept it. Respect what God is doing even if you see only by faith at the present time.

*"So husbands ought to love their own wives as their own bodies; he who loves his wife loves himself"* (Eph. 5:28). If your husband does not love you the way you feel he should, perhaps the problem is not with you but with him. The Scripture says that he who loves his wife loves himself. If a husband has a love failure toward his wife, couldn't it be the result of a love failure toward himself? How can a man who doesn't respect himself love his wife? I suggest, wives, that you, with God's vision, take another look to see how your husband feels about himself. With God's vision you can look past his façade, the image he tries to present, and really see how he feels about himself.

Ladies, if you are not feeling lovable, what is it you really need? Isn't it love? If your husband does not have self-respect, what is it he really needs? Isn't it respect? It is respect the Scripture tells you to give. You may have to kill some pride and climb over a lot of hurt to do it, but it is obedience to God. When you obey God in this manner, you can actually position yourself to receive the healing you need. Just as importantly, your respect could help bring "increase" to his self-respect, which would return to you by way of his love.

Ladies, as you think about the way you want your husband to love you, you must also think about how he needs to be respected. Don't you want him to love you unconditionally even in those times you are not very lovable? So most assuredly, there are times when your husband needs respect even when he has not been very respectable.

Respect and disrespect are attitudes. Attitudes are not just communicated with words. Demeanor and behavior communicate attitudes as loudly, if not louder than words. I believe that if you really take a good look with God's vision at your husband and his life, what you see can change your heart, resulting in a right attitude toward the man you fell in love with at the beginning.

All interaction with the husband should be void of attitudes and words of disrespect. Honesty doesn't give the freedom to debase or demean. Anger, disappointment, and hurt need to be expressed and can be expressed without having to be disrespectful. We all have heard, if not been personally told, "You shouldn't feel that way." This is another lie that has to be destroyed. Feelings are not wrong, and it is not wrong to express them. Wrong comes in when feelings are expressed inappropriately. It is wrong to condemn, belittle, degrade, and harm others no matter how we feel. Men need to understand that expressing feeling is not meaning disrespect. I believe it is a good practice in all kinds of relationships that when we feel it necessary to speak a negative or a correction, that we also speak a positive or a compliment. When someone is affirmed in doing something right, they can more easily hear when something is not right. Moms and Dads, that goes for our children too.

In fact, the marriage relationship in a home is the classroom where the children learn who they are, what they believe about themselves, and how they are to act and interact in relationships. What they witness daily in the home is what they absorb into their belief structure and their identity. They will learn more from what they witness than what they are being told.

## YOU ARE A WOMAN OF GOD

You are a woman of God. Be it! You do not have to prove it, justify it, or excuse it. Above all, you do not have to flaunt it. When God's life dwells in you; when you have come out of the cave of the carnal gender mentality; and when you have come into God's order, being a godly woman is just being natural. No longer are you bound and limited by religious and social laws. No longer do you have to labor to perform the "right" behavior. You are free just to be natural and do what is in your heart to do. You are free to live your life to the fullest.

As you grow in knowledge and intimacy with your God, you will discover and learn wonderful things about yourself. You will become more than you ever thought possible. One day you will realize that you are absolutely comfortable with yourself and enjoy your own company. This is wholeness. Now you are ready to become a godly wife.

## YOU ARE THE INITIATOR

Women alone have the decision of remaining in or coming out of the carnal gender mentality cave. Although a belief system has been set up by religion that has permeated society, women have the power to come out by changing how they believe. No person has control over what another person believes. The wife does not need the husband to change or do anything for her to free herself from the bondages and limitations that come from cave life. But her coming out of the cave will not automatically result in moving marriage into the multiplication dimension. Moving into the multiplication dimension will depend totally upon the husband. Husband, you are still the man. You are the initiator. The wife presents (submits) herself to you and then becomes the responder. God says it this way, "*Therefore shall a man leave his father and his mother, and shall cleave unto his wife: and they shall be one flesh"* (Gen. 2:24 KJV). It is the husband who initiates by leaving his father and his mother, and it is the husband who initiates by cleaving to his wife. If the husband initiates nothing, then the wife has nothing to respond to.

What is leaving his father and his mother? During Jesus' time on earth, it was customary for the groom to build a room on to his father's house that was to be for him and his wife. When everything was ready, he would go get his bride and bring her back to his father's house where they would live. Jesus also went to prepare a place for His Bride and will bring her back to His Father's "house" (see Jn. 14:2-3). The Hebrew word for *leave* is a primary root meaning "to loosen." Therefore, *leave* does not necessarily mean the physical leaving of his father's and his mother's presence. The husband is to loosen himself from his dependence upon Dad and Mom and begin to establish his own domain where his wife becomes the other one of the equation to bring increase and productiveness. He is to cleave to her just like one (1) has to cleave to one (1) to make one: $1 \times 1 = 1$. Which 1 is more important? Remember $1 \times 0 = 0$ and $1 \times \frac{1}{2} = \frac{1}{2}$. Again, the husband initiates to make multiplication happen. We are seeing *cleave* is more than just being committed. Commitment says, "I will always be there for you." Cleave says, "I am going to take you somewhere with me."

*Cleave* cannot happen within the carnal gender mentality. Cleave does not stereotype the wife into a certain place of being and functioning with certain expectations of how she is to make the husband's life better. Cleave is the husband saying, "If you yield yourself to me, I will cleave to you, giving up my life to increase your life, not just making it better, but making it full in every dimension of your being." Cleave is the husband saying, "I am going to pursue you to know you and to learn you in all that you are so I can increase you and take you to heights we could never reach alone." Isn't this what Jesus says to us, His Bride?

*"Husbands, love your wives, just as Christ also loved the church and gave Himself for her, that He might sanctify and cleanse her with the washing of water by the word, that He might present her to Himself a glorious church, not having spot or wrinkle or any such thing, but that she should be holy and without blemish"* (Eph. 5:25-27). As a result of Christ giving Himself for His Bride He says, *"Most assuredly, I say to you, he who believes in Me, the works that I do he will do also; and greater works than these he will do, because I go to My Father. And whatever you ask in My name, that I will do, that the Father may be glorified in the Son"* (John 14:12-13). His Bride increases Him in the earth.

*When the husband gives up his life to cleave to and increase his wife, his wife will in turn increase him. This is multiplication.*

*"But I want you to know that the head of every man is Christ, the head of woman is man, and the head of Christ is God"* (1 Cor. 11:3). *"For the husband is head of the wife, as also Christ is head of the church; and He is the Savior of the body. Therefore, just as the church is subject to Christ, so let the wives be to their own husbands in everything"* (Eph. 5:23-24). First Corinthians 11:3 would have been better translated, "The head of every husband is Christ; and the head of the wife is the husband." Surely it does not need to be said that men in general do not have any headship over women. These Scriptures are talking about the marriage relationship, not the church, and not business. The Corinthian believers were trying to establish a system of headship in the church that was meant only for marriage. A careful study of this entire text reveals that Paul was refuting this attempt.

There is a principle of God that I would like to bring to our attention at this time: *"One witness shall not rise against a man concerning any iniquity or any sin that he commits; by the mouth of two or three witnesses the matter shall be established"* (Deut. 19:15). And again in Second Corinthians 13:1b, *"By the mouth of two or three witnesses every word shall be established."* One witness alone is not sufficient evidence to make a judgment on any matter. I have found that I can use this principle consistently when studying the Word of God. If I think I am seeing a truth in a Scripture, I wait until I have seen it in two more places in Scripture before I accept it as truth. God's Word interprets itself.

Where in Scripture does it say that the husband is to "govern" his wife? We have already clarified Genesis 3:16. Besides this clarification, if God had really said that the husband was to rule over the wife, once she was redeemed that should have ended. She wasn't just partially redeemed; her redemption was total. The same Spirit that raised Christ from the dead dwells in her too, so if she is to be governed, He will do it. Otherwise, the Holy Spirit in her would have to be subject to a man.

It was very common for the New Testament writers to use the physical body and the body parts to illustrate the principles of how the "Body" of Christ or the Church works. When Paul says the husband is the "head," he is talking about the physical body, not government with a head of state. The most frequently used example of this is First Corinthians 12:12: *"For as the body is one and has many members, but all the members of that one body, being many, are one body, so also is Christ."*

Christ is the Head and the Church is His body. I find it interesting that He made His current ministry in the earth dependent upon His Body. It is not that He can't do it by Himself, but He chose to do it through His Bride coming into oneness with Him. When Jesus returned to His Father, He sent His Spirit to earth to dwell in the heart and mind of each believer. He made His ministry dependent upon cleaving to and becoming one with each believer individually and then all believers corporately as He brings them into oneness with each other.

Let's look at the relationship between the head and the body of a human person. Are they not dependent upon each other? If a person should become brain-dead, the body would be able to do nothing. There might be absolutely nothing wrong with the body as such, but without the brain functioning, the body could not function. On the other hand, if the body is disconnected from the head by the severing of the spinal cord as with a paraplegic, there would again be no function. The brain could still think, reason, and have good ideas, but would be totally helpless to act on them because of its disconnection with its body.

How does headship work between Jesus and His Body? He makes it work. He is the initiator; He is the pursuer; and He is the enabler. His Body yields and responds to Him. This is how He will accomplish His purpose in the earth.

How does headship work between the husband and his wife? The husband makes it work. The husband is the initiator; the husband is the pursuer; and the husband is the enabler. The wife yields and responds to her husband.

Several years ago, a close friend gave me a book written by Myles Monroe. Somewhere in that book he said that the graveyard is the most resourceful place in the earth. That is where all the unpainted pictures, the unwritten books, poems, and songs, and all other kinds of works of art never completed, along with inventions never invented, are buried. This touched something in my head that said, "Carol, you cannot let this happen to you. If God put ability in you, it is not just good stewardship but it is your duty to Him to develop them for His glory and pleasure."

My head, the head on my shoulders, recognized that there was ability in my body that had not been developed. My head could have said, "Carol, you have no talent. There is nothing you can do that is worth anything." And that would have been the end of that. My head has the ability to increase me or decrease me according to what it chooses to believe about me. My head can be for me or against me. However, it is to my head's advantage to support the rest of me because it cannot go anywhere without me. On the other hand, my body can do nothing without my head working with it.

Cleaving is the husband (the head) saying, "I cannot be all that is in me to be and I cannot do all that is in me to do without you in oneness with me. I am going to take you with me, not only into my future of hopes and dreams, but also into a greater dimension of who we are. Together we are going to grow into an increased life of potential and abundance." *It is not governing. It is multiplying.* And it is for marriage.

Jesus gave Himself and became nothing to make His Bride infinitely more than what she could possibly be alone. *"Therefore God also has highly exalted Him [Jesus] and given Him the name which is above every name"* (Phil. 2:9). Isn't that what you are looking for, gentlemen? Isn't there something in you telling you that there is a higher existence than where you are living? Energy, effort, and time that should be spent on marriage and family are off other places striving for identity with purpose and value. Are you looking for identity and value in all the wrong places?

In society today, there is a lie that has attached itself to humility. Many times I had spoken to the men in our ministry, "There is a lie that has attached itself to humility. That lie is that to humble yourself is to diminish you as a man." I thought that seemed simple and clear enough to make my point. The men would sort of respond with, "Oh yeah, sure." One day something rose up in me that was rather out of character for me, but I said, "There is a lie that has attached itself to humility. The lie is that if a man should humble himself, he is kissing a__." That did it. That was something they could relate to. Now they knew what I was talking about. Please do not be offended by my bluntness. But it is very necessary that a man see humility the way he should, because God requires it from him.

Jesus took on the form of a servant. Can you? Are you believing a lie that is preventing you from humbling yourself? Would it be demeaning or diminishing to you as a man to serve your wife? Do you feel like you would become her victim and she would take over? If humbling yourself is intimidating to you, will you continue to ignore the prodding of the Holy Spirit in you and continue to do what you have been doing? That's your choice, but nothing will change—at least not for the better.

Because of the misunderstanding of Genesis 3:16, religion has required the wife to serve the husband. Jesus came as the last Adam to set things back into order. He came as a servant to serve and now requires the husband to follow His example. If through this writing you have received any vision of great possibilities for your marriage, please know that you can only get there by coming into God's order and following Christ as the example set before you. By focusing on your wife to make her gloriously great, you will be opening the way to your own greatness. *"Then said Jesus unto His disciples, If any man will come after Me, let him deny himself, and take up his cross, and follow Me. For whosoever will save his life shall lose it: and whosoever will lose his life for My sake shall find it"* (Matt. 16:24-25 KJV).

Serving the wife also includes taking care of her and protecting her. Jesus came to destroy the works of the devil and to break the power of sin for His Bride (see 1 John 3:8). He positioned Himself between His Bride and her enemy to free her from his power to steal, kill, and destroy (see John 10:10a).

God told Adam he was to tend to and keep the Garden of Eden (see Gen. 2:15). The Hebrew word for keep is *shamar*, which means to hedge about, guard, protect, and attend. It is the same word used in Genesis 3:24 when God placed angels to "keep" the way to the tree of life. The first Adam was also to position himself between his bride and the enemy. Eve was to have been safe inside the garden as Adam kept satan out of the garden, the same as the angels were to keep trespassers out of the garden.

Husband, do you "keep" your home and the environment in which your family lives? Is the enemy allowed to trespass into your domain? Jesus has defeated satan, but satan is the father of lies and uses deception to trespass where he is allowed to roam. How does a husband know when the enemy is trespassing? Look around, husband. Is there any stealing, killing, or destroying going on in your family? Is your family being robbed of provision and the righteousness, peace, and joy that is the Kingdom of God? Is God's life-flow to and among your family members being killed before it can produce the life and health that it is intended to give? Do you see more destruction of purpose than increase and multiplication? Are you still blaming people and circumstances and refusing to see how real satan is and how real satan's power is working through people and circumstances?

It is time for husbands to recognize and accept their place to "keep" and guard their realm of domain. Although wives have the same power and authority against satan in the spirit realm, they should not have to bear the responsibility of the family alone. It is time for husbands to learn how to take this position. It is time for husbands to pick up the sword of the Spirit, which is the Word of God, and begin to wield it against their enemy. It is time for husbands to learn how to speak to powers they cannot see to establish and maintain a safe and peaceful environment for their family to live and grow in wholeness and purpose.

So what am I saying? God's order is not wives serving and taking care of their husbands. God's order is husbands serving and taking care of their wives. Is this not consistent to God's nature and the example of Jesus? Tell me, what is your example of a real man? Jesus? Or is it the egotistical, know-it-all, iniquity-hiding man that can't be honest and thinks that honoring and taking care of his wife looks like he is being henpecked? To choose Jesus as his example can make the man feel like he is losing something of himself. The truth is, he is losing something. He is losing his independence; he is losing his aloneness; he is losing his self-centeredness; he is losing his pride; but he is not becoming a loser. The real man who makes Jesus his example will soon find a nurturing wife whose natural response will be to love, honor, respect, and serve him.

## Do You Know Your God?

Gentlemen, the key to this relationship with your wife, the key to your marriage is your relationship with God. If you are commanded to humble yourself so that you can properly serve and love your wife as Christ loves the Church, how are you going to do it without knowing Christ? He is your enabler. I don't mean knowing about Him. I mean *knowing* Him. Our teenagers can sit in a drivers' education class and learn all about the mechanisms and mechanics of driving a car; they can learn all about the laws of yielding, stopping, and parking; but until they get behind the wheel of a car, they do not *know* how to drive.

I have a daughter-in-law who took drivers' education in high school and passed the written test, but when it came time to take the driving test, intimidation got the better of her and she "put off" going. After she and our son married, he began to take the time to encourage her and build her confidence not only in her driving ability but also in herself as a person. She was not a failure. Intimidation was the enemy trying to keep her less than what she was in her abilities and her identity.

Gentlemen, intimidation is your enemy trying to keep you less than what you are in your abilities and your identity as a husband and a father. It causes you to "put off" what you should do. Why are you intimidated? Because you don't know what to do much less how to do it. God's Word says, *"Likewise, ye husbands, dwell with them according to knowledge, giving honor unto the wife, as unto the weaker vessel, and as being heirs together of the grace of life; that your prayers be not hindered"* (1 Pet. 3:7 KJV). The New King James Bible says, *"Husbands, likewise, dwell with them with understanding...."* Is that intimidating or what? How many times have you said, "I don't understand her. I don't know what she wants." Face it. You don't understand your wife; you don't know what to do; and you are intimidated.

If God's instruction to you is to live with your wife with understanding, then it is possible to do so. To not do so hinders your prayers. You may remember that we stated somewhere earlier that God never intended for man to fulfill God's purposes without God's empowerment. Yes, you can live with your wife with understanding, but *not* without the empowering ability of the Holy Spirit working in you. It's not going to be a one-time thing either. It will have to be an everyday relationship with Him to know how to live with your wife every day with understanding.

You may not like the thought of having to put forth the time and effort you think this might mean. In fact, it might sound like a "big hassle." Guys, that's the problem. The carnal gender mentality has made it a "big hassle." Its belief structure dictates that man is to put all his efforts and energy into his work and then come home to rest and relax. He should be able to do at home whatever he wants even if it means doing nothing. His wife should have his "castle" ready for him with all the amenities. *She* should live with *him* with understanding. She should know when he wants her to stay out of his life and to know when to be generously ready when he wants her in his life or bed. Please do not take offense. I don't want to be offensive. But this is the belief structure of the carnal gender mentality. Hopefully, any of that mentality you may have had is being pulled down and you are being filled with visions of great possibilities.

Remember, insanity is doing the same things over and over again while expecting to get different results. Are you doing the same things over and over in your marriage, yet finding that they are not working? How many times have you walked away having made the decision, "There is nothing else I can do"?

Guys, you may be trying to respond to your wife by "reading" her logically. That means you see what she does and how she is acting, then you interpret it as such and such and that is how you respond. The problem is that you interpret it from a man's perspective. She is not a man. She is not one of the guys. How many times have you communicated disapproval or disgust with her behavior when she was just thinking and acting "like a woman"? Whatever you may be thinking and feeling right now, can we at least agree that something needs to change? Something has to be done differently, and that takes us right back to relationship with God. *He is the only Source of finding the difference that is going to work.*

I challenge each man reading these words: Are you in this thing with God and your wife, totally committed, and willing to give whatever it takes? Being *mostly* committed and giving only up to a certain point will not work, nor will having a "pick and choose" mentality. If your answer is "yes," then I congratulate you on taking the step that will bring you into a life that will, at the least, surpass anything you have ever yet hoped for. If your answer is "no," then it is only reasonable that you cannot expect any more from your wife. Jesus is the initiator and His Bride, the Church, responds. You are the initiator and your wife is the responder. Even if you choose not to initiate, in essence, you are still initiating. Just as doing nothing is really making a choice to do something that provokes a response. To not initiate is really initiating negatives that will most assuredly get negative responses. Nothing will change, at least not for the better. Of course, once you have seen the truth and then reject the truth, things could get worse.

I am going to assume that your answer is "yes." So where do we go from here? First of all, you are to love your wife as Christ loves the Church. The name *Christ* means the "Anointed One" and is one of several names given to Jesus. Each one of Jesus' names, including *Jesus*, has certain meaning and when used in Scripture is significant to its context. It is not Jesus, the Savior, who is the example of how husbands are to love their wives. Husbands are not their wives' saviors. Isn't that good news?

Those who feel the sense of lack and want in their lives usually are subconsciously looking for someone to rescue them and finally make them feel good about themselves. Falling in love can deceive us into believing the rescuer has come. For a while the old feelings of need may be overwhelmed with the new feeling of being in love. But sooner or later, the old feelings will return because no human can rescue us. So, husbands, you are not the rescuer, but you are anointed to bring the Rescuer into your wife's need.

What did Christ's anointing mean? *"The Spirit of the Lord is upon Me, because He has anointed Me to preach the gospel to the poor; He has sent Me to heal the brokenhearted, to proclaim liberty to the captives and recovery of sight to the blind, to set at liberty those who are oppressed; to proclaim the acceptable year of the Lord"* (Luke 4:18-19). As a Christian husband with Christ as your example, you are anointed to bring the anointing of Christ to your wife; anointed to encourage her with His good news that she needs to hear in whatever circumstances she finds herself; anointed to bring His healing to her broken heart; anointed to bring His power to set her free from all oppression, hindrances, and bondages; anointed to help her see beyond her blinding circumstances; anointed to bring His liberty to her captivity in the cave of the carnal gender mentality; and anointed to bring her to the day when her hope will become a Tree of Life.

Therefore, the husband's thinking has to change from, "I don't know what to do" or "There is nothing I can do" to "I am anointed to do something to bring her Savior into her situation." Easier said than done? I believe God has shown me three responses that men tend to have when they are intimidated by not knowing what to do. Perhaps we need to identify them and see them for what they really are to better understand how thinking needs to change.

The first is to simply retreat into his aloneness. Usually loners have never really seen, or at least never accepted, that they have any other part in their marriage relationship other than making a living and faithfully showing up at home at the end of the day. They shrug their shoulders and say, "I don't know what to do" and walk away. Jesus literally took on the form of His Bride and became a human so He could get involved with her. Even though she was a total mess and "ugly as sin," He still came to get involved with her. To love your wife as Christ loves the Church means getting involved with her. It means thinking differently and facing the intimidation of not knowing what to do, instead of walking away. It means thinking (and praying), "I don't know what to do, Lord, but You do. I am not going to walk away but stay and get involved with this situation until we have found Your provision." It means taking the time to think it through and talk it through with your wife. It doesn't mean you are going to hear a booming voice from Heaven. But somewhere in the thinking and talking it through, you will find your solution, or at least the first step toward solution. That's how God works. He lives in you and knows how to subtly direct your thoughts to see your solution—that is, if you are not already occupying your thoughts with, *I don't know what to do.*

> *If any of you lacks wisdom, let him ask of God, who gives to all liberally and without reproach, and it will be given to him. But let him ask in faith, with no doubting, for he who doubts is like a wave of the sea driven and tossed by the wind* (James 1:5-6).

The second response men can have when they don't know what to do and are intimidated is to judge the situation and/or his wife as making an unreasonable or foolish demand of him. Then he puts up a wall, or retreats behind the wall he has already constructed with his thoughts of, *This is not my problem. She wants me to do everything for her. She expects too much. This is her problem. When she gets her act together, she won't be this way. Until then, she is on her own.* This is pure abdication any way you look at it. It is refusing to take your place in the marriage relationship, abandoning the wife.

*No temptation has overtaken you except such as is common to man; but God is faithful, who will not allow you to be tempted beyond what you are able, but with the temptation will also make the way of escape, that you may be able to bear it* (1 Corinthians 10:13).

"Temptation" here is from a root word that means to be put to the test. When you are in any situation that is testing and trying you, you have a safe place to go. God will be faithful to keep you from being overwhelmed and will provide you a way to escape from it or to solve it. That's how He loves the Church.

Does your wife find a safe and faithful place in you? For example, if your wife wrecks the car and it is her fault, can she run to you knowing you will not allow her to be overwhelmed and that you will take care of it and her? Are you her safe place, even when she has blown it, or would she rather lie or hide it from you because of what else she will have to endure from what you dump on her with tongue lashings, silence, or "giving her what she deserves"—whatever that means. Few wives go out to have a wreck on purpose.

We see from this example that the abdicator may need a lot of mind-renewing to follow the example of loving his wife as Christ loves the Church. It starts by thinking (and praying), *"My wife's problems are my problems. My wife's concerns are my concerns. God has called me, authorized me, and anointed me as her husband to be her safe place in her environment. I will be faithful to help her find a solution or find a way out. I take off all the judgments I have placed on my wife. She is no longer on her own."*

The third response is to "try harder" or "do better." This is another dead-end way of thinking. To try to change or improve behavior without changing thoughts in the belief structure is only adding stress and vain labor to life. It puts the husband into a position of following instead of leading. It is the burden of performing where nothing really changes and creates the feeling that nothing you do is good enough. The truth is that nothing we do apart from the Lord is good enough. *"I am the vine, you are the branches. He who abides in Me, and I in him, bears much fruit; for without Me you can do nothing"* (John 15:5). *"For with God nothing will be impossible"* (Luke 1:37). *"Unless the Lord builds the house, they labor in vain who build it; unless the Lord guards the city, the watchman stays awake in vain"* (Ps. 127:1). The meaning of the word "house" in this Scripture includes family, which again takes us right back to relationship with God. If we are going to labor, it would be best to do so by finding out what and how God wants our family to be built and our relationship to work, and changing our thinking to agree with Him.

Instead of striving to "do better," we start thinking (and praying), *"I do not possess the ability to do better. I always fall back into the same rut of failure. God is not giving me the grace to try harder. He wants to renew my mind, change my belief structure, and change my thinking. I am anointed and will take the leadership position in my home. I am no longer to strive in my circumstances and relationships, but I am to seek God and obey Him. I will cease striving and yield to the mind of Christ within me."*

If loving your wife is an obligation to you, then your relationship will simply be a performance. Loving your wife should be what is in your heart to do, not what you *have* to do. I can understand the not knowing how to, but the "want to" should be a strong motivation that causes you to learn "how to." Is your marriage more about what she is doing or not doing? Did you get married to love or only to be loved? Are your thoughts and your prayers more about what's wrong with her and how she should be, without honestly looking at yourself? Just because you are trying doesn't mean you are doing it right. Just because you didn't mean to hurt her doesn't mean you didn't hurt her. Your starting place toward a healthy marriage is *you*. It is humbling yourself and giving up your life for Jesus' sake and for her sake. It is you becoming honest in your relationship with God to discover your wrong thinking and then change it. It is seeing the truth from God's perspective and then agreeing with it.

## DON'T LIE TO YOUR WIFE

We see it and hear it often on the television sitcoms: "Men are liars." Of course, all men are not liars, but it is prevalent enough for men to be stereotyped as such. As a minister, one of the most common complaints I have heard from wives is, "My husband lies to me." Does Christ lie to His Bride?

If a husband is living a second secretive life, then I can understand his need to lie to his wife. If he is having an affair or affairs, then he would lie. But these wives who have complained are married to godly men who faithfully come home to them. So why do they lie? What do they have to hide?

We have already discussed at length the Adamic tendency of men to hide their iniquity rather than be honest about their actions and the motives of their hearts. Hiding always creates the need to lie. However, a man who has come face-to-face with his God no longer has to hide. The man who has seen who he is in Christ can accept his weaknesses and imperfections and no longer has to hide. The man who has come to peace with himself no longer has to present to his wife or anyone else a façade and then protect it with lies. The man who has become secure in his own manhood no longer has to blame his wife and her behavior for his need to lie.

Sir, do you have any idea what it does to your wife to lie to her? It demeans and devalues her. It shuts her out of intimacy with you. If she has any spiritual intuitiveness, she knows you are lying. At first, she tries to give you the benefit of the doubt. But when it happens again and again, she knows without any doubt that you are lying. She may confront you with it, and you can look her right in the face and still lie. She may back off, not because she believes you, but because she has no proof of the lie to push the issue.

Your wife will probably continue to love you because she has the ability to cover your lying with love. But to continue to respect and trust you is another matter. Do you expect your wife to continue to respect you when you do not have enough self-respect to deal with the issues in your life that cause you to lie, making you less than the man she knows you really are? Do you expect your wife to continue to trust you when you do not have enough trust in her to be honest with her?

> *These six things doth the Lord hate: yea, seven are an abomination unto Him: a proud look, a lying tongue, and hands that shed innocent blood, an heart that deviseth wicked imaginations, feet that be swift in running to mischief, a false witness that speaketh lies, and he that soweth discord among brethren* (Proverbs 6:16-19 KJV).

This Scripture is very clear about how God views lying. What more do we need to say, other than the son that God loves will be chastised (see Heb. 12:6)? *"Blessed is the man whom Thou chastenest, O Lord, and teachest him out of thy law; that thou mayest give him rest from the days of adversity"* (Ps. 94:12-13a KJV). You have the choice to deal with your issues in the private intimacy of your relationship with the Lord, or you can wait until the Lord brings them out in the open to deal with them. Sooner or later, they will be dealt with because the Lord loves you.

How do you deal with lying and the issues that cause you to lie? You deal with them and destroy them by exposing them. It appears that some men would rather lie, lose their family, and even die than expose their weaknesses and imperfections. Does that describe you? Sir, you will never know the great enabling power of God's grace or the great strength of your wife's love until you take a step out of your control and self-protection, make yourself vulnerable, and put them to the test.

## Living With an Emotional Being

Women are different from men, and *God made them that way.* Women are more emotional and intuitive than men, and

*God made them that way.* No man has a right to be critical or judgmental of these facts. Certainly there is no justification for a man to demean his wife. I would suggest that men listen to the things they say around their peers on the job, in the locker room, on the golf course, and elsewhere. What kind of comments do you make about your wife or women in general? Do you speak highly and complimentary of her or them? Or do you make comments like, "Just like a woman!" "Sounds like my old lady." "Oh boy, if she is going to the mall, you had better take the checkbook away from her." "She has to cry over everything." "Talk, talk, talk," "Nag, nag, nag"? Of course I could give much worse examples with vulgarities and sexual slurs. I have heard men jokingly make comments about their wives that aren't even true about them. It is just the funny, expected thing to say (ha, ha, ha). It sounds like her worth is not even above rhinestones much less rubies (see Prov. 31:10).

*"Brood of vipers! How can you, being evil, speak good things? For out of the abundance of the heart the mouth speaks"* (Matt. 12:34). If you speak it, then it is coming from somewhere in your heart. In other words, there is something in your belief structure that agrees with what is coming out of your mouth or you wouldn't be saying it. If it is mean, ugly, or just not complimentary, it is not just joking. (Special alert: Some men may not be saying these things because of how they feel or what they believe about their wives. It may be coming out of what they believe about themselves.)

Men, likewise, have to face up to wrong beliefs and attitudes they may have in their mentality or belief structure. Men have had strong female influences in their lives from the day they were born that have affected their attitudes toward women. These attitudes were already established before marriage, and very likely the wife had little to do with them. A man can also develop attitudes and beliefs from how his father treated his mother. Some men may have good, healthy attitudes, and some men may have bad, harsh, and even perverted attitudes. As we have learned, what is in a man's belief structure is how he treats his wife and approaches his marriage.

I have said many things to come to the point I now want to make: A man has to totally and completely accept the emotional part of his wife as a good and right thing necessary to their relationship, before he can begin to live with her with understanding. Assuming that you agree, I would like to give you some general information about the emotional being of a woman that can help us move on from here.

The female man receives information through her emotional being first. Therefore, isn't it obvious that there could often be varying degrees of animated and verbal responses to things she hears? You men call it "going bananas" or "going berserk" or "getting crazy." Granted a spiritually mature woman should be ruling her emotions, but that does not mean she will act like a man. She is still a woman just like she should be, and there will be responses that come from her emotional being. *Don't take it personally!* Allow her to be who she is. Give her the time and space, without abandoning her, to process what she has to process the way she has to process it.

If you take her responses personally or think she is, by her response, blaming you, you will feel justified in not sharing information with her. *Wrong!* If your wife is not maturing emotionally, then perhaps you should begin to encourage her. Tell her that instead of her growing into a helper to you in this area, she is acting like she wants to be a little girl needing a daddy. Now you say to me, "She doesn't want to hear that. It will just make her mad."

Guys, you are appointed by God to be the head of your wife. That means there will be times you *have* to say things that don't want to be heard. The result may be anger and/or silence for several days. Anticipating a negative reaction from you wife should not be the judge of your wisdom or obedience to God. What does God say is best for your marriage and home? Obey

Him and leave the result to Him. *Important! Important! Important!* Once you have spoken the truth to her in love, no matter how she reacts, do not withdraw from her or withdraw your security, acceptance, and value of her. *Stay consistent* to how you are in love with her. If you react with anger, she will feel she doesn't have to listen to you because you are just as bad. Nothing will be accomplished.

On the other side of the coin, you have not been appointed by God to always point out what is wrong with her. You are not to be her critic. It is the Holy Spirit's work to deal with her heart. At times God will use you to confront her and speak to her. As with all people, we are to speak the truth in love and then let God do the "heart" work.

*"Husbands, likewise, dwell with them with understanding, giving honor to the wife, as to the weaker vessel..."* (1 Pet. 3:7a). God says you are to honor your wife as the weaker vessel. A vessel is a container; therefore, what is weaker is the container in which the person of your wife lives. One way the vessel is weaker is that the woman's body has not been created with the intensity or the endurance of strength as the man's body has been. He can lift and push more weight. That means, husbands, you are better equipped to carry things and lift things. More and more, I am seeing wives walk into a building, behind their empty-handed husbands, carrying the infant seat with the infant, the diaper bag, her purse, and whatever else she needs.

There is another way her vessel is weaker. She cannot carry within her a large amount of emotional stress and turmoil. Husbands, God made you to be able to handle your emotions differently than women. There are times when men have to be able to execute hard and sometimes gut-wrenching tasks. Men have the ability to fight wars and kill enemies without being devastated emotionally. As Ecclesiastes 3:8b says, there is *"a time of war, and a time of peace."*

Women can handle only so much emotionally before something has to give. A husband who lives with his wife with understanding can learn to know when his wife is starting to overload and can learn to know what to do about it.

I was 28 years old and pregnant with our first son. I had spent four years in college, three years supporting myself while on my own, and now after three years of marriage we were having a baby. We had put a lot of time and work into preparing ourselves to deliver our son naturally. It was a Wednesday, and I was at the doctor's office for my weekly visit. At that time, the baby was two weeks late. The doctor checked me and decided to x-ray. Her suspicions were confirmed by the x-ray that the baby was coming headfirst, but instead of his chin being tucked in, his head was tilted back and he was coming nose first. Normally, the doctor would have ordered a C-section, but knowing how dedicated I was to giving birth naturally, she gave me the option of letting her and another doctor try to change the baby's position. I rested on the table using the breathing techniques I had learned as they pushed and pulled and shoved. I left the clinic with the instructions to walk, walk, walk to help keep the baby in its new position. Around midnight that night, labor started and with it came an intense back pain that never let up between contractions and lasted until the baby was born.

The whole time I was pregnant, I was consumed with the joy of having a baby. Being the oldest of six children I knew how to care for a baby, so there was no fear or insecurity in bringing our new son, Tory, home from the hospital. But I had been through a lot emotionally during this whole process. I had been thrown a couple of hard curves. Then when we came home, I experienced some difficulty in nursing. I was coming very close to the point of not being able to handle any more emotionally. My husband recognized my emotional overload and went into action. He called my mother to come take care of Tory and told me to get ready to go out for dinner and a movie. Those three hours of distraction with my husband was all I needed to release the emotional load. I was then ready to come home to my baby.

Gentlemen, it really doesn't take much to help free your wife from emotional overloads, especially if you are living with them with understanding. You first have to see that there are things you should do and can do instead of walking away saying, "I don't know what to do." Sometimes all you have to do is tell her she doesn't have to bear the load anymore because you are taking it from her. Tell her you will bear it and take the full responsibility of it. Isn't this what Jesus does for us? Maybe she should not have to be the one to face a cranky neighbor, deal with an overcharge on a bill, deal with a child having trouble at school, or handle_____ (You fill in the blank.).

Just remember, you are to give them honor as the weaker vessel. Don't tease them or belittle them. You give them honor. The person who lives in that vessel is not the weaker. She is the one (1) that matches your (1) that makes 1 x 1 = 1.

## Do You Listen to Your Wife?

Does your wife say you don't listen to her? Do you listen to her? Why does she say you don't? Has your wife ever pulled the "you don't listen to me" test on you? It's the test where she stops talking in the middle of a sentence or maybe in the middle of a word and you never notice. Do you think this is enough reason for her to believe you don't listen to her? What do you think it does to a person's security, acceptance, and value when they stop in the middle of a sentence to find they are not being listened to? Do you sit looking at her face and hearing her words and then tomorrow can't remember what she said? When she comes to you to help her make a decision concerning household business, do you question her later about why she made such a decision? In all honesty, is she justified in believing you don't listen to her?

To you husbands who do listen to your wives, we thank you. However, listening is the normal courteous thing to do and should not warrant special acknowledgment.

I know the excuses: "She uses too many words and she takes too long." How long does it take her? Two or three minutes? How about ten, fifteen, or twenty minutes? There are twenty-four hours in one day, and you think it is too long to give her twenty minutes?

"She always wants to talk when I am engrossed in watching something on television." Let's see now, she is engrossed in preparing, serving, and cleaning up dinner until about 7:00 in the evening. So tell me when are you not engrossed in watching television from about 7:00 till 10:00 p.m. or bedtime? Actually, is there any time when you are at home that you are not engrossed in something other than your family? You tell her she is the most important thing in your life, yet television gets more of your listening attention than she does. Is she going to believe that she is really that important? Can you leave the television for sex?

"She is important to me. I am just not interested in the things she wants to talk about." She is usually not interested in the things you want to talk about either, but she listens because she is interested in *you*. If I were not married to Richard Peet, I would know about half, if that, of what I know about government today. Government is in my husband's heart. He loves government, has taught government, and serves in government. He can quote most of the U.S. Constitution. I have received his seed, and now government is part of me and important to me. Now, what should his interest be toward me?

The carnal gender mentality has told us that the wife's daily routine and interests are not that important. She should be giving her attention to her husband and the things that concern and interest him. Is this the example of Christ loving the Church? Jesus, "*being in the form of God, thought it not robbery to be equal with God: but made Himself of no reputation, and took upon Him the form of a servant, and was made in the likeness of men"* (Phil. 2:6-7 KJV). Why did He do it? Because He was totally interested in *her*. Gentlemen, this is your wife's only time to live on this earth. Every day, week, and year that goes by in which she is being ignored is wasting her life. She has a right to be listened to and valued each day. God values every moment of her life as highly as He does yours.

The husband who cannot listen to his wife, no matter how long she wants to talk or when she wants to talk or what she wants to talk about, has not totally given himself to the marriage. The independence he is holding onto does not want to *bother* with what he has judged as the nonessentials. Saying she is the most important thing in his life is simply lip service, because in reality, she has been third, fourth, or fifth on his priority list.

But the husband who has received the vision of multiplication possibilities will give up his independence, remove his judgments, and start listening so he can learn how to live with his wife with understanding. Listening to the wife is more than just listening to her words; it is hearing her heart. What are the things that are important to her? What are her greatest concerns? Are there things she is worried about? What are the desires of her heart? What would she like to see happening. What would she like to change? What is she hoping for? What does she believe is her greatest asset? Where does she believe she has failed? What is her greatest success? Husband, do you know these things about your wife? Should you? What is living with your wife with knowledge and understanding if it is not knowing the things in her heart? You *must* listen in order to know them. The best teacher on the subject of your wife is your wife. Listen to her.

That beacon of warning and insight that operates in the wife's emotional being won't work effectively if the husband is not listening. Throughout the Bible God used wives to speak warnings and helps to their husbands. God told Abraham to listen to the voice of his wife and to do what she said (see Gen. 21:9-12). God even used the wife of the heathen Pontius Pilate to give him warning about Jesus (see Matt. 27:19).

So you say that you are going to "do better" and "try harder" to be a good listener to your wife. *Wrong!* You may be sincere, but with that response you will continue to fail. What do you have to do? *Change your belief structure!* If you continue to believe she uses too many words and that that is not a good thing; if you continue to believe that her conversation is not interesting; or if you continue to believe it is a bother—necessary—but still a bother, you will stay in the same mind-set. It will be impossible to "do better."

How do you make yourself believe something that you don't really believe? This prayer might help you: "Father, I see and admit that I have been a poor listener. I have failed my wife in listening to her, hearing her, and learning to know her heart. I ask You to forgive me and start the work of changing me into the listening husband that my wife rightfully deserves. I want to make her first priority in my life. I pull down the lie from my belief structure that my wife uses too many words when telling me something. If it takes that many words for her to say something, then it is all right with me. I totally accept it and will learn to enjoy listening to her. I turn my eyes from the things in life which I have made more interesting than my wife, and I choose to focus on her, making her the most interesting thing I could possibly see. I denounce my selfishness that has made listening and conversing with my wife a bother, when I can be totally engrossed for two hours or more in a football game or a movie on television. Help me readjust my belief structure so I can honestly be the godly husband that is in order the way You say it should be. Amen, so be it."

Now your energy should be spent on "thinking straight," not "doing better." You have control over your thoughts. You can stop your mind from going down channels of the same negative thinking about your wife that has become normal to you. It might also be a good idea to go to your wife and apologize for having failed her. Don't tell her you are going to do better. Just tell her that with God's help you are doing some readjusting in your thinking and that the results will be beneficial to your marriage.

## REMOVE YOUR BLAME

We have already discussed Adam's blame of his wife and how blaming has become a tendency passed on in Adam's heritage to his sons. How and where does blaming come into your life as a husband to your wife? What do you blame her for? Missed opportunities, not getting to "go places," being tied down, spending too much money, getting pregnant, wanting everything her way, not making you feel man enough, all your failures, the kids getting in trouble, not being attractive enough, not giving you enough sex?

One day when I was feeling totally shut out of my husband's life, I came to the realization that I had become chained by his blame. If I disagreed with him, I was against him. If I expressed hurt, I was making him feel like a heel. If I expressed anger, I was attacking him. If I stayed silent, he would say to others, "I don't know what's wrong with her. She won't talk to me." I couldn't win for losing. I couldn't get past his blame to communicate with him. He couldn't get past the blame to listen to me. It was like living with a porcupine. Every time I would try to get close to him in relationship, I would get poked with a quill. It appeared all he wanted me to be was a cheerleader on the sidelines of his life telling him how wonderful he was. I couldn't talk to him about the real issues in our marriage.

If your wife is the worst wife in the whole world, you are still commanded by God to love her as Christ loves the Church.

Christ didn't just remove the blame from her, He took her blame as His own. I have heard men say, "I will take my own blame, but I'm not going to take her blame." Aren't you glad that wasn't Jesus' response? Jesus did it because He knew who He was with His Father. You may say, "Sure, but He was God." Let's look at Philippians 2:7 again. The New American Standard says that Jesus emptied Himself and took on the form of a bond-servant. The New International Version says that Jesus became nothing, taking the very nature of a servant. That means He emptied Himself of His God-part and left it with His Father. He made Himself just like the first Adam. The only God-part He had in Him was the Holy Spirit, the same God-part that believers have in them today. Jesus said, *"I can of Myself do nothing. As I hear, I judge; and My judgment is righteous, because I do not seek My own will but the will of the Father who sent Me"* (John 5:30). Then Jesus says to us, *"I am the vine, you are the branches. He who abides in Me, and I in him, bears much fruit; for without Me you can do nothing"* (John 15:5). *"But if the Spirit of Him who raised Jesus from the dead dwells in you, He who raised Christ from the dead will also give life to your mortal bodies through His Spirit who dwells in you"* (Rom. 8:11).

This means that He has made available, by His Holy Spirit, all the power you need to live in obedience to God. This was all Jesus needed to accomplish the course that was set before Him. It is all you need to obey God and follow your course with a godly gender mentality. Therefore, I repeat, if your wife is the worst wife in the whole world, you are still commanded by God to love her as Christ loves the Church.

In an earlier chapter, we explained how the first Adam had a brief moment, before he ate the forbidden fruit, when he could have stepped between Eve in her deception and God, and interceded on her behalf. *"Wherefore He [Jesus] is able also to save them to the uttermost that come unto God by Him, seeing He ever liveth to make intercession for them"* (Heb. 7:25 KJV). The last

Adam intercedes for His Bride. Do you intercede, or do you blame your wife?

Women tend to be guilt prone. When things go amiss, they too quickly feel they have done something wrong, or at least in some way, it is their fault. Too often they take on guilt when there are absolutely no grounds for it. They already have a Savior who has taken care of their guilt before God. What they need is a husband who is delegated by the Savior to help them stay in the place of feeling guilt free. The husband is in the position to see and recognize the encroachment of illegal guilt trying to trespass into areas of the wife's life. The husband is anointed and authorized to step between this villain and his wife, to thwart its purpose and block its intent.

The husband has the power to take the guilt from her and for her, unless he is too busy blaming her. He can't operate or function in his anointing and authority if he is lining up and being a cohort with the enemy.

Sir, if your wife is really guilty of an offense in your life, then it is time to forgive her. It is time to deal with it and end it. Your blame is hindering the best gift God has given to you next to Himself in salvation. It is standing as an "iron curtain" or a "great wall" of separation that prevents oneness and any hope of entering into the multiplication dimension.

Do you want to see her punished? Do you feel that if you forgive her and let it go that she will be "getting away" with something? Haven't you been set free without being punished? Jesus took your punishment and has let you go free. Yes, maybe she continues to do whatever awful thing it is for which you are holding her guilty. Well, what awful thing are you still doing—lying, cheating, stealing? How about just plain disobedience to God? Forgiveness doesn't start with perfection. Jesus came to die and provide forgiveness for us even while we were yet sinners. How many more days, weeks, and even years are you going to waste away waiting for your wife to "get her act together" before you are willing to obey God? You may have to set her free before she changes. Let me restate this: You *will* have to forgive her and set her free before you can ever hope for her to change.

So what do you want? Do you want a real marriage with a oneness relationship with your wife that can take you into the multiplication dimension? Earlier in this book, I quoted from my brother, Skyler Smith. He has also written a poem that I believe is a great work of art inspired by the Holy Spirit. Every husband who is serious about taking his marriage into the multiplication dimension should consider the contents of this poem in a very personal way. It could be your prayer. It could be your confession or statement of intent. It could be a love letter to your wife.

## CREATED IN AN IMAGE

Forgive me, my wife...my bride.

Forgive me for not recognizing my place because of my pride.

You confessed your sin that you were deceived, but I hid mine in my bosom.

I left my first love. Wisdom says she loves those who love her.

She would have led us on the path of life, but without her, death has come.

With this death, separation also has entered our environment.

The veil has fallen between our God and us, between you and me, and between the spirit and the soul.

God, being responsible for our survival, always provides everything we need.

He said it's not good for man to be alone so He took us, one man created in His image, and made two and told us to become one.

One egg times one seed becomes one...one nurtured in your womb, until the appointed time and then you will give back one.

One that will take its place in a quiver...an arrow to be aimed and shot to extend our boundaries.

You will give one that will feed a nation during a drought, one that will become a deliverer of a nation, one that will become a king of a nation and finally, One to become all of these and so much more!

Forgive me, my wife...my bride.

Forgive me for not understanding the other dimensions of us becoming one.

I am to come out of my aloneness. Aloneness is silence.

I am to be one who speaks and declares into places prepared for seed.

To give you seeds in the form of words to connect and be received by you.

Seeds in the form of my hopes, my dreams, my desires, and even my fears and weaknesses.

I will trust you to nurture and bring life to my hopes, my dreams, my desires, and my fears and weaknesses!

You will make them have purpose and become greater than I could have in my aloneness, in my silence.

I have seen those women with barren wombs.

They cry out to God in agony with such desire for their wombs to give birth.

They are perceived as drunk, even in their prayers.

I try to understand the pain of having a barren womb.

When I work the ground and after I plant the seed, I wait for the rain to bring life to the seed.

Day after day…week after week and then painfully months go by without rain.

There is nothing I can do. It is out of my hands…my control.

I watch as the ground becomes hard…too hard, even to receive rain.

Cracks develop and grow bigger with each passing day.

The grass turns yellow and the leaves wither and fall to the ground.

Yes, I try hard to understand the agony.

With those with a barren womb, each month they are reminded of their barrenness.

Their months turn into years until the day comes when they no longer have the ability to receive seed.

Forgive me, my wife…my bride.

Forgive me for not taking responsibility for your actions.

Forgive me for blaming you…blaming you over and over again.

I knew what God said and yet…in silence, I watched you eat from the tree of the knowledge of good and evil.

Created in the image of God, I lifted myself up to be equal with God and did not humble myself and we died after I ate, out of disobedience, at the tree.

Because I ate when I should not have, I was told the ground would produce thorns.

I was told that by the sweat of my brow I would eat my food.

However, this came as no surprise to God because from the foundation of the world there was one slain...the last Adam!

When He was tempted, He did not eat and even became obedient in two more areas of temptation.

He, being in the very nature of God, did not consider equality with God something to be grasped, but made Himself nothing, taking the very nature of a servant, being made in human likeness.

And being found in appearance as a man, He humbled Himself and became obedient to death—even death on a tree.

After He died for His Bride, God exalted Him to the highest place.

He took responsibility for her actions and put those actions on Himself.

He never blamed her...He just loves and forgives her over and over.

In a garden, He sweated from His brow redemptive blood that brings me rest in my thought life.

In the purpose of the last Adam, the death process produced a crown of thorns for His head where that same redemptive blood was shed.

Today, doubt and unbelief will not keep me from entering the garden...the rest, again.

I will let the angel with the flaming sword do as God's will says.

The flames will serve their purpose and the sword its purpose.

I will love and follow wisdom on the path that leads to the Tree of Life.

Skyler S. Smith

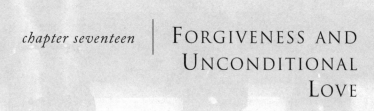

| FORGIVENESS AND
UNCONDITIONAL
LOVE

*L*ove and *forgiveness* are the two words we hear most about
in church, and rightfully so. Love and forgiveness is what
God is and what He is all about. If we are in the process of
being restored to His image, in which we were created, then love
and forgiveness should be what we are and what we are all about.

Many years ago, I went through an experience where I was
totally rejected by people I loved and cared a lot about. It was my
first time facing right-out open rejection. I was gravely wounded
and cried and cried to the Lord. Then He began to show me
about the kind of "love" that we as man, male and female, pass off
as love. If this kind of "love" could talk, it would say, "If you look
the way I want you to look and act the way I want you to act and
talk the way I want you to talk, then I will love you. I need you to

look, act, and talk 'right' so I can always feel safe and secure, loved and accepted, and valued by you. If you don't look, act, and talk 'right,' then I won't 'love' you anymore." This isn't real love. It is control, manipulation, and using people. It is another subtle form of witchcraft.

Then God told me, "This is the kind of love on which man builds relationships. It is really building on sand, and when the storms of circumstances come, the building will fall" (see Matt. 7:24-27). In this case the buildings are relationships. Then He said, "I never build on or with what man has built. I tear down man's building before I begin to build" (see Jer. 1:10). I said to myself, "Praise God! He is going to teach them how to love me." Knowing at the time that forgiveness is essential to living in relationship with God, I honestly and truly forgave those who had rejected me and continued to be consistent in my friendly behavior toward them.

Two or three years went by when I was asked to give my testimony at a women's gathering in a neighboring city. In preparation I was prayerfully thinking through my life asking my Father what He wanted me to share. This incident of rejection came to my mind and He said, "It wasn't their love I was working on."

Can you see from this example how "real love" and forgiveness cannot be separated from each other? If I had not forgiven, then my heart would have been hardened to God building His real love in me. Forgiveness and real love go hand in hand. What I am calling "real love" is God's *unconditional love,* and if this real love could talk, it would say, "It doesn't matter how you look, I will always love you. If you get fat or skinny, lose your hair, lose your breasts, or lose your legs, I will always love you. No matter how you act I will always love you. If you should fail and get into trouble or get desperate and do something stupid, I will always love you. You do not possess the words in your vocabulary that can stop me from loving you. You may wound me, you may disappoint and fail me, but I will forgive you and never stop loving you." Does this kind of love appear impossible? It is impossible for man. But with God all things are possible. Unconditional love is God's kind of love, and it is the only kind of love that makes a marriage work.

How do we get this kind of unconditional love to work in our lives? It starts with the individual first, making a commitment. Man's love is based on feeling, emotion. It is only real if you feel it. God's unconditional love is based on commitment—being committed to it whether it is felt or not. So, each individual starts by making a commitment to love unconditionally. Then God sets to work making it real in the individual's heart. I believe I can best illustrate it by using the example of Peter.

Then Jesus said to them that Thursday evening of the Lord's supper:

*"All of you will be made to stumble because of Me this night, for it is written: 'I will strike the Shepherd, and the sheep will be scattered.' But after I have been raised, I will go before you to Galilee." Peter said to Him, "Even if all are made to stumble, yet I will not be." Jesus said to him, "Assuredly, I say to you that today, even this night, before the rooster crows twice, you will deny Me three times." But he spoke more vehemently, "If I have to die with You, I will not deny You!" And they all said likewise* (Mark 14:27-31).

The account in Luke adds more detail to this event.

*And the Lord said, "Simon, Simon! Indeed, satan has asked for you, that he may sift you as wheat. But I have prayed for you, that your faith should not fail; and when you have returned to Me, strengthen your brethren." But he said to Him, "Lord, I am ready to go with You, both to prison and to death." Then He said, "I tell you, Peter, the rooster shall not crow this day before you will deny three times that you know Me"* (Luke 22:31-34).

I have no doubt that Peter meant what he said. In the way Peter saw and knew himself, he really believed he could and would die with Jesus. Then something happened that threw him into a place where he didn't know how to function. It happened when the guards came to get Jesus in the Garden of Gethsemane. *"Then Simon Peter, having a sword, drew it and struck the high priest's servant, and cut off his right ear. The servant's name was Malchus. So Jesus said to Peter, 'Put your sword into the sheath. Shall I not drink the cup which My Father has given Me?'"* (John 18:10-11). Matthew's account reads, *"And suddenly, one of those who were with Jesus stretched out his hand and drew his sword, struck the servant of the high priest, and cut off his ear. But Jesus said to him, 'Put your sword in its place, for all who take the sword will perish by the sword. Or do you think that I cannot now pray to My Father, and He will provide Me with more than twelve legions of angels? How then could the Scriptures be fulfilled, that it must happen thus?'"* (Matt. 26:51-54). Then Jesus put the servant's ear back on and healed it.

All who are acquainted with the Peter who walked with Jesus as told in the four Gospels know that he was *not* a fearful man. He was the man who got out of the boat in a storm and walked on the water. He was a "take charge and get the job done" sort of man. And that is what he did when the guards were trying to take Jesus. He was ready to kill or be killed to defend Jesus. I believe he was being consistent to the commitment he had made—to even die with Jesus. But it was Jesus' response to his efforts that threw him. Jesus healed the servant's ear and admonished Peter. It threw Peter totally out of his control. If what he did to defend Jesus wasn't the right thing, then what in the world was he supposed to do?

Have you ever been in a situation where you found yourself totally out of control? It can hinder and even stop you from thinking and functioning. If you are used to being in control and then lose control, you can do some pretty stupid things.

At a distance Peter followed Jesus and the guards and began to witness the proceedings. And as it goes, he was "accused" three times of being "one of them." As Jesus had prophesied, three times Peter denied having any part with Jesus. I don't believe Peter did it out of fear of dying. It was the fear of being out of control. He was always in control. His security, his value, and strength all rested in being in control. The vulnerability of being out of control was more than what he could handle. It was one thing to die fighting, but to walk up and say, "Here I am—kill me," was another matter, so he failed Jesus three times.

After Peter had denied Jesus the third time and the cock had crowed the second time, "*the Lord turned and looked at Peter. Then Peter remembered the word of the Lord, how He had said to him, 'Before the rooster crows, you will deny Me three times.' So Peter went out and wept bitterly*" (Luke 22:61-62).

I am sure Peter now thought it was all over. Even if Jesus got out of this thing alive, it was all over for Peter. He blew it. He failed. How could he ever be worth anything to God again? For the first time, Peter was really seeing himself. Just like Peter, we never really see ourselves; we do not really know ourselves until we are out of control. It took the "sifting" by satan for Peter to see the truth about himself, but what he didn't know as he left weeping bitterly was that the best was just beginning.

On that first Easter morning, the women went to anoint Jesus' body for burial. When they arrived, the tomb was open, Jesus was gone, and there was an angel who told them Jesus had risen. "*But go your way, tell His disciples **and Peter** that He goeth before you into Galilee: there shall ye see Him, as He said unto you*" (Mark 16:7 KJV, emphasis added).

Can you imagine what Peter must have felt when the women came to the disciples with the message from the angel? Here again I put myself into Peter's place feeling a total failure. He had failed Jesus to whom he had committed his life, and he had failed himself. Then in the dark, ugly emotional pit of the reality of what he had done, he heard the women say, "Tell the disciples and *Peter*...." Did the angel really say his name? Perhaps he even asked the women to repeat it. Yes, he really did say, "Peter."

Why did the angel specifically speak Peter's name and Peter's name only? Out of all the disciples it was Peter that satan had asked for to "sift" as wheat. All the disciples had experienced the tumult and tragedy of the previous events, but it was Peter who had gone on the catastrophic journey of facing the reality of himself. Jesus had told him, *"But I have prayed for you, that your faith should not fail; and when you have returned to Me, strengthen your brethren."* The angel spoke Peter's name because Peter needed to hear his name, and God wanted him to know he was still included.

The third time that Jesus appeared to His disciples after He had risen from the dead, He had a conversation with Peter. Before we look at this conversation, we need to understand two Greek words that mean "love." The first is *phileo*, and it means "brotherly love, friendship love" and is within man's ability to do so. The second is *agape*, and it is God's "always faithful, never failing, and unconditional love with no hidden agenda," which only becomes possible in man through his relationship with God. Now let's look at Jesus' conversation with Peter. I have written the Scripture using the original Greek words for "love" as they are found in the original text.

> *Jesus said to Simon Peter, "Simon, son of Jonah, do you* **agape** *Me more than these?" He said to Him, "Yes, Lord; You know that I* **phileo** *You." He said to him, "Feed My lambs." He said to him again a second time, "Simon, son of Jonah, do you* **agape** *Me?" He said to Him, "Yes, Lord; You know that I* **phileo** *You." He said to him, "Tend My sheep." He said to him the third time, "Simon, son of Jonah, do you* **phileo** *Me?" Peter was grieved because He said to him the third time, "Do you phileo Me?" And he said to Him,*

*"Lord, You know all things; You know that I phileo You."* Jesus said to him, *"Feed My sheep"* (John 21:15-17, emphasis added).

From the vantage point of our present-day revelation and understanding, we can see that Jesus was not just confronting Peter, He was also identifying three levels or dimensions of ministry. Allow me to amplify and paraphrase this Scripture:

*Jesus said to Peter, "Simon* [which means harkening], *son of Jonah* [which means dove, a symbol of the Holy Spirit] [Jesus is speaking here to Peter's identity], *do you unconditionally love Me more than everyone else?"*

It is obvious that Jesus is not speaking to the same arrogant, in-control, and take-charge Peter who declared he would die with Him. Peter is now facing Jesus with a broken and contrite heart. *"The sacrifices of God are a broken spirit, a broken and a contrite heart—these, O God, You will not despise"* (Ps. 51:17). *Contrite* means "deeply sorry, penitent." And Peter is now speaking to Jesus at the most gut-level honesty he has ever spoken about himself. Peter is speaking to Jesus stripped naked of his façade of control, arrogance, justification, and logic reasoning as he answers, "Yes, Lord, I love You as my best friend, but isn't it obvious that I do not love You unconditionally?" Jesus says, "You have given a right answer; therefore, I send you to feed my Word to my spiritual babies." This is the first level or dimension of ministry.

*Then Jesus asks a second time, "Harkening* [Simon], *son of the Spirit* [Jonah], *do you love Me unconditionally?" And again Peter answers, "Yes, Lord, I love You as a best friend, but I do not have the ability to love You unconditionally." Jesus says, "You have again given the right answer; therefore, I send you to take care of My followers who are growing into maturity."*

This is the second level or dimension of ministry.

Jesus asks Peter a third time, but His question is a little different:

*"Harkening, son of the Spirit, do you phileo Me?" Peter was now grieved, probably thinking Jesus was not pleased with only phileo. Then Peter gives another excellent answer, "Lord, You know. Lord, You know everything. You knew when I was "showing off" in my arrogance and control that I really didn't love unconditionally. You know now that I am speaking the truth when I say I love You as my best friend."*

Yes, Jesus knew that where Peter was in his spiritual growth, *phileo* was all he had and all he could give, and He was willing to meet Peter at that place. Jesus also knew that because of Peter's broken and contrite heart and because of Peter's honesty with himself, that his heart was no longer fallow ground. The "soil" of his heart had been broken up and worked by the trial he had been through and was now rich and ready to receive the spiritual seed of agape, the seed of real unconditional love. Jesus knew Peter would quickly grow into a man of agape. Because of what Jesus knew, He sent Peter to do third-dimension ministry, "Feed my mature followers."

We are seeing here that, at least to God, honesty about our love is more important than the quality of our love. When there is honesty, there is also a heart in which God can plant and establish His agape, the unconditional love that we really want to be able to give. But the most important thing I want us to see from this illustration is, *we cannot have or give unconditional love until we know God's unconditional love for us. We cannot know God's unconditional love for us until we have failed.* It amazes me how we can be blind to our lack of unconditional love and yet see other's lack so clearly.

Jesus did not condemn or reject Peter because of his love failure. Jesus didn't turn His back to Peter telling him that he should get what he deserves. Jesus allowed Peter his "tearing down" time and then met him with love, acceptance, and restoration on the other side. Jesus had said to him, *"when you have returned to Me, strengthen your brethren"* (Luke 22:32b). Peter experienced God's unconditional love.

Let us emphasize again that before Jesus was taken a prisoner, Peter really believed he had the real kind of love. We believe we have it, but the hidden agendas in our love are so hidden we don't even realize they are there. I challenge you to a test. What is it that you are about to do or are planning to do for someone that needs to be done? Don't do it. If it really needs to be done, give it to someone else to do, but don't do it yourself. Do you have an objection to me telling you not to do it, other than it needs to be done? Would you struggle not doing it or giving it to someone else to do? Why would you struggle? *"Because they would think I didn't care."* That's the give-away answer. Do you not see the hidden agenda in it? We use our "love" to be sure we get what we need in return, and at least for a Christian but not limited to Christians, it usually has to do with how we need others to see us.

This way of loving is very unhealthy. It causes us to placate and avoid certain issues because it "might hurt someone's feelings." *Placate* means "to make somebody less angry, upset, or hostile, usually by doing or saying things to please him or her."[12] I don't see anything in this definition about truth and honesty. This love is based on fear; hence, we cannot afford to be truthful and honest because someone might get mad at us or disapprove of us or even reject us. Isn't this simply loving and protecting self? It really is a selfish, self-centered love that is supposed to make everyone think we are nice, kind, and wonderful so we can feel safe.

On the other hand, unconditional love is sacrificial love. This love puts self at jeopardy to help and/or protect someone else. "Well, in all honesty, I haven't met too many people, if any, who deserve a sacrifice on my part to be loved." Isn't that pretty much the attitude we encounter daily in others and ourselves?

Then one day, when totally broken in weakness and the inability to come through for yourself and God, God will come through for you. He will engulf you in Himself and in a personal way you will see and experience His sacrificial love for you. As a result, you will be different. You will no longer even see what people deserve. Mercy and compassion start to become familiar companions, and your love will no longer require conditions.

So how do we get unconditional love working in our lives? It starts with each individual making a commitment to love unconditionally. Then God sets to work, making it real.

The first work God does to plant unconditional love into our hearts is to teach us to forgive. The Lord's Prayer asks our heavenly Father to forgive us in the same way that we forgive others (see Matt. 6:12). You can't pray that prayer very often without getting serious about forgiving. There is no person who has lived life without, at some time, suffering deep wounds and severe pain by the words or behavior of another person. It is inescapable. We know the indescribable suffering that Jesus endured at the hands of men. Mel Gibson's movie, *The Passion of the Christ*, has made it very real to us. Why would His Father not only allow but also require Him to go through such suffering? One reason was so that He could, at the height of His suffering, say, "Father, forgive them...." We are forgiven; surely we can forgive.

Forgiveness starts with a decision, "I will forgive...." Then it is standing on that decision, confirming it whenever necessary until it becomes a finished work in the heart.

There was another time in my life, when weighed on my scales of justice, was many times worse than the example I gave earlier in this chapter. I can even see the very spot I stood when I prayed a prayer worded something like this: "Father, everything in me that is me wants to hate. I want to strike back. I want them to get what they deserve, and I want them to hurt just like they have hurt me. I know this does not please You, but I do not have the power to keep anger and resentment from consuming me. If I get through this, it will be by Your grace alone. I can say that I choose to forgive, but there is nothing in my being that feels it or even wants to. I choose to forgive only because I love You." I am still awed by God's faithfulness to me. He took the smallest mite that I offered Him and made it enough to do a complete work in me. But if I had not offered it to Him, I would today be bitter with resentment and still be fretting over "how I was treated." My heart would have been hardened, not allowing any seed of God's Word to penetrate and take root. Forgiveness is a requirement to knowing unconditional love. Forgiveness is a requirement to receiving and giving agape—God's always-faithful, never-failing, unconditional love with no hidden agenda.

As we have said, we cannot give unconditional love until we have known God's unconditional love for us. To know God's unconditional love, we have to have failed in our ability to give love so that we need God to love us unconditionally. Until then, we really believe in some ways we are measuring up. We *say* we don't deserve God's love, but we have done things "right," and we give of ourselves lovingly, so we are sure God is going to faithfully love us. Subconsciously this is how we operate and then we expect others to do the same. When they don't do things "right" or give of themselves as they should, then in some way, either with words or "pulling away" from them, we have to show or communicate our disapproval so they can learn to do better. We certainly can't approve of their misbehavior. I say—Phooey! Hogwash! That is *not* unconditional love. It is religious self-righteousness which brings embarrassment and shame down on those who aren't able to be as good as we *think* we are. Anyone who thinks this way needs to go stand by the cross from about noon to 3:00 on Good Friday.

The term "unconditional" can be misleading to those who already have misconceptions about love, so let's talk about some more things that love is *not*. Love is not—letting others control you because they might get angry if you refuse to do what they want.

Living a life pleasing to God will not conform to other's control, and it will make them angry. Their anger is their problem, not yours. For adult children, this includes parents. Even for minor children, parents are to rule them, teach them, guide them, and discipline them, but they are not to control them. Think about it.

Now, on the other hand, parents, you have got to get a grip on your children. Love is not—letting your children do what they want because they might get mad if you say "No." Children almost always get mad when told "No." They have to learn to take "No" for an answer. Life is not always going to say "Yes" to them. I thought "The Cosby Show" was, for the most part, a good example of parents not afraid to say "No" and at the same time still allow their children the freedom to express their thoughts, feelings, and individuality. Children should be allowed this freedom of expression. Saying "No" sets the safe boundaries that gives them the security they need first and foremost. Children do not know what is safe and good for them. They have to be disciplined to conform to what is safe and good for them. *Discipline*, which is defined in the Strong's Concordance with words such as "warning, instruction, restraint, correction, and rebuke" is unconditional love in action. You are not your children's friends; you are their parents, and they will get mad at you often. Unconditional love is about the children, not about you and how they feel about you. Your children will get over their anger because their security and health is in *your* discipline. Parents are to tell children when to go to bed, what they should or should not eat, when they are to take their medicine, where they are to play, etc. This has to do with health and security. However, parents should not force their children to conform to the parent's preferences. I have seen major battles over things such as the color of a shirt, a barrette in the hair, sitting on Santa's lap, kissing somebody, riding the horse, or petting an animal. I have seen small children terrorized by their parents forcing them to do something that has nothing to do with the child's safety or well-being.

I do not term *punishment* as part of *discipline*. Jesus took the punishment for all our sins, including our children's. Our children need to know that. But I do believe there are to be consequences when children step outside the boundaries parents have set. Those consequences may look the same as punishment, but the terminology and concept should not be punishment. The truth is that wrong choices bring about bad results, which is something we never outgrow. However, if we suffer our own punishment, why do we need the sacrifice Jesus gave?

Unconditional love does not mean we have to allow ourselves to be used, abused, or taken advantage of. Yes, there are times when God asks us to "turn the other cheek" or carry another's load a second mile or give more than another is requiring (see Matt. 5). But we are to do these things as a free choice. If you have the free choice to walk out of your disadvantaged situation today, but the only reason you are staying is because it is where the Lord wants you, then you best stay and let God complete the work He is doing. But there are also times when unconditional love requires us to speak the truth and exercise the authority of God by speaking life into dead, unhealthy, and even abusive situations. In other words, unconditional love does not mean we always have to keep our mouths shut because someone might get angry and it might stir up trouble. Unconditional love does not mean keeping the peace at any cost. If freedom is the cost we have to pay to keep the peace, then peace is already lost. It is not peace we are preserving; it is control.

Now let's bring unconditional love into the marriage. Hopefully, you have seen that unconditional love must start with the individual first. It is your love and your love only that God will deal with first. When your love is right, you can easily love your spouse because unconditional love is giving love without conditions. It frees your spouse to give to you what is in his or her heart to give, not what is required. Then, when both spouses are giving love unconditionally... *Wow*...what a marvelously fertile garden this marriage becomes. Fruitfulness will be unlimited, and the expression of the Father will be so powerful that any words we would use to try to describe it would only limit it.

*chapter eighteen* | # COMING INTO AGREEMENT

"Can two walk together, unless they are agreed?" (Amos 3:3). Two people walking together imply that they are going some place together. It then becomes obvious that there are several issues that must be agreed upon: Where are they going? When are they leaving? How fast should they travel? What do they need for the journey?

Notice that these are not moral issues. They are not issues of "right" or "wrong." These are issues of goals and purposes. When two people, with individual goals and purposes, start living together, there can be a lot of opinions and desires that begin to immerge. This is where a married couple can start getting into trouble. One thinks it should be this way and the other thinks it should be that way. One has always wanted to do this, and the other has always wanted to do that.

There are issues that should be discussed and agreed upon before marriage, such as church, careers, and children. But regularly there are other goals and purpose-related decisions that come up after the wedding that were unforeseen. It can be common for one to see it from one perspective and the other to see it from a different perspective. Coming to agreement can turn into a painful, ugly battle that can cause much damage to the marriage relationship.

Of course, the carnal gender mentality can easily solve such situations. The wife is to give up her opinions, desires, and whatever else necessary to allow the husband to do what he wants. I have seen talented and resourceful wives give up and sacrifice to follow their husbands down one dead-end road after another. Because she doesn't realize that she has as much to contribute and say about the marriage, the couple functions like a bird with only one wing. The best they can do is fly in circles.

One solution to help married couples come into agreement is to take turns in being "right." Perhaps a "possession light" that is used in basketball games should be incorporated into every married couple's home décor. The possession light is a short box about five or six inches deep and about two to three feet long with a light on each end. Whichever light is turned on indicates which team gets the ball the next time two players grab it at the same time.

The one that we use in our homes could have a pink light on one end and a blue light on the other end. Let's say that the wife gets to be "right" first and the husband has to agree with her. Then the blue light is turned on so that both know the next time the husband gets to be "right" and the wife has to agree with him. Then after that time, the pink light is turned on, and so on.

Yes, I am being facetious. Even though it is a ridiculous solution, it would be better than the arguing, the anger, and the bitter stalemate that can result when it is necessary to come to an agreement.

I do believe God has a better way. In fact, He always has a way. He even makes a way where there seems to be no way (see 1 Cor. 10:13). His way is better than the wife's way, and His way is better than the husband's way. The best solution would be for the wife and the husband both to give up their ways, their opinions, their desires, to God. Instead of spending their energy in fighting each other, they could be spending it finding out God's way.

There is only one God. The God who lives in the husband is the same God who lives in the wife. God always agrees with Himself. He will not say or lead the husband in one way and then say or lead the wife in another way. If both the husband and the wife really want God's way, they will find it because God will make it known. When God's way is discovered, there will be agreement.

God is not about the business of making one spouse right over the other. This exercise is *not* about finding out which spouse God is going to say is "right." It is about finding out what God's will is and giving up our opinion and giving up our way to agree with Him. His way is always the best and greater way. Why would anyone want to hold on to being "right" when they can have the better way?

If both the husband and the wife are not competing and if they both have given up their victim mentality, then there is no need to strive against each other as to who is right. When there is nothing left that has to fight for self, then the motive of the heart will naturally be for the other. Finding God's way and agreeing will be much easier.

Wife, if you have submitted yourself to your husband, and husband, if you have left your father and mother to cleave to your wife, then you are going someplace together. To get there you have to agree. You have to agree with God as to where you are going. You have to agree with God on how fast you will travel. You have to agree with God as to what you are going to need for the journey. As long as the two of you are agreeing with God, you will be able to walk together.

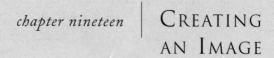

| CREATING
AN IMAGE

Now that we have learned how we come into agreement in a marriage, I want to describe two great giants that literally take positions between the husband and the wife, causing division. These are humongous giants dressed in full armor with swords and knives and scourging whips, hungry for battle and ready to strike out at any moment. These enemies, unless defeated and *totally* annihilated, will prevent agreement.

We have emphasized throughout this writing that God created man, both the male man and the female man, in His image. Then God said it was good. Even though man has done a great job messing up that image, God has made a way for His image to be restored to "good." God is God, and because He is God, He gets to create images. The image God has created in man is not a god; therefore, the image does not get to create other images. I am not talking about art forms or reproducing images here. Let me explain.

Throughout history, men have created their own religions and then created images from wood or metal or stone to represent their religions and be their gods. What they have done is create idols, which in turn, rule them. They lock themselves into dead religions with dead gods on which they spend their lives and sacrifices, getting no results. Christians know how much God has hated this, because it pulls mankind away from the living God (who can and will do something for them) toward a dead god that leaves them in their helplessness.

So what does this have to do with the carnal gender mentality and marriage? It has a lot to do with marriage, because husbands and wives both create images. Stay with me as I explain.

Usually I do not watch daytime television. But one day while I was ironing, I turned the television on to help pass the time. I settled on a channel where they were doing makeovers with new clothes, new hairstyles, and facial makeup. When that program ended, another program began, showing a young man being helped to set up the perfect time, place, and environment to ask the girl of his dreams to marry him. Throughout the episode, he would make such comments as, "She is a wonderful person. She is so kind and giving. She adds so much to my life. She makes me feel I can do anything. I couldn't find anyone more perfect." Suddenly I was brought to attention by the response I heard coming out loud from my mouth, "Sure, I would like to hear what you have to say in about two years." Realizing God was getting my attention, I began to examine why I had made such a statement.

I have mentioned earlier how we come into marriage with preconceived mind-sets and certain beliefs about the opposite sex. We have also formed beliefs about marriage itself and what married life should be. Out of these beliefs come expectations. Some expectations we can be very aware of, discussing them and understanding them together as a couple before the wedding date. But there can be some very strong and demanding expectations that are so obscure before marriage that they are not really seen or felt until they have been violated after marriage.

We will use a hypothetical couple with whom hopefully we all can relate. They are so in love with each other and believe they have found the only person in the whole world with whom they want to spend the rest of their lives. They talk about each other just like the young man talked about his girlfriend on the television program I viewed. Considering how they feel about each other, surely they are going to live "happily ever after."

However, it is not long after the wedding when they each begin to violate one of the obscure expectations. He comes home late one evening, but never called to say he would be late. She can't believe he could be so inconsiderate of her, and she files it away as a love failure and a strike against her value to him. Maybe the fact that he didn't call was inconsiderate, but he was only not doing what he had never done and didn't even think about doing. He certainly can't understand why it was inconsiderate. When she accuses him of being inconsiderate, he then refuses to see it as inconsideration. So now a pattern of behavior has been established. Her expectation gets violated, and he refuses to give it any credibility by neglecting to take any responsibility for his actions, which only serves to reinforce what she has filed away in her mind that eventually becomes a belief in her belief structure. She begins to believe that he does not really value her or care for her feelings. When this happens, she changes the image of her husband. She is now picturing him as what she is feeling about him, not what is truth about him. This image becomes an idol because it begins to "rule" her.

In the meantime, the husband is thinking how ridiculous she is in "overreacting" to such a little thing. So what if he didn't call?—He was going to be home soon anyway. He knows that he held no inconsiderate intentions toward his wife. Then he makes judgments that he files away in his mind, "She always wants things her way. I was not being inconsiderate. She is just too demanding." As the pattern repeats itself, eventually what he has filed away becomes a belief in his belief structure even though it is not the truth. He, too, is changing the image of his wife into the judgments he has made about her. Likewise, this image becomes an idol because it begins to "rule" him.

How do these idols "rule" them? Both the wife and the husband begin to see each other and respond to each other according to the images they have created, and they begin to *expect* the other to act like the image. They approach the other in a defensive mode as if they really are the image. The real person, the real image gets lost behind the created one.

I have given you just one example of one issue. There can be several different types of issues that are used to establish a pattern of beliefs that change the spouses' images in each other's minds. The result can be the creation of two great giants, so out of proportion to the truth and ready to destroy anything that should challenge its reality.

Have you ever watched "Divorce Court" on television? (I really don't recommend it.) What we often see is one of the spouses accusing the other of being and doing something horrible. The other spouse appears shocked at being accused of such a thing and vehemently denies it and then throws out accusations of his or her own. Now, it is the first spouse's turn to be shocked and counter-deny. I believe what we are seeing are the two created giants at war with each other. Truth isn't even the issue. Truth has been eaten up by the giants. Isn't this a form of idolatry? And as long as the giants are allowed to live, there will be no winner. The couple will either have to totally separate or destroy one another.

When giants have been created, the only way the marriage can be healed is to kill the giants. Each has to kill his own giant by seeing the truth about the image that was created and then removing it from the belief structure. Each spouse has to go back to see and embrace the truth about who the person they married really is. No, they are not perfect. Yes, they do have flaws and failures. And by this stage of the marriage both the husband and the wife could have done some very ugly and mean things out of anger and resentment. But we owe it to our wedding vows to work through the "junk" to be able to see the true heart of the one we married. This is a very difficult thing to do. Once giants have been created, it is almost impossible to do. It most definitely requires God's help and maybe even some help from a godly counselor. But it can be done.

The size and strength of your giants will be determined by how long you have been married and how you have dealt with issues in your marriage. Again, it has been my goal in this writing to give you vision of a marriage possibility that is worth the fight to kill your giant. It is worth humbling yourself, admitting to the truth of having created a giant, and becoming resolved that you will recapture the true image of the person you fell in love with and to whom you made a vow until death do you part.

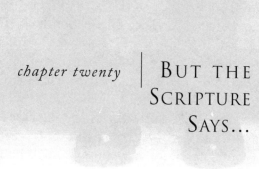

| # BUT THE SCRIPTURE SAYS...

A s I have made various points throughout this writing, I have almost heard these words floating toward me on the airwaves of the future, "But what about the Scripture that says...?" "But Paul said..." "And what about this Scripture...?" So now, let's take a look at these Scriptures.

Before we delve into the Scriptures that appear to place and keep women in the carnal gender mentality cave, let's set some groundwork. First of all, all truth comes from God. God created the heavens, the earth, and all that is in the earth. He was the One who set all of it into operation. God is truth; therefore, all that He does and all that He says is truth. Our logic and our understanding, without God, is limited to our perceptions of what we have experienced—what we have seen, heard, and felt. Mankind in its arrogance and pride has always tried to impose upon God's truth what his logic reasons from his experiences. When we look at it this way, we must agree how foolish mankind can be.

We observe the world's ways with its perverted "truth" about abortion, euthanasia, same-sex marriages, and peace at the cost of freedom, to name a few, and wonder how truth got so lost. But when we are in church with the mixture all around us that religion has added to truth, it is much more difficult to see our own perversions. In fact, when something that is not truth has been added to truth, then truth is no longer the truth. It has become a lie. Lies bring bondage. Truth makes free. Even if most of what we believe is the truth with a little mixture, that little bit that is not the truth can handicap all the truth we do believe. *"Do you not know that a little leaven leavens the whole lump?"* (1 Cor. 5:6b). For example, you can believe all the truth about God's faithfulness to take care of us and His great abundance to provide for us, but if you doubt that you are truly and completely forgiven, then you will be handicapped in your faith that God will always come through for you. Doubt is a lie that taunts us when we are in the greatest need for the truth.

The Word of God interprets the Word of God. The Bible does not contradict itself. If it appears to contradict itself, then we are not seeing it correctly. We are not seeing it the way God means it. Truth is consistent throughout the Bible. God says of Himself, *"For I am the Lord, I do not change"* (Mal. 3:6a). Jesus said to the devil, *"It is written, 'Man shall not live by bread alone, but by every word that proceeds from the mouth of God'"* (Matt. 4:4). If God does not change, then truth does not change. But we must remember that revelation and understanding of truth is progressive. Seeing and understanding truth is a journey that we will travel throughout our entire lives on earth and even perhaps throughout eternity. Therefore, we will have to change our belief structure many times as we grow spiritually, move into greater intimacy with our Father God, and develop in our understanding of His Word.

The goal in studying God's Word is to learn how to read out of it what God means and not read into it what we think we understand. This is one reason the Holy Spirit must be active in our coming to understand the Word. Jesus told Peter that the gates of hell shall not prevail against the Church (see Matt. 16:18). We used to believe this meant that God was going to protect the Church by preventing the gates of hell from breaking open, allowing hell to prevail against the Church. Since learning God's truth is a progressive journey with the Holy Spirit actively at work in the hearts of believers, man began to see and understand this Scripture differently. It really means that God so empowers the Church that the gates of hell cannot keep the Church from breaking through to take dominion.

There have been many times I have had to change my mind, change my belief structure to agree with something different God had shown me through His Word and by His Spirit. It is not easy to do. When a concept has appeared as truth for so long, to give it up as a lie can feel like yielding to deception. As I face the issues of life in this world, I hold on to what I believe is truth with a death grip; but when I study God's Word and sit in His presence, I hold truth openhandedly. Only truth makes free. I want God to remove or change anything I believe if it is not the truth, the whole truth, and nothing but the truth.

I have heard it said that Paul, the writer of most Scriptures that religion uses to "govern" women, had a problem with women, never married, and therefore, didn't understand what he was writing about. I don't believe this. I believe Paul, writing by the inspiration of the Holy Spirit, got it right. It has been the translators that have gotten it wrong. Let me give you an example.

The Greek word *diakonia* was used by Paul many times in his writings of the letters that are included in the New Testament. At least seven times he used the word to identify his "ministry" to the saints or to the Gentiles or to the Corinthians, etc.

He also used the term to identify the "ministry" of Timothy, of the Colossians, and of those of the house of Stephanas. He used it several times to identify "ministry" in general, and in Romans 12:7, he used it to identify "ministry" as a spiritual gift.

Luke also used the word more than once to identify the "ministry" of the apostles. The Hebrew writer used it to identify the "ministry" of the angels. However, let's look at Romans 16:1-2 in the King James Version. *"I commend unto you Phoebe our sister, which is a **servant** of the church which is at Cenchrea; that ye receive her in the Lord, as becometh saints, and that ye assist her in whatsoever business she hath need of you: for she hath been a succourer of many, and of myself also."* The same word *diakonia,* which was translated "ministry" or "ministering" in the many Scriptures I mentioned above is translated "servant" in this Scripture. Please notice that in this Scripture, it is in reference to a woman. The translators took Phoebe's "ministry" and diminished it to a servant. Yes, ministry can be *"serving* the Lord." It is the inconsistency that is objectionable because it is misleading to true understanding.

The word translated "succourer" in relation to Phoebe is *prostates* in the Greek, which is the feminine term of the word *proistemi.* The Strong's Concordance defines this word "to stand before, to preside, to practice: maintain, be over, and rule." This kind of "rule" is not that of a dictator. It is the God-given authority to bring the person's realm of influence into God's order. That is God's order by God's definition of order. *Proistemi* is used in the following Scriptures with emphasis added:

> *One that **ruleth** well his own house, having his children in subjection with all gravity; (for if a man know not how to **rule** his own house, how shall he take care of the church of God?)* (1 Timothy 3:4-5 KJV, emphasis added)

> *Let the elders that **rule** well be counted worthy of double honor, especially they who labor in the word and doctrine* (1 Timothy 5:17 KJV, emphasis added).

*Or he that exhorteth, on exhortation: he that giveth, let him do it with simplicity; he that **ruleth**, with diligence; he that showeth mercy, with cheerfulness* (Romans 12:8 KJV, emphasis added).

We see in these Scriptures the word in question is translated "rule." The Romans 16 Scripture is the only place *prostates* is translated "succourer." We can now see that Phoebe's ministry was a leadership ministry, and Paul approved of it and received from it. She ministered with godly authority that brought order to the church.

Also, the word "business" in this Scripture is translated from a Greek word that means "deed." Phoebe didn't need those in Rome to assist her in business she needed to do; Paul was instructing them to do the deeds that would help her do her ministry.

A more accurate rendering of this Scripture would be, "I commend unto you Phoebe our sister, which is a minister of the church which is at Cenchrea: that ye receive her in the Lord, as becometh saints, and that ye assist her in doing whatever deeds she hath need of you: for she hath been a leader of many, and of myself also."

It is translation that has been the culprit in causing misunderstanding about the place of women in life and in the church. Remember, it was the mistranslation of the word *teshuqa* as "desire" in Genesis 3:16 that set the stage for Scriptures about women to become twisted in understanding.

Let us again bring attention to the principle of God concerning two or three witnesses. "*One witness shall not rise against a man concerning any iniquity or any sin that he commits; by the mouth of two or three witnesses the matter shall be established*" (Deut. 19:15). And again in Second Corinthians 13:1b, "*By the mouth of two or three witnesses every word shall be established*." One witness alone is not sufficient evidence to make a judgment on any matter. We should use this principle consistently when studying the Word of God. If we think we are seeing a truth in a Scripture, we wait until we have seen it in two more places in Scripture before we accept it as truth.

Jesus came to fulfill the law of God given through Moses. So how do we relate to the law today? Jesus gave us two commandments: *"The first of all the commandments is: 'Hear, O Israel, the Lord our God, the Lord is one. And you shall love the Lord your God with all your heart, with all your soul, with all your mind, and with all your strength.' This is the first commandment. And the second, like it, is this: 'You shall love your neighbor as yourself.' There is no other commandment greater than these"* (Mark 12:30-31 KJV). All the commands of God are included in these two. *"For all the law is fulfilled in one word, even in this: 'You shall love your neighbor as yourself' "* (Gal. 5:14). If you love God totally and completely, you live to please Him. You don't need a commandment to keep you legal. You are governed by love. Love wouldn't allow you to go outside the boundaries of what is right in His sight. If you love your neighbor as yourself, you don't need commandments to tell you how to treat him. Love would never violate or wound him.

This is what the New Testament covenant is all about. It is God bringing us into a love relationship with Him through His Son who fulfilled the law for us. We are no longer bound by the law. We are only bound by love. Everything read in the Epistles of the New Testament must be read in the light of love, not law. Jesus didn't free us from the law and then instruct the apostles to give us new laws. The Epistles teach us God's ways. It is love that motivates us to live and walk in His ways.

Now we are ready to look at the Scriptures.

## JUDGES 4:4-24

*Now Deborah, a prophetess, the wife of Lapidoth, was judging Israel at that time. And she would sit under the palm tree of Deborah between Ramah and Bethel in the mountains of Ephraim. And the children of Israel came up to her for judgment. Then she sent and called for Barak the son of Abinoam from Kedesh in Naphtali, and said to him, "Has not the Lord God of Israel commanded, 'Go and deploy troops at Mount Tabor; take with you ten thousand men of the sons of Naphtali and of the sons of Zebulun; and against you I will deploy Sisera, the commander of Jabin's army, with his chariots and his multitude at the River Kishon; and I will deliver him into your hand'?" And Barak said to her, "If you will go with me, then I will go; but if you will not go with me, I will not go!" So she said, "I will surely go with you; nevertheless there will be no glory for you in the journey you are taking, for the Lord will sell Sisera into the hand of a woman." Then Deborah arose and went with Barak to Kedesh. And Barak called Zebulun and Naphtali to Kedesh; he went up with ten thousand men under his command, and Deborah went up with him. Now Heber the Kenite, of the children of Hobab the father-in-law of Moses, had separated himself from the Kenites and pitched his tent near the terebinth tree at Zaanaim, which is beside Kedesh. And they reported to Sisera that Barak the son of Abinoam had gone up to Mount Tabor. So Sisera gathered together all his chariots, nine hundred chariots of iron, and all the people who were with him, from Harosheth Hagoyim to the River Kishon. Then Deborah said to Barak, "Up! For this is the day in which the Lord has delivered Sisera into your hand. Has not the Lord gone out before you?" So Barak went down from Mount Tabor with ten thousand men following him. And the Lord routed Sisera and all his chariots and all his army with the edge of the sword before Barak; and Sisera alighted from his chariot and fled away on foot. But Barak pursued the chariots and the army as far as Harosheth Hagoyim, and all the army of Sisera fell by the edge of the sword; not a man was left. However, Sisera had fled away on foot to the tent of Jael, the wife of Heber the Kenite; for there was peace between Jabin king of Hazor and the house of Heber the Kenite. And Jael went out to meet Sisera, and said to him, "Turn aside, my lord, turn aside to me; do not fear." And when he had turned aside with her into the tent, she covered him with a blanket. Then he said to her, "Please give me a little water to drink, for I am thirsty." So she opened a jug of milk, gave him a drink, and covered him. And he said to her, "Stand at the door of the tent, and if any man comes and inquires of you, and says, 'Is there any man here?' you shall say, 'No.' " Then Jael, Heber's wife, took a tent peg and took a hammer in her hand, and went softly to him and drove the peg into his temple, and it went down into the ground; for he was fast asleep and weary. So he died. And then, as Barak pursued Sisera, Jael came out to meet him, and said to him, "Come, I will show you the man whom you seek." And when he went into her tent, there lay Sisera, dead with the peg in his temple. So on that day God subdued Jabin king of Canaan in the presence of the children of Israel. And the hand of the children of Israel grew stronger and stronger against Jabin king of Canaan, until they had destroyed Jabin king of Canaan.*

I have heard it stated right from the pulpit that the only reason that God used Deborah, a woman, was because He couldn't find a man willing. First of all, Deborah was a prophetess and a judge sometime before Barak came on the scene. Nowhere is there any indication that God couldn't find a man willing to be a prophet and a judge. God knows long before time what and who He is going to use. Instead of deciding on the spur of the moment, God raises up individuals to fulfill His purposes. Abraham, Moses, Joshua, Samuel, David, Esther, and even Deborah are examples. If God had wanted a man to do what Deborah did, then He would have raised up a man.

God raised up Barak to lead the fighting men in battle. He was not a prophet or a judge, but he wanted the prophet to go to the battlefield with him. It was not uncommon for the prophets to go with armies to battle, because godly leaders of armies wanted the ears and mouthpiece of God to be at hand. Deborah did tell Barak that God would give the enemy, Sisera, into the hands of a woman, but that woman was not Deborah. It was Jael, a foreigner.

Let's look at the conditions in Israel when God made Deborah prophetess and judge. Because the Israelites had begun serving other gods, the Lord sold them into the hands of Jabin, a king in Cannan, whose army commander was Sisera. In verse 3 of chapter 4 it says that, *"Jabin had nine hundred chariots of iron, and for twenty years he harshly oppressed the children of Israel."* In chapter 5 we are told that the roads were abandoned because the travelers took roundabout ways, and that village life had ceased because of the cruel treatment against the Israelites.

In these circumstances and in this environment, God still chose a woman to oversee His nation of Israel. If God's Word does not allow for women to be prophets, judges, and leaders of nations, then God broke His own Word when He used Deborah. If God broke His Word, then the whole foundation of biblical Christianity is faulty. Our faith is established on the fact that God is true to His Word. *"Forever, O Lord, Your word is settled in heaven. ... The entirety of Your word is truth, and every one of Your righteous judgments endures forever"* (Ps. 119:89, 160). Now if God did not break His Word when He chose Deborah, then His Word allows women to be prophets, judges, and leaders of cities and nations. He used women then, and He will use women now.

For those who would discredit Deborah as being relevant because she is in the Old Testament, let me remind you that the only "Bible" Jesus used was the Old Testament. The only "Bible" the apostles had was the Old Testament. They built the New Testament Church on the Old Testament Scriptures along with a living Messiah who *had* come and fulfilled the law. Also as First Corinthians 10:6 tells us, these things of the Old Testament were given to us as examples.

## SCRIPTURES IN FIRST CORINTHIANS

There are several things we need to understand about the Book of First Corinthians before we look at the specific Scriptures that speak to our interest. First of all, all Scripture, both the Old and the New Testaments were written without punctuation marks. There were no periods, commas, question marks, or quotation marks. There were also no capital letters or paragraph indentions. There were no indicators to show where a sentence or a paragraph began or ended. This has caused great challenges for Bible translators.

Secondly, First Corinthians is a letter Paul wrote to the church at Corinth in response to a letter he had received from them. It appears there were divisions within the church in Corinth. They were having problems with those who wanted to add Jewish laws and traditions to the pure gospel Paul had taught them. Some of the issues in question were eating food sacrificed to idols, communion, circumcision, operating in spiritual gifts, marriage, and the place of women in the church.

It has been discovered that from chapter 7 of First Corinthians through chapter 14, there are times when Paul quotes from the letter to which he is responding. Remember that since there were no quotation marks to indicate quotes, it has taken study and the guidance of the Holy Spirit to see it. I quote from a writing almost 100 years old, "Professor Sir William Ramsay, the most widely accepted authority on St. Paul in the present day and known for his researches in the history of the early church in Asia Minor, an extensive writer about St. Paul, his epistles, and journeys says, 'We should be ready to suspect Paul is making a quotation from the letter addressed to him by the Corinthians, whenever he alludes to their knowledge, or when any statement stands in marked contrast either with the immediate context, or with Paul's known views.' "[13]

Let me give you a simple example: *"Now I praise you, brethren, that you remember me in all things and keep the traditions just as I delivered them to you"* (1 Cor. 11:2). It is obvious that Paul is quoting something to them which they had written to him, "We remember you in all things and keep the traditions just as you delivered them to us." "Traditions" is the word that really sticks out here. Paul was always battling Jewish traditions. Notice how Paul starts out the next verse by saying, *"But I want you to know...."*

Here is another example: *"Therefore when you come together in one place, it is not to eat the Lord's Supper. For in eating, each one takes his own supper ahead of others; and one is hungry and another is drunk"* (1 Cor. 11:20-21). How do we know this is a quote from the Corinthians' letter? How did Paul know such things were going on in the Corinthian church if they had not written it to him in their letter? He was quoting back to them what they had written. We see Paul's response as we look at the next verse. *"What! Do you not have houses to eat and drink in? Or do you despise the church of God and shame those who have nothing? What shall I say to you? Shall I praise you in this? I do not praise you"* (1 Cor. 11:22).

With all of this in mind about First Corinthians, let us look at the Scriptures.

## First Corinthians 14:34-39

*Let your women keep silence in the churches: for it is not permitted unto them to speak; but they are commanded to be under obedience, as also saith the law. And if they will learn any thing, let them ask their husbands at home: for it is a shame for women to speak in the church. What? came the word of God out from you? or came it unto you only? If any man think himself to be a prophet, or spiritual, let him acknowledge that the things that I write unto you are the commandments of the Lord. But if any man be ignorant, let him be ignorant. Wherefore, brethren, covet to prophesy, and forbid not to speak with tongues.*

"*...for it is not permitted unto them to speak; but they are commanded to be under obedience, as also saith the law.*" Says what law? What law do women have to obey that commands them to be silent, and forbids them to speak in the church? There is not one law that says so in the whole Bible. This is the only place. Remember, "*by the mouth of two or three witnesses every word shall be established*" (2 Cor. 13:1b).

Let's look at Psalm 68:11. The Amplified Bible and the New American Standard Bible are two versions that translate this Scripture correctly. "*The Lord giveth the word: the **women** that publish the tidings are a great host*" (emphasis added). If there had been a law in the Old Testament Law that commanded women to be silent, then according to this Scripture, there was a great host of women who didn't obey the law. They took the Word the Lord gave and published it. The only way the women of that time could have published the Word of the Lord was to speak it forth.

On the day of Pentecost, who was in that upper room?

*Then returned they unto Jerusalem from the mount called Olivet, which is from Jerusalem a sabbath day's journey. And when they were come in, they went up into an upper room, where abode both Peter, and James, and John, and Andrew, Philip, and Thomas, Bartholomew, and Matthew, James the son of Alphaeus, and Simon Zelotes, and Judas the brother of James. These all continued with one accord in prayer and supplication, with the **women**, and Mary the mother of Jesus, and with his brethren* (Acts 1:12-14 KJV, emphasis added).

Both men and women were present on the day of Pentecost.

*And when the day of Pentecost was fully come, they were all with one accord in one place. And suddenly there came a sound from heaven as of a rushing mighty wind, and it filled all the house where they were sitting. And there appeared unto them cloven tongues like as of fire, and it sat upon each of them. And they were all filled with the Holy Ghost, and began to speak with other tongues, as the Spirit gave them utterance* (Acts 2:1-4 KJV).

They were all, both men and women, filled with the Holy Ghost, and they all, both men and women, began to speak with other tongues.

Peter stepped up to preach the first sermon of the New Testament Church and said,

*This is that which was spoken by the prophet Joel; and it shall come to pass in the last days, saith God, I will pour out of My Spirit upon all flesh: and your sons and your **daughters** shall prophesy, and your young men shall see visions, and your old men shall dream dreams: and on my servants and on my **handmaidens** I will pour out in those days of My Spirit; and they shall prophesy"* (Acts 2:16-18 KJV, emphasis added).

Please notice that daughters and handmaidens shall prophesy. God's Word has given women the freedom and the right to speak publicly and in church where believers gather. No man has a right to tell them to be silent.

Paul himself refers to women praying and prophesying in chapter 11 of this same Corinthian letter. Why would he, three chapters later, be telling women to keep silent? He also says just two verses before we read women are to be silent that, *"For you can all prophesy one by one, that **all** may **learn** and **all** may be encouraged"* (1 Cor. 14:31, emphasis added). This verse also contradicts verse 35: *"And if they will learn any thing, let them ask their husbands at home"* (KJV). If all can prophesy in the church and all can learn in the church, then why would he say if women learn anything, they have to learn it from their husbands at home? Then why would he write in his letter to Timothy to let the women learn? (see 1 Tim. 2:11).

To top it all Paul says, *"For it is a shame for women to speak in the church."* Tell me, reader, is this not contradictory. Obviously, something is not right. I have heard it said that this is referring only to church business. Please tell me where in the context of this whole chapter is church business mentioned? Where are the other Scriptures that forbid women from getting involved in church business? "The great German lexicographer, Schleusner, in his Greek-Latin Lexicon, declares that the expression *"as also saith the law,"* refers to the Oral Law of the Jews."[14] Also, let me quote from the Talmud, "It is a shame for a woman to let her voice be heard among men."[15] The Talmud is "a collection of books and commentary compiled by Jewish rabbis from A.D. 250–500. The Hebrew word *talmud* means 'study' or 'learning.' This is a fitting title for a work that is a library of Jewish wisdom, philosophy, history, legend, astronomy, dietary laws, scientific debates, medicine, and mathematics."[16]

"At some points during Jewish history, traditions and the Talmud have been considered equal to or better than the Scripture itself. Jesus encountered such an attitude among the Pharisees even before the existence of the Talmud (Matt. 15:3). Christians must be careful not to make the same mistake in regard to our own traditions."[17]

There was only one law that "saith" and that was the Jewish Oral Law, which eventually became written into the Talmud. The Talmud is a work of men not inspired by the Holy Spirit of God.

I do not believe that from the very start of the Christian church, God has limited women to learning spiritual things from their husbands. How absurd! How about single women and widows who have no husband? How about all those wives whose husbands are either in bed, in front of the TV, or out on the golf course on Sunday mornings?

I believe we have shown enough contradictions to prove that in verses 34 and 35, Paul was again quoting from the letter he had received from the Corinthian church. If you still have any doubt, look at the next verses, verses 36-38: "*What? came the word of God out from you? or came it unto you only? If any man think himself to be a prophet, or spiritual, let him acknowledge that the things that I write unto you are the commandments of the Lord. But if any man be ignorant, let him be ignorant*" (KJV).

Evidently, there were those in the Corinthian church who were "prophesying" that women were to be silent in the church. Paul makes it very clear that they were the only ones in the entire Christian church speaking such a thing. Then he discredits it by saying that only what he had written to them were the commandments of the Lord, and that anything they would add to it was ignorance.

Concerning this Scripture, First Corinthians 14:34-35, I would like to quote Dr. Adam Clarke, a biblical expositor of the late 19th century. He said that it is "the only one in the whole Book of God which even by a false translation can be made prohibitory of female speaking in the Church. How comes it then, that by this one isolated passage, which according to our best Greek authorities, is wrongly rendered and wrongly applied, woman's lips have been sealed for centuries, and the 'testimony of Jesus, which is the spirit of prophecy' silenced, when bestowed on her? How is it, that this solitary text has been allowed to stand unexamined and unexplained, nay, that learned commentators who have known its true meaning, as perfectly as either Robinson, Bloomfield, Greenfield, Scott, Parkhurst, or Locks, have upheld the delusion, and enforced it as a Divine precept binding on all female disciples through all time? Surely there must have been some unfaithfulness, 'craftiness,' and 'handling the word of life deceitfully' somewhere. Surely the love of caste and unscriptural jealousy for a separated priesthood has had something to do with this anomaly. By this course, divines and commentators have involved themselves in all sorts of inconsistencies and contradictions; and worse, they have nullified some of the most precious promises of God's Word. They have set the most explicit predictions of prophecy at variance with apostolic injunctions, and the most immediate and wonderful operations of the Holy Ghost, in direct opposition 'to (supposed) positive, explicit, and universal rules.' "[18]

## FIRST CORINTHIANS 11:3-16

*But I want you to know that the head of every man is Christ, the head of woman is man, and the head of Christ is God. Every man praying or prophesying, having his head covered, dishonors his head. But every woman who prays or prophesies with her head uncovered dishonors her head, for that is one and the same as if her head were shaved. For if a woman is not covered, let her also be shorn. But if it is shameful for a woman to be shorn or shaved, let her be covered. For a man indeed ought not to cover his head, since he is the image and glory of God; but woman is the glory of man. For man is not from woman, but woman from man. Nor was man created for the woman, but woman for the man. For this reason the woman ought to have a symbol of authority on her head, because of the angels. Nevertheless, neither is man independent of woman, nor woman independent of man, in the Lord. For as woman came from man, even so man also comes through woman; but all things are from God. Judge among yourselves. Is it proper for a woman to pray to God with her head uncovered? Does not even nature itself teach you that if a man has long hair, it is a dishonor to him? But if a woman has long hair, it is a glory to her; for her hair is given to her for a covering. But if anyone seems to be contentious, we have no such custom, nor do the churches of God.*

This is another Scripture that Bible interpreters have greatly misunderstood. Again I reiterate that people can see only what is in their scope of experience and understanding. If Bible interpreters understood women within a certain religious stereotype, then how they interpreted Scriptures about women would naturally have had to fit into that concept. As you read this Scripture, hopefully you saw the contradictions it contained within itself.

The first contradiction is that if it dishonors the husband's head (Christ) to cover his own head, then why doesn't it dishonor the wife's head (husband) to cover her head? Why is it one way with the husband and the other way with the wife? It doesn't make sense. If the woman should wear a sign of her husband's authority over her head, then why shouldn't a Christian man have to wear a sign of Christ's authority over his head? We must also note that Christ is the head of the Christian man only.

Another contradiction is in verse 7: *"For a man indeed ought not to cover his head, since he is the image and glory of God; but woman is the glory of man."* But we know it says in Genesis 1:27, *"So God created man in His own image; in the image of God He created him; male and female He created them."* The male man alone is not the full and only image of God. The woman most specifically is also the image of God. The wife may be the glory of her husband, but *first* she is the glory of God. So again, why must he uncover and she cover? Both the Christian male man and the Christian female man are on the same level and have the same relationship with their Creator. They both have the same redemption through the same shed blood from the same Savior. And it is the same Holy Spirit with the same anointing and power that dwells in them both. As a Christian, Christ is also her head, so surely she too can approach Him with her head uncovered.

It is time that we renew our minds and accept the truth that just because Adam walked this earth alone before God brought Eve out of him doesn't mean she is less or less important with less ability of giving glory. *Eve was not an afterthought!* God had a plan. His plan was a people, a Body of believers He identified as the Bride, created and prepared for that part of Himself He identified as the Son. His whole plan was centered around and focused on the *Bride.* God created and then formed Eve specifically the way He did to identify her as a type and shadow of the Bride. Adam, the male man, was formed first because he was to be a type and shadow of Christ, at which he failed. Then he had no additional importance other than he was part of the Bride. "But," you say, "man is still supposed to be a type of Christ in the earth today." Yes, he is. So is the woman.

Let's start by explaining why both the Jewish men and the Jewish women covered their heads in the first place. The men wore head coverings called "talliths." Although it was not required by the Old Testament law, the reason they wore them was to show before God and man their condemned sinful state. Then Jesus came to be the perfect sacrifice given once and for all, making the way for man to be redeemed. Once a man was redeemed, he was no longer in a condemned state, for there is now no condemnation to those who are in Christ. Therefore, to wear the tallith when standing publicly praying before God dishonored what Jesus had done for them in their redemption. Paul was not saying that it was wrong to wear hats before God; it was just wrong to wear this particular hat because of the reason it was being worn. It was being worn for a spiritual reason that no longer was true for the Christian man. We can now recognize how it would dishonor Christ as the perfect sacrifice.

The reason Jewish wives wore veils had nothing to do with religion. It was a social custom. When a woman married, she began to veil herself. It was to show all other men that she "belonged" to a husband. She honored her husband as the only man allowed to look upon her. Only dishonorable women appeared in public without their heads covered. Therefore, it became a social stigma for wives to go out in public without their heads covered. *There was no spiritual significance in women covering or uncovering their heads.*

We can use the example of wives in our western culture today who wear wedding rings. A ring is put on the wife's finger by her husband during their marriage ceremony. God's Word in no way commands such a custom. It is a man-made custom that has nothing to do with spirituality. However, if I should take my wedding ring off and leave it home when I went out in public, my husband, in a very personal way, would feel dishonored. Although, today being married and going without a wedding ring would not present me as a dishonorable woman; therefore, neither my husband nor I would suffer the social stigma the Jewish husbands and wives would have suffered when Paul wrote this letter.

Let's look first at verse 10: *"For this reason the woman ought to have (a symbol of) authority on her head, because of the angels.* Please notice the words that I have enclosed in parentheses. They are not in the original text. And the Greek word translated "on" in this Scripture has been translated "over" in 49 other Scriptures in the New Testament. Therefore, a more accurate reading would be, *"For this reason the woman ought to have authority over her head, because of the angels."* For what reason? Because she was made for the man (vs. 9). She was in man and was separated from man being made of his very substance. She was made for man to be a joint-ruler in taking dominion. She is a joint-heir with man of all God has to give. Therefore, she is equal and has equal authority. She ought to have her own authority over her own head to choose to veil or to choose to unveil. As verse 11 indicates, it is between her and her husband. After all, as verse 15 says, God has already given hair to her as a natural covering for her head. Since veiling was a social custom, it was none of the church's business to tell her what to do. *"But if anyone seems to be contentious, we have no such custom, nor do the churches of God"* (vs. 16).

*"Take heed that you do not despise one of these little ones, for I say to you that in heaven their angels always see the face of My Father who is in heaven"* (Matt. 18:10). If the angels can always look into the face of God without a veil, then women, who are redeemed by the blood of the Lamb and are joint-heirs with Christ, can also, and should be allowed to, stand face-to-face unveiled before God's presence.[19]

Now as to verses 5 and 6, *"But every woman who prays or prophesies with her head uncovered dishonors her head, for that is one and the same as if her head were shaved. For if a woman is not covered, let her also be shorn. But if it is shameful for a woman to be shorn or shaved, let her be covered."* We must again apply our principle of two or three witnesses. The only other place in the entire Scriptures where shaving a woman's head is mentioned is in Deuteronomy 21:10-12: *"When you go out to war against your enemies, and the Lord your God delivers them into your hand, and you take them captive, and you see among the captives a beautiful woman, and desire her and would take her for your wife, then you shall bring her home to your house, and she shall shave her head and trim her nails."* This Scripture applies only to a foreign woman and has nothing to do with covering or uncovering her head. It has nothing to do with honoring or dishonoring the husband or God.

Once again, we have to go to an outside source to find a "law" for women to cover their heads. "It is a fact that the Oral Law decreed that if a Jewess did not cover her head, she should be 'shorn'—the very greatest 'shame' that was possible to a Jewish woman—so much so that a Jew might divorce his wife if she was seen abroad with her head uncovered...."[20] Certainly Paul was not affirming that wives were to live by the Oral Law. He was again quoting or repeating to the Corinthians what they had written to him. He was repeating it so they would know exactly what he was about to speak to.

When we see it in light of the truth, we recognize that Paul was giving the married women freedom to unveil in public worship before the Lord, but also recognizing from his knowledge of the Oral Law the ramifications and possible results of doing so. Since her veiling or unveiling had nothing to do with her relationship with God, Paul was not making it an issue.

That day when Jesus died on the cross, there came darkness, rumbles, and thunderous sounds, and the earth shook. The veil in the tabernacle that was made of several layers of different materials and that kept man separated from God's presence was torn from top to bottom. Only God could have done it, because it was a feat impossible for human hands. God Almighty had accepted the sacrifice. His judgment was satisfied. And God, Himself, ripped open the veil making free access to His presence for all believers. No man, not even a husband, has a right to place another veil between a woman and her God. Let's restate this sentence so it applies to the real issue at hand: No man, not even a husband, not even a minister, has a right to place his authority between any woman and her God! *Selah! Pause* and think about this.

"But," you say, "there is no authority that does not come from God." No, but there are imposters. There is the counterfeit "authority" of the flesh, the counterfeit "authority" of prejudice, and the counterfeit "authority" of religion. I have put "authority" in quotation marks because *they have no authority!* They have set themselves up as gods and have imposed their illegitimate authority.

God's authority is delegated authority. Just because a man (or woman) has been placed by God into a position of authority, doesn't mean he gets to make the rules and say how it is to be. A person in such a position is no different from Jesus, who only did what He saw and heard from His Father God.

So why did God place these Scriptures in the Bible if they were going to get us so messed up? It was because God really wanted to say something to us that has been totally obscured by the misunderstanding and misinterpretation.

## FIRST TIMOTHY 2:8-15

*I desire therefore that the men pray everywhere, lifting up holy hands, without wrath and doubting; in like manner also, that the women adorn themselves in modest apparel, with propriety and moderation, not with braided hair or gold or pearls or costly clothing, but, which is proper for women professing godliness, with good works. Let a woman learn in silence with all submission. And I do not permit a woman to teach or to have authority over a man, but to be in silence. For Adam was formed first, then Eve. And Adam was not deceived, but the woman being deceived, fell into transgression. Nevertheless she will be saved in childbearing if they continue in faith, love, and holiness, with self-control.*

This Scripture, more than all the others we are writing about, has been wrongfully violated. Every time I read verse 15, I shudder. Since when has love, holiness, and self-control become requirements for being saved? *"For by grace you have been saved through faith, and that not of yourselves; it is the gift of God, not of works, lest anyone should boast"* (Eph. 2:8-9). If love, holiness, and self-control are necessary to being saved, it should apply to men also. These are qualities of God that He works in us by His Spirit after we are saved.

The words, *"she will be saved in childbearing,"* take us back to Genesis 3:15. It is through Eve's Seed that salvation has come to mankind, both the female man and the male man. We will give further explanation to verse 15 later.

Once again, we see that Adam appears to be made more important because he was formed first. It is true that Adam was not deceived. He knew exactly what he was doing. So why does it appear that Eve's deception was worse than Adam's blatant disobedience? The intent of this Scripture was to point out the opposite. Eve fell into the transgression because of deception while Adam chose to disobey. Because he was formed first and because he had been given instructions personally from God to keep the garden and not to eat from the forbidden tree, he had the responsibility of protecting Eve from satan and the deception. It is the same responsibility Jesus holds for His Bride.

Although sources vary as to the specific date Paul wrote this letter to Timothy, they all state somewhere between A.D. 63-67. It was during these years that Nero was the Roman emperor. In the year A.D. 64. the great fire of Rome erupted and burned for a week. "The confused population was searching for scapegoats and soon rumors held Nero responsible. Nero had to engage in scapegoating of his own and chose for his target a small sect of reputed misanthropes called Christians. Caius Gornelius Tacitus, a Roman historian, has preserved a record of this affair. We quote the following from his Annals (XV. 44): 'And so, to get rid of this rumor, Nero set up (i.e., falsely accused) as the culprits and punished with the utmost refinement of cruelty a class hated for their abominations, who are commonly called Christians. Christus, from who their name is derived, was executed at the hands of the procurator Pontius Pilate in the reign of Tiberius. Checked for a moment, this pernicious superstition again broke out, not only in Judea, the source of the evil, but even in Rome.... Accordingly, arrest was first made of those who confessed; then, on their evidence, an immense multitude was convicted, not so much on the charge of arson as because of (their) hatred for the human race. Besides being put to death they were made to serve as objects of amusement; they were clothed in the hides of beast and torn to death by dogs; others were crucified, others set on fire to serve to illuminate the night when daylight failed."[21]

"Severus, a historian of those days, who informs us: 'This was the beginning of severe measures against the Christians. Afterwards the religion was forbidden by formal laws, and the profession of Christianity was made illegal by published edicts.'" Sir William Ramsay writes, "When Nero had once established the principle in Rome, his action served as a precedent in every province. There is no need to suppose a general edict or formal law. The precedent would be quoted in every case where a Christian was accused. Charges such as had been brought against Paul in so many places were certainly brought against others; and the action of the Emperor at Rome would give the tone to the action of the provincial governors"[22]

The Book of Timothy was a personal letter Paul was writing to Timothy, not to a church. Paul had left Timothy in charge of a work he had started in Ephesus. Realizing he would not be returning as soon as he had hoped, Paul was giving Timothy some instructions and guidelines as Timothy continued in this work in the midst of the cruel and horrendous injustices that awaited Christians even in Ephesus. It is important to note that Paul was not giving Timothy "new laws" that were to be followed for all time. If these instructions were to be new laws, then Jesus would have taught them as such. Jesus fulfilled the law freeing us to live by the Spirit, which simply means when the Spirit says, "Don't do it," then we don't do it, and when the Spirit says, "You can do it," then we can do it, and when the Spirit says, "Do it," then we do it. The apostles were to carry out only what they had been taught by Jesus. I will quote an example: "Because Paul says to Timothy in this same letter, 'Use a little wine for the stomach's sake,' no one is so foolish as to believe that all Christians for all time are expected to drink wine. He was not so hampered by his inspiration that he could not, like the rest of us, give advise of temporary use only, advice unsuitable for all individuals to practice under all circumstances. Expositors who cannot see a difference between God's inexorable laws, or eternal principles of justice and righteousness, as described in personal epistles, and practice or advice suitable for the emergency only, are too literal in their mental make-up to be useful teachers for their age and generation."[23]

Some people will ignore this Scripture of drinking a little wine, totally refusing to drink wine under any circumstances and then go to the drugstore and buy an over-the-counter "drug" for their stomach. Some people will drink wine anytime and any place saying, "If it was all right for Timothy, then it is all right for me." And so, we see that mankind "hears" and applys Scripture according to their preferences and prejudices, while ignoring the Holy Spirit who is the only true interpreter of Scripture. Of course, it is easier to see in the case of this Scripture, but much more difficult when reading Scriptures concerning women.

Because of the tyrannical rule of Nero, the Christian church at the time Paul was writing to Timothy was in a state of emergency. I will refer to this point several times in this chapter.

Jesus was and still is the Liberator of women. Jesus and the truths of His Word free women from the "laws" of religion and society that have absolutely nothing to do with their spirituality or their relationship with Him. Women are accepted by God the same as men and have the same access to Him as men. As with men, their dress, their hairstyle, their public and social life do not have to conform to certain guidelines to prove their spirituality or to be acceptable to God. Yes, there is a certain standard of decency and modesty that should be a fruit of true spirituality, but it applies to men as well as women. There should be no double standard. If godly men can step into the style of the day, then godly women can do likewise.

I observed something back in the late 70s and early 80s. There were denominations, and still are, who restricted women in their dress and outward appearance. They believed godly women were not to cut their hair, wear makeup or jewelry, or dress stylishly. At this time, at least in my part of the country, God started showing up and using women with short hair, wearing makeup, all manner of jewelry, and the latest fashions. Little by little, Jesus began to liberate some of the ladies in the more restricted denominations. Little by little, they began to cut their hair, wear a bit of makeup, and then wear a little more. Gradually, they began to look like a part of society in which they belonged—which is not wrong. We are a peculiar people, but not because of how we look. It should be because of our heart, our faith, our mannerisms, and our godly behavior.

The point I am trying to make here is that when women are liberated, it shows up in their physical appearance. I believe the Christian women in Paul's day were beginning to look different from the traditional Jewish women. If they were still veiling themselves, how did anyone know they were braiding their hair?

I love beautiful things. I love color. I like to wear beautiful things and make my home beautiful. One day while I was laying my heart before the Lord, checking my motives in this area,. Father said to me, "Look at My creation." As I began to consider His creation, I became overwhelmed with its beauty. I considered the massive mountains enhanced with magnificent giant boulders, rocks, and crevices, surrounded by the deep forest-green color of the evergreen trees and the silvery-green color of the aspens with occasional glimpses of the great waterfalls and rapidly running streams. I considered the great plains with "corn as high as an elephant's eye,"[24] with "the waving wheat that sure smells sweet when the wind comes right behind the rain,"[25] and, where the coyotes roam, the cattle graze and "the deer and the antelope play."[26] And I considered the miles and miles of seashore with sandy beaches in a vast array of colors decorated with seashells, grass and seaweed, and crabs and water birds. I considered the beauty of a peacock, a parrot, a turkey, and a blue jay, a tiger, a giraffe, and a zebra, a whale, an octopus, a rainbow trout, and the fish in a tropical aquarium, a Great Dane, a Poodle, a Dalmatian, and the family mutt. I considered my flower bed and realized that the Great Creator also loves beauty. He also loves color. It is in His nature and He created me in His image. It is only natural that I should love beauty and want to surround myself with beauty. To desire beauty is not worldly or carnal. All that God created in this world's environment, He created for mankind to use and enjoy. Are only the ungodly allowed to enjoy the beauty of ruffles and lace, of silk and chiffon, of curls and braids, and of gold, silver, gems, and jewels?

So what was Paul meaning when he wrote, *"that the women adorn themselves in modest apparel, with propriety and moderation, not with braided hair or gold or pearls or costly clothing, but, which is proper for women professing godliness, with good works"*? I believe he was dealing with one of two issues or perhaps both issues. The first issue was safety. Because of her liberty, it was becoming easier to pick out the Christian woman in a crowd. Since Christians were being persecuted and executed almost daily, it would have been much safer for the Christian women to not be so obvious. Exercising their liberty could endanger their lives and, if with a group of Christians, could endanger others' lives.

The second issue was making their witness more effective. Sometimes subtlety is less intimidating, especially for the specific women to whom Paul was referring. In verse 10 Paul wrote about women who were *"professing godliness."* The Greek word translated "professing" in this Scripture is *epaggello,* pronounced ep-ang-el'-lo. (In the Greek "gg" is pronounced as "ng.") According to the Strong's Concordance it means, "to announce upon; to engage to do something; to assert something respecting oneself: to make a promise." It comes from a word that means, "to bring tidings; a messenger (an angel); by implication, a pastor," which in turn comes from a primary verb that means, "to lead."

These women who were "professing godliness" were not housewives who were just confessing their faith in Jesus. These were women who were witnessing and speaking publicly as preachers and evangelists.

"To make a promise" is part of the definition of *epaggello*. Promise is so connected with the gospel that they are almost one and the same. John 3:16 is the gospel message in only a few words and it includes a promise: All who believe will have everlasting life. Ministers of the gospel are ministers of a promise.

Now let's go back to the beginning of this Scripture and talk it through verse by verse. *"I desire therefore that the men pray everywhere, lifting up holy hands, without wrath and doubting"* (verse 8). "Everywhere" would certainly include public places. Lifting up hands while praying and worshiping God was very much part of the Jewish Old Testament worship. A Christian man praying to and worshiping Jehovah with hands uplifted would look no different from the traditional Jewish worshiper. Other than using the name of "Jesus," he also would not sound much differently. Why did Paul include "without wrath and doubting"? If a person has to deal with wrath, anger, or doubt, while praying, it would mean that what they are praying about or for, is being greatly challenged. What could be a greater challenge than the great persecution they were experiencing as a result of their faith in Jesus Christ? Read the first three verses of this chapter 2. Isn't it true that the more difficult the circumstances in which we find ourselves, the more we struggle with anger and doubt?

Verse 9: *"in like manner also, that the women adorn themselves in modest apparel, with propriety and moderation, not with braided hair or gold or pearls or costly clothing."* Remember, there were no punctuation marks in the original texts. So when we read "in like manner also," we must discover in like manner to what? It is obvious that Paul was not telling the men to not braid their hair or over-adorn themselves with gold and pearls. Therefore, we go back to verse 8 and recognize that Paul was saying that the women were to, in like manner as the men, pray everywhere, lifting up holy hands without wrath and doubting. Once again, this was not uncommon to see among the Jews, even the Jewish women. But for the sake of their safety in perilous times, he encouraged them to keep a low profile. They were to do what they had to do so that unnecessary attention would not be drawn to themselves. Paul was not establishing a law that was to be imposed upon all women at all times in every generation. These were instructions to help them deal with their present time.

The Greek word translated "modest" in this verse 9 commands our interest when we read its definitions. The Strong's Concordance states the meaning as "orderly, i.e. decorous." It comes from another interesting word meaning, "orderly *arrangement, i.e. decoration*; by implication the *world*." The Encarta Dictionary defines decorous as, "conforming to what is acceptable or expected in formal or solemn settings, especially in dress or behavior."[27] It means dressing to fit in, not dressing down to some pious or religious attire that would make a woman stand out and draw attention. Of course, it would also mean not overdressing.

Everyone appreciates a woman who presents herself attractively, but a woman "over-done" in her dress, accessories, and makeup can be a distraction. Attention can too easily be drawn away from her words to her appearance. Paul was simply giving Timothy a warning in this writing. At least for the Jewish culture, it was difficult enough to accept listening to a woman much less a woman dressed "fit to kill." Words may have been more easily received from a more modest physical presentation.

Actually, the same distraction can exist with a woman who is "under-done" and presents herself unattractively. I was in a department store recently in a west Texas city when my attention was drawn to two young married couples leisurely shopping. It was obvious the two handsome husbands were cowboys. They wore the typical cowboy hat and had the cowboy haircut. I could tell because there was not much hair showing beneath the wide brims. They had on bright-colored western shirts, starched and ironed, and wore the typical cowboy blue jeans that fit quite snuggly. They certainly didn't need their leather belts with the nice-sized shiny silver buckle to hold their pants up. Their cowboy boots made their outfits complete. By their physical appearances no one would know that they were Christians much less belong to a religious sect. It was their wives who revealed it.

These two pretty young ladies wore the cotton-print, shirt-waist dresses with the collars, sleeves, and full skirts at a very respectable length. On their feet were anklets (socks) and modest lace-up tennis shoes. Their uncut hair was pulled up into some type of bun that was covered with a small cap made of the same cotton print with strings that could tie around the neck, but were just hanging loose. I appreciate these ladies' dedication and attempts to please God, but if they were dressed like that so as not to draw attention to themselves because of their *propriety and moderation*, they were greatly failing. They drew attention to themselves wherever they went. I don't believe it is the kind of attention that glorifies God.

Women look at them and think, *If I have to look like that to be godly, then I don't want to be godly.* Married men think, *If my wife began to look like that, I'm gone.* Unmarried men think, *I would rather stay single than to marry a woman who looks like that.* I don't mean to be disrespectful; I just want to point out that to those who don't know the Lord, this appearance, this witness is not drawing them in God's direction. It is pushing them away.

We must recognize that Paul was giving advice that was appropriate to the culture and the circumstances of that time. He was not setting down rules that were to be followed at all times. It is with wisdom and by the Holy Spirit we take Paul's words and apply them to our time. It is with wisdom and by the Holy Spirit that each woman discovers what is personally appropriate for her in her dress and physical appearance.

Here in verse 9 the word translated *"propriety"* in the New King James Bible is translated *"shamefacedness"* in the King James Bible. There is only one other place in the New Testament this Greek word is used, and that is in Hebrews 12:28. *"Wherefore we receiving a kingdom which cannot be moved, let us have grace, whereby we may serve God acceptably with **reverence** and godly fear"* (KJV, emphasis added). In this Scripture, the word is translated *"reverence."* Would it be appropriate to use "shamefacedness" here instead of "reverence"? We are certainly not to serve God with shamefacedness. The redeemed no longer have anything to be ashamed about, and we are not to go around looking like or acting like we are ashamed. But once again, when it came to women, the translators went above and beyond their reasonable duty.

In the Strong's Concordance, the meaning of the Greek word translated "moderation" in verse 9 means, "soundness of mind." *"God has not given us a spirit of fear, but of power and of love and of a sound mind"* (2 Tim. 1:7). Therefore, First Timothy 2:9 could be read, "that the women adorn themselves in decorous apparel that causes her to look like she fits in with her environment, with reverence and soundness of mind without fear."

Verse 10: *"but, which is proper for women professing godliness, with good works."* According to Strong's Concordance, the word "proper" would be better translated "appropriate." These female ministers were to dress appropriately as they went about in this threatening environment doing the good works that God had called them to do.

*"Let a woman learn in silence with all submission"* (verse 11). At least in Timothy, the translators allowed the women to learn;

whereas, in Corinthians, *if* they learned anything, they were to ask their husbands at home. The word translated "silence" in this Scripture is used only three times in Scripture—twice in this chapter of First Timothy and once in Acts 22:2. It means "stillness," and it's from a word that means to be "undisturbed, peaceable," which in turn comes from a root word that means "boldness, courage." Paul was not saying that women were to be silent; rather, he was encouraging them to not worry or be fearful of the possible danger surrounding them, but to boldly and courageously continue to learn in the attitude of *"be still, and know that I am God"* (Ps. 46:10 KJV).

They were to learn with all *"submission."* Submission to whom? Why is it that anytime the word "submission" is used in any female context, it is automatically assumed it must be submission to a husband or a human man? First of all, there is nothing in these Scriptures to indicate submission to a husband. Secondly, Paul is referring here to women functioning in ministry, not functioning in a marriage. It is possible that some of them were not married. Therefore, this submission is to God and should have no more requirements then the submission to God required from men functioning in ministry. The word translated here as "submission" and in the King James Bible as "subjection" is the identical Greek word Paul used in Ephesians 5:21-28, which we dealt with in the chapter entitled, "To the Woman," under the subtopic of "Submission."

*"And I do not permit a woman to teach or to have authority over a man, but to be in silence"* (verse 12). After all that has been explained thus far, we can understand why Paul would give Timothy such advice. The social repercussions of women teaching men or exercising any kind of authority over men would be difficult enough for these women, but to also have the threat of a torturous death over their heads if caught doing so, was more than Paul thought necessary. He was not making laws to restrict or limit women in ministry. He was trying to protect them. Why didn't he just say so? He had to be cautious in his correspondence.

Mail wasn't as private as it is today. Timothy, also living in life-threatening circumstances, knew and understood well what Paul was communicating to him. Paul was *not* forbidding women to ever teach men or to ever exercise authority over men.

Generation after generation, century after century, it has been mostly the women, the mothers, who have taught their sons. They have taken these small infants and taught them through their most informative years. They have taught these young "men" morals, values, standards, godliness, and, if they knew how, to read and write. I do not intend to diminish the value and the roles of fathers in establishing the foundations on which their sons would build their lives. I just want to recognize how much influence women have had in these "men's" lives before they ever reached the age of a man. How can we then say that after a certain age, it is wrong to teach the man? Teaching should be based upon knowledge, ability, and calling—not on gender as the carnal gender mentality would dictate.

What is teaching anyway? And what is learning? Where do we draw the line between relating to one another, communicating with one another, and teaching? I have learned many things in general conversation. If I, being a woman, would happen to know something that a man does not know, should he be so bound by law that he should refuse to learn it from me? Of course, the carnal gender mentality would tell me to shut up or "be silent." It would be my responsibility to see that no man learns from me. Does this not sound foolish?

Let's look at the word "silence" in verse 12. It is the identical Greek word used in verse 11. It brings the same meaning and the same intent Paul was communicating in verse 11 right into verse 12. Paul didn't want to shut the woman's mouth or shut the woman down spiritually. He just wanted to protect her and encourage her. Is this not more consistent to the nature of our God?

Should a woman exercise authority over men? *"Let every soul be subject to the governing authorities. For there is no authority except from God, and the authorities that exist are appointed by God. Therefore whoever resists the authority resists the ordinance of God, and those who resist will bring judgment on themselves"* (Rom. 13:1-2). How can a woman exercise authority over men if God hasn't given her authority to exercise? Therefore, the question is not, should a woman exercise authority over men? The question is, does God delegate authority to women? We have already looked at Deborah to whom God gave authority to lead and judge the nation of Israel, which, of course, included men. In fact Barak, the leader of the army, was in submission to her authority. We have already stated that God never breaks His Word. If His Word allowed Deborah His delegated authority, then God will consistently give other women His delegated authority. Let's look at a second witness to God delegating His authority to a woman.

> *Thus it happened, when the king heard the words of the Law, that he tore his clothes. Then the king commanded Hilkiah, Ahikam the son of Shaphan, Abdon the son of Micah, Shaphan the scribe, and Asaiah a servant of the king, saying, "Go, inquire of the Lord for me, and for those who are left in Israel and Judah, concerning the words of the book that is found; for great is the wrath of the Lord that is poured out on us, because our fathers have not kept the word of the Lord, to do according to all that is written in this book." So Hilkiah and those the king had appointed went to Huldah the prophetess, the wife of Shallum the son of Tokhath, the son of Hasrah, keeper of the wardrobe. (She dwelt in Jerusalem in the Second Quarter.) And they spoke to her to that effect. Then she answered them, "Thus says the Lord God of Israel, 'Tell the man who sent you to Me, "Thus says the Lord: 'Behold, I will bring calamity on this place and on its inhabitants, all the curses that are written in the book*

*which they have read before the king of Judah, because they have forsaken Me and burned incense to other gods, that they might provoke Me to anger with all the works of their hands. Therefore My wrath will be poured out on this place, and not be quenched.' " ' But as for the king of Judah, who sent you to inquire of the Lord, in this manner you shall speak to him, 'Thus says the Lord God of Israel: "Concerning the words which you have heard—because your heart was tender, and you humbled yourself before God when you heard His words against this place and against its inhabitants, and you humbled yourself before Me, and you tore your clothes and wept before Me, I also have heard you," says the Lord. "Surely I will gather you to your fathers, and you shall be gathered to your grave in peace; and your eyes shall not see all the calamity which I will bring on this place and its inhabitants." ' " So they brought back word to the king.* (2 Chronicles 34:19-28).

According to Second Kings 22:8 Hilkiah was the high priest. So both the high priest and the king submitted to Huldah's God-delegated authority. Therefore, whatever verse 12 of First Timothy 2 means, it must be consistent with the whole Word of God, including the examples of Deborah and Huldah along with the example of Phoebe. God does delegate authority to women, and as it says in Romans 13:2, *"Therefore whoever resists the authority resists the ordinance of God, and those who resist will bring judgment on themselves."*

By whose authority does a man, any man, stand behind a pulpit or before the masses declaring the Word of the Lord? If it is not by God's authority, he has no business speaking and should remain "silent." Neither a man nor a woman should operate outside the delegated authority of God. It is God who chooses how to delegate His authority. He chooses to whom He gives His authority. It is neither for a man nor a woman to tell another that they can or cannot operate in God's authority. God will prove His own authority through the person to whom He delegates it.

Because God does delegate authority to women, there will be women who are allowed by God's Word to exercise authority over men.

The word "usurp" used in the King James Bible is not even in the original text.[28] "Usurp" means moving in and taking over someone else's authority. It is something men can do as well as women. Of course, it is wrong, but it doesn't apply to this Scripture and to what Paul is communicating to Timothy.

Why are men so afraid of women taking over? Perhaps we should go back and reread the chapter entitled, "Who's the Victim?" If God is the One who has delegated authority to a man, if God is the One who established a man in His authority, then how can a woman possibly come along and "take over." If the man operating in God's delegated authority is secure in who he is in God and is secure in his delegated authority, no one can take it over. If God delegates it and God establishes it, then it is God who secures it and protects it. I have seen it and experienced it over many years that the men who are secure in who they are in God are not threatened nor intimidated by the authority God has delegated to me. On the other hand, the insecure ones use their authority to oppose me.

Let's return to First Timothy 2:15: *"Nevertheless she will be saved in childbearing if they continue in faith, love, and holiness, with self-control."* Why did Paul make such a statement? We know he was not adding love, holiness, and self-control as requirements to salvation. First of all, according to Strong's Concordance *holiness* means "purity," which is having and keeping a right heart before God, and *self-control* is the same identical Greek word translated "moderation" in verse 9 and means a "sound mind." Remember *"God has not given us a spirit of fear, but of power and of love and of a sound mind"* (2 Tim. 1:7). Paul was saying that they were saved through the childbearing of Eve down through the generations to the childbearing of Mary; that the same God who was faithful to fulfill His promise of salvation through childbearing would be faithful to these women facing the rejection of religious tradition and the persecution with possible torture and death from an insane emperor; and that if they would continue to walk in faith, love, and holiness or purity with a sound mind, they would surely have the comfort of His saving power present with them at all times.

The God who is no respecter of persons, the God in whom there is no male or female is bringing us up out of the carnal gender mentality to free us, both women and men, to be able to stand side by side to finally accomplish the work He gave to mankind on the sixth day of creation—*"Be fruitful and multiply, subdue the earth and have dominion."*

*chapter twenty-one* | WOMEN IN
MINISTRY

I t would seem that after all that has been said on the pages of this book, there would be little left to say about women in ministry. Ministry belongs to God. It is God who calls a person, male or female, into ministry. Actually, all Christians are called into ministry. It may be as a Christian doctor, a Christian law enforcer, a Christian secretary, a Christian teacher, a Christian laborer, or whatever occupation in which one can serve. As every Christian takes the Father's unconditional love and Jesus' righteousness into his or her realm of influence, we are taking dominion.

The ministry I would like to focus on now is what has been termed the fivefold ministry of the apostles, the prophets, the evangelists, the pastors, and the teachers (see Eph. 4:11). Yes, women can function in all five areas of ministry, if God has called them to do so. If He has called a woman, He will authorize her and anoint her.

I would like to point out a rather obscure Scripture: *"Greet Andronicus and Junia, my countrymen and my fellow prisoners, who are of note among the apostles, who also were in Christ before me"* (Rom. 16:7). I sat before Dr. Fuchsia Pickett at a women's gathering many years ago as she brought this Scripture to our attention saying that *Junia* was a woman apostle. She was not only an apostle, she was chief among them. When I came home, I wrote the name *Junia* on a piece of paper. I gave the paper to our middle son and asked him to take it to his high school Latin teacher to inquire of him if the name was for a male or a female. Later that evening, my son called to me from another room, "Hey, Mom, that was a woman's name." Since that time I have read the attempts of several sources to explain it away. Those of you who want it to be true that God calls and appoints women as apostles will accept this wholeheartedly. Those of you who do not want this to be true will explain it away. Those of you who just want to know the truth, will ask God, and He will show you the truth. You may have to wait for it, but He will show it to you in a way that only God can do.

We know that it takes a man and a woman, a father and a mother to bring a baby into this world. Wouldn't we also agree that it takes a man and a woman, a father and a mother to raise that baby and bring it into the wholeness and the maturity necessary to live life on its own? Yet in the church we say it should only be the man in ministry—only men are to bring spiritual babies into maturity. Think about it.

Men are mental and strongly logical. Women are emotional and strongly intuitive. True parenting takes both. Why doesn't true ministry take both? How did the church get so infiltrated and, in many cases, dominated by religion? Maybe it is the result of the "homospirituality" in the church. Isn't it true that in religion, women are delegated to limited spiritual lesbianism? Think about it.

When I was about 24 years old, I was a single teacher, teaching in a parochial school of my denomination. That year I attended the annual pastor/teacher conference in Austin, Texas. Being young and single, I was not ready to spend my evenings alone in my hotel room, so I would go to the hospitality room to visit. Of course, there were not many women visiting in the hospitality room. This one particular evening, I was visiting with some younger male pastors and teachers, when a pastor at least 20 years my senior, confronted me with, "What are you trying to prove?" I didn't have a clue what he meant so I asked him. He replied, "I remember a time when the female teachers didn't even speak to the male teachers much less the pastors." Tell me why this isn't second-dimension homosexuality in the church? It is men (ministers) giving seed, and it is men (ministers) receiving the seed; and the result has been sterile religion.

It has been men interpreting the Scriptures; it has been men translating the Scriptures; and it has been men establishing the doctrines, the teachings, of their denominations. The Protestant denominations have taken it one step further than the Catholic church by allowing their ministers to marry, although the wife is to remain silent and learn only from her husband at home.

God has been faithful to give women spiritual seed by anointing the limited truths that have been spoken by the "homospiritual" priesthood. In my youth there were still churches that required the women to be separated from the men and to sit together on one side of the church. There may still be those who do so. Other than perhaps the women's prayer meetings, women have mostly had the responsibility of the church socials and dinners and taking care of the missionaries.

I have made the point over and over again that God is requiring marriage to come into order the way He intended it to be, the way He created it to be. I believe it is the same for ministry in the church. I believe God is saying that it is time for ministry through women to take its place alongside the ministry through men, to establish the full image of God in the priesthood. I am not just talking about a husband and wife who are in ministry together. I am talking about the realization of the need for and the full acceptance of ministry through women at every level and in every type of ministry to bring balance and to manifest the whole image of God.

I know there were no women who served in the priesthood in the Old Testament. That was because the Old Testament priesthood was a type of the ministry of Jesus. The priesthood was carried out by males because Jesus was a male who was the *Son* of God, the *Son* of man, and the *Bridegroom* who *was yet to come*. God didn't exclude the woman because she was less or because of her deception in the garden. He excluded her because she was the type and shadow of the Church for whom Christ came. God chose men in the Old Testament, not because they were better and certainly not because their sin of outward disobedience weighed less on the scales of justice; God chose men because they were the type and shadow of the male Christ. But, *Jesus has now come* and fulfilled His ministry, and then He left His ministry to His Bride, *the Church, in which there are both men and women.* It really should be said, *"In Christ there is no male or female"* (Gal. 3:28 paraphrased). Actually, Jesus turned His ministry over to the woman, His Bride. We have seen God raise up some great ministries through women such as Dr. Fuchsia Pickett, Iverna Thompkins, and Joyce Meyer. But we have yet to see them and accept them as a necessary counterpart to the ministry of men.

There is a belief that says because of Eve's deception, women cannot be trusted with leadership and need headship to keep them from deception. If this is the case, couldn't it be argued that men cannot be trusted with leadership because of Adam's disobedience and casting his blame on another? Who is in charge over men to ensure that they do not knowingly disobey God and then refuse to own their own choices? Again, we have a double standard. If the Spirit of God dwelling in the man is sufficient to deal with a man's disobedience, then the Spirit of God dwelling in the woman is sufficient to protect her from or deal with her deception.

In my earlier days when God began to show me new revelation, I used to fret and worry about falling into deception. I would prostrate myself on the floor begging and then waiting for God to show me any deception. There was no "man" in my life, not even a pastor, who I could go to who was searching out God's truths beyond his denominational doctrine. I prayed repeatedly for God to give me a pastor who could see beyond his religion and who could hear my heart when I shared the new things I was seeing from God's Word. One day God asked me a question, "If you cannot know the truth apart from My Spirit revealing it to you, then how can you know deception without My Spirit revealing it to you?" I knew I could then rest because I could trust my faithful Father to cause me to know truth and to cause me to know deception. Only those who refuse to see beyond what they already believe as truth and those who want truth to conform to only what they want to believe are susceptible to deception. Because I wanted to know God and His truth more than the approval of man, I no longer worried about deception.

However, I strongly believe in submission among those God has put together in relationship. I do not recommend that anyone travel alone on his or her journey of truth. There is safety, security, and accountability in "jam sessions," and the discussions of new understanding of truth that is emerging out of darkness and coming into the Light. Safety, security, and accountability through submission is God's order and, therefore, important and necessary, but it has nothing to do with gender.

For many years in my life, because of the carnal gender mentality thinking, I thought I had to have a male man, a male minister, to give my ministry credibility. It is one thing to be in submission to those with whom we are in relationship, but it is another thing to believe we need another human to give us credibility. Credibility comes from God, and it comes from God through our inner man. *"A man's gift makes room for him, and brings him before great men"* (Prov. 18:16). *"Every good gift and every perfect gift is from above, and comes down from the Father of lights, with whom there is no variation or shadow of turning"* (Jas. 1:17). Our gift that is within us, that comes from our Father, and is finally (through process) released through us gives us spiritual credibility. *"Now when they saw the boldness of Peter and John, and perceived that they were uneducated and untrained men, they marveled. And they realized that they had been with Jesus"* (Acts 4:13). We see again that their spiritual credibility came from what was within them as a result of having been with Jesus. *"While Peter was still speaking these words, the Holy Spirit fell upon all those who heard the word. And those of the circumcision who believed were astonished, as many as came with Peter, because the gift of the Holy Spirit had been poured out on the Gentiles also. For they heard them speak with tongues and magnify God. Then Peter answered, "Can anyone forbid water, that these should not be baptized who have received the Holy Spirit just as we have?" And he commanded them to be baptized in the name of the Lord"* (Acts 10:44-48a). It was the gift within them that was manifested with speaking in other tongues and magnifying God that gave these first Gentile Christians at Cornelius' house spiritual credibility.

I would like to say to every woman who believes God has called her into the ministry, "You do not have to make anything happen." God will get you from here to there. It is a hard thing to be in ministry. You will be tried and tested. It is necessary to bring quality and strength into your ministry. You will be rejected and lied about. It is also necessary. It is all about you being tried with fire so you can be sent as a vessel that contains only Him; so you will have nothing to say except the words that come from Him and so you can manifest the Father in His unconditional love to all people. If you are truly called, you may actually come to a time when you wonder if it is worth the preparation and may think about trying to run from it, but trying to run will be like those dreams where you put all your effort into running but can't get anywhere. You can't help it, if you are truly called. Just remember that weeping lasts for a night, but joy comes in the morning (see Ps. 30:5). The "night" can last for months and even years, but you will find the morning to be more than your dreams and visions dared to show you.

Every ministry should be like Elisha who was related to and served the ministry of Elijah or like Timothy and Titus who was related to and served the ministry of Paul. *"Behold, I will send you Elijah the prophet before the coming of the great and dreadful day of the Lord. And He will turn the hearts of the fathers to the children, and the hearts of the children to their fathers, lest I come and strike the earth with a curse"* (Mal. 4:5-6). This Scripture is the very last statement made in the Old Testament. It is something God said He was going to do, and God always keeps His Word. Many people read this verse and are encouraged by the promise from God to restore families. But as we look further to grasp its full meaning, we see that God is also going to restore to ministry the generational blessing of the priesthood that was passed from a spiritual father to his spiritual son. Elisha was not Elijah's natural born son, but he served Elijah; he saw the same things Elijah saw; he called Elijah father. And when God took Elijah, Elisha received Elijah's anointing in a double portion. For more understanding of this concept, I recommend Dr. Mark Hanby's book entitled, *You Have Not Many Fathers.*

*chapter twenty-two* | CONCLUSION

We made the statement in the beginning of this book that it was to a married couple that God gave the commission to subdue the earth and take dominion. We also said that God did not give this commission to government or to the Church. The commission Jesus gave to the Church is, *"Go therefore and make disciples of all the nations, baptizing them in the name of the Father and of the Son and of the Holy Spirit, teaching them to observe all things that I have commanded you; and lo, I am with you always, even to the end of the age. Amen"* (Matt. 28:19-20). However, if we see this first married couple God placed in the Garden of Eden as a type and shadow of Christ and His Bride, then we must include the Church. Actually, we could say that God gave the commission (to subdue and take dominion) to marriage—the marriage between a husband and wife and the marriage between Christ and the Church. It is bringing natural life together with spiritual life, causing us to see another kind of marriage we could call Kingdom marriage or third-dimension marriage.

Are you seeing that we can no longer bypass our marriage relationships with our spouses and expect the Church to ever become the powerful institution of making mature disciples equipped to subdue the earth and take dominion? How can we run the race in the Church when we are lame and wounded in our homes? How can we have a healthy and prosperous marriage with Christ when we have a sick and poor marriage in our homes? I believe First Timothy 3:5 asks the same question, *"For if a man does not know how to rule his own house, how will he take care of the church of God?"*

So what did God see when He looked at Adam and said, *"It is not good that man should be alone"*? *He saw Himself.* After God brought all the animals before Adam to name and there was not found among them a suitable helper comparable to him, God saw Himself. There was nothing in God's whole realm of existence that was comparable to Him, so He made something *like* Him in His own *image* (see Gen. 2:18-20; 1:26-27). God wanted relationship with a living being that was comparable to Him. God didn't want a servant, a maid, or a sex partner. He wanted a relationship and created a plan to form and make someone like Himself. Because God was one Being alone, He formed man, both male and female together, as one being alone. Everything that was both male and female was in that one being just like it is all in the one Being of our triune God. Because mankind's life came out of God as a breath, and because the Bride of Christ came out of Jesus' side as redemptive blood and cleansing water, God took the man's relationship partner out from his side and then told them to become one.

Husbands, you can no longer be about the business of the church, your careers, or your jobs when your marriages and homes are out of order, when you are still living your alone life without coming into intimate relationship with your wife. You cannot expect God to prosper you. You are the initiator. You have found on the pages of this book some excellent tools with instructions on how to use them, but what happens now is between you and your God. Hopefully, you have seen that there is no one you can legally blame nor is there any legitimate excuse to keep you in the same monotonous place of doing the same things over and over expecting to get different results. If it hasn't worked before, then it certainly is not going to work now. You can no longer expect everyone else to change and then when they don't, conclude that there is *"nothing I can do."* There is plenty you can do. Anyone who seeks God with their whole heart will find Him, and He has every answer, every solution, and all provision (see Heb. 11:6). Stop hiding because of your insecurities and inadequacies. Get honest. Your destiny is at stake and your wife and family need you to stand in and to function in that place God has ordained for you and only you. Your wife is not your mother. She is a woman who is coming out of the cave of the carnal gender mentality, and you are her man. What are you going to do with her? What are you going to do for her? Whatever you want is not going to happen automatically. You will have to get involved.

We all have heard it said, and I have said it myself, "Being a wife and mother is a 'divine calling.' " The last time I said it I started getting that "nagging sense" we get when the Spirit of God is telling us something is amiss. I also realized that the statement kept coming back to my mind. I couldn't get away from it. So I asked Father what was wrong. "It is not a divine calling. It is the natural process of human life." Defining the roles of wife and mother as a divine calling is not scripturally founded. We cannot legally put a spiritual definition on something God has not so defined. It is spiritual manipulation to keep women in the carnal gender mentality cave.

Being a wife and mother is something Buddhist women do, Hindu women do, Muslim women do, and even heathen women do. And many of them do it with just as much dedication and love as Christian women do. Being a husband and a father and being a wife and a mother are ways that humans live life. It is the expression of life. Life is relationships and procreation. The only divine part about it is that God created it and established it in the first place. Life as God created it is wonderful, and it is awesome that we should get to live it and experience all parts of it and know the fullness of it. But we cannot make it what God does not say it is.

It is a "divine calling" to be one saved by grace. It is a "divine calling" to be a member of the Body of Christ where every member is fitted into its place to allow the manifestation of the full life of Christ in the earth. It is a "divine calling" to be a part of the Bride of Christ with whom He shares the intimacies of His truths and the purposes and desires of His heart. It is a "divine calling" to die to the self-life and let Jesus live His life through us. It is a "divine calling" to develop our gifts and talents to maximize our potential for the life of Christ in us.

For the third time, I state in this book that I give the place of wife and motherhood the highest respect. I appreciate the dedication and effort that goes into the functioning of these two positions. I always wanted to be a wife and mother and am very glad I stayed home those years to help raise our sons. But God is liberating women from a restricted mentality to now be able to live life to the fullest as a wife and mother and also function in their "divine calling." Each woman's "divine calling" may be manifested through her life in different and unique ways. God doesn't conflict with Himself. He moves in harmony with Himself. When women dare to step out of the carnal gender mentality cave, God can make life and "divine calling" come together and work together with the same unifying harmony that is in His nature.

Anytime man begins to stray from God's order, man will begin to reap problems in that area from where he has strayed. Straying from God's order is really man lifting his knowledge and thoughts above God's truth. The result will always be problems. After a while, that area then becomes defined by its problems which are thought to be innate and natural to this situation or area of life. However, they are lies that have simply come from abandoning God's order. Coming back into God's order will eradicate the problems.

Education is an excellent example of becoming defined by the problems. There is nothing simple about teaching in a public school today. Education used to be teaching reading, writing, and arithmetic with history and science. Today's education, because of the problems, includes drugs, values, morals, and sex. There are now many programs that have been established just to take care of all the "problems." There are "students at risk" programs, alternative high schools, in-school suspension programs with teachers available so troublemakers can continue their class work. Isn't it just possible that the problems are not *the* problem? The problems are the symptoms of the problem of man abandoning God's order in education.

My second example has been written on the pages of this book. Man, the male man and the female man, deviated from God's order of marriage, which has resulted in an over 50-percent divorce rate and many couples abandoning marriage altogether. Yet we religiously keep cramming our concept of marriage down the church's and society's throats, and then blame the wives and husbands for not making it work. Isn't it time that we back up and take a good look and ask the Lord what He says about it? If you can't agree with anything I have written here, can't you at least agree that something is seriously wrong and only God can reveal what's right? Of course, we can always blame satan, stick our heads in the sand of our self-righteousness, and go on as usual, beating a dead horse. I for one refuse to make satan bigger than God. God's order and His ways work. If marriage and today's gender mentality were in God's order, *it would be working.* Satan is not bigger or more

powerful than God. He can*not* overpower anything that is operating in God's will by God's order.

God began showing me these truths back in the 1970s. I
have lived them, walked in them, and taught them to others.
God's order, His way and His truth *works*. I know it; I have
experienced it myself; and I have seen it in others. God's order
*works*. It not only heals and makes a marriage whole; it produces righteousness, peace, and joy, which are the fruits of the
Holy Spirit and the manifestation of the Kingdom of God in
our lives.

Adam and Eve abandoned God's order for marriage. It is
the problems that resulted that have defined marriage today
and created a carnal gender mentality that has robbed us of
the beauty of marriage with its fruitfulness and prosperity and
its power of multiplication. It has also diminished women in
their individuality and their full potential physically, mentally,
emotionally, socially, and spiritually. Because the women have
been diminished, the men have also been diminished because
$1 \times \frac{1}{2} = \frac{1}{2}$.

I have such great expectation. I don't know what living in
God's order is going to fully look like. I have only glimpses of a
world where marriages are whole functioning in the multiplication dimension, with husbands and wives living in the full
potential of who they are in Christ, individually and as one. As
we learn and grow in our spiritual marriage with Jesus, we will be
learning and growing in our earth marriage with our spouse;
therefore, I can only imagine the kind of power God will give to
families and to the Church who know how to function God's way
in marriage.

Throughout history, at least for the most part, women
have literally had to fight for rights that were already theirs by
virtue of their creation. We have proven that it was not God,
their Creator, who took their rights from them. Eve gave them
up, and because of ignorance facilitated by satan, women

throughout the generations have lived as second, third, and even fourth-class citizens. Now is the time for the final battle to be fought so that women can be fully restored to their rightfully created place.

This battle is not to be fought against flesh and blood. The enemy is not people. The enemy is the carnal gender mentality, which is a principality. By definition, a *principality* is "the territory ruled by a prince." The carnal gender mentality is the territory, and satan is the prince who rules through the mentality. As we recapture the territory, bring it into God's order by ordering our thoughts to agree with God, and make Jesus its Lord, satan will be left powerless. Ultimately, the lies of the carnal gender mentality must be destroyed from the minds and belief structures of all mankind in every nation.

How do we destroy such an enemy that is so deeply rooted and guarded by the monstrous giants of religion, tradition, prejudice, culture, and custom? It starts with each individual. If you are a Christian, if the living God dwells in you by His Spirit, then you are commissioned to "have dominion." As you recognize the lies in your own belief structure and begin to battle them with the truth of God until the truth has replaced the lies, you will be taking dominion. Having dominion is first having dominion over your thought life. Once you have dominion over your thought life, you will begin to take dominion over your physical life and then move out into the whole realm of your influence. Having dominion means you, as a delegated representative of Jesus Christ, have taken over and are now ruling the territory that satan had occupied.

We are not to rule people or tell them what to do. It is when they see the righteousness, the peace, and the joy that is the Kingdom of God manifested in our lives (because we are no longer bound by lies that oppress), that they, too, will want to know the truth that makes them free. This is how we defeat and destroy this enemy. Remember, the battleground where we are to fight is the mind. After that, the battle is the Lord's.

I have written all that I believe God has instructed me to write. I send it out as an arrow shot into the atmosphere aimed at the heart to fatally wound the carnal gender mentality. I prophesy its death once and for all. I send release to all women to know their God as He created them in chapter 1 of Genesis, to recapture their full inheritance as the female man, to discover the multifaceted purposes of their lives, to move into the dimension of multiplied fruitfulness, and to fulfill their destiny in the Kingdom of God. I release you to discover your God-appointed place in the Body of Christ and free you to follow the call of God on your life and to do what is in your heart to do.

I send release to men of the false responsibilities and burdens placed on them by the carnal gender mentality. I release them to discover their true place as a godly man and a godly husband. I release them from their aloneness, to leave their father and their mother, to receive and cleave to the "help" that God has given to them, and to learn how to initiate the power of multiplication in their marriages.

I send release to the Body of Christ, the full Body of Christ in which there is *"no male or female."* I release you to the full expression of Kingdom marriage.

*Now the body is not made up of one part but of many. If the foot should say, "Because I am not a hand, I do not belong to the body," it would not for that reason cease to be part of the body. And if the ear should say, "Because I am not an eye, I do not belong to the body," it would not for that reason cease to be part of the body. If the whole body were an eye, where would the sense of hearing be? If the whole body were an ear, where would the sense of smell be? **But in fact God has arranged the parts in the body, every one of them, just as He wanted them to be. If they were all one part, where*** *would the body be? As it is, there are many parts, but one body. The eye cannot say to the hand, "I don't need you!" And the head cannot say to the feet, "I don't need you!" ...If one part suffers, every part suffers with it; if one part is honored, every part rejoices with it (1 Corinthians 12:14-21,26 NIV, emphasis added).*

# ENDNOTES

1. Penn-Lewis, Jesse, *The Magna Charta of Woman* (Minneapolis, MN: Bethany Fellowship Inc., 1975 edition, originally published in 1919), 66.

2. Merrill F. Unger, *Unger's Bible Dictionary* (Chicago, IL: Moody Press, 1979 edition), 1147, 1149.

3. Katharine C. Bushnell, *God's Word to Women* (Mossville, IL: God's Word to Women Publishers, 1998, originally published in 1923), 62.

4. Penn-Lewis, 71.

5. Bushnell, 62.

6. *Ibid*, 45.

7. Albert Einstein Quotes. *Brainy Quote* (accessed August 4, 2005). http://www.brainyquote.com/quotes/a/alberteins133991.html.

8. *The Encarta Dictionary* (Redmond, WA: Microsoft Incorporated, 2004).

9. Joshua Dressler, *Cases and Materials on Criminal Law*, 3rd Ed. (St. Paul, MI: West Group, 2003) 392-396.

10. *Ibid*, 405.

11. *Ibid*, 413-415.

12. *The Encarta Dictionary*.

13. Penn-Lewis, 24-25.

14. Bushnell, 90-91.

15. *Ibid*, 91.

16. Thomas Nelson, ed., *Nelson's Electronic Bible Reference Library* (Nashville, TN: Thomas Nelson, Inc., 1997).

17. *Ibid*.

18. Penn-Lewis, 33-34.

19. *Ibid*, 42.

20. *Ibid*, 38.

21. *Brainy Encyclopedia* (Boston: Free Software Foundation 2002). (accessed April 29, 2005). http://www.brainyencyclopedia.com/encyclopedia/n/ne/nero.htlm

22. Professor Sir William Ramsey, *Church in the Roman Empire* (New York and London: Mansfield College Lectures, G.P. Putnam's Sons, 1912), 243-245.

23. Bushnell, 140.

24. Oscar Hammerstein, *Oh What a Beautiful Morning* (New York: Williamson Music, 1943).

25. Oscar Hammerstein, *Oklahoma* (New York: Williamson Music, 1943).

26. Dr. Brewster Higley, *Home on the Range*. 1876.

27. *The Encarta Dictionary*.

28. Bushnell, 157.

# MINISTRY CONTACT PAGE

Carol Peet Ministries
P.O. Box 2100
Pampa, Texas 79065

www.carolpeetministries.org

## UNDERSTANDING YOUR POTENTIAL

### *by Myles Munroe*

This is a motivating, provocative look at the awesome potential trapped within you, waiting to be realized. This book will cause you to be uncomfortable with your present state of accomplishment and dissatisfied with resting on your past success.

**ISBN 0-7684-2337-6**

## SECRETS OF THE MOST HOLY PLACE, VOL.1
### *by Don Nori*

Here is a prophetic parable you will read again and again. The winds of God are blowing, drawing you to His Life within the Veil of the Most Holy Place. There you begin to see as you experience a depth of relationship your heart has yearned for.

ISBN 1-56043-076-1

## SECRETS OF THE MOST HOLY PLACE, VOL. 2
### *by Don Nori*

This book is about realizing the fullness of God's love and forgiveness so the dream He has dreamed for each of us can come to pass.
You will experience God's loving mercy and will be free to do the will of God with joy, personal fulfillment and anticipation of His Presence every day.

ISBN 0-7684-2175-6

Additional copies of this book and other book titles from DESTINY IMAGE are available at your local bookstore.

Call toll-free: 1-800-722-6774.

Send a request for a catalog to:

**Destiny Image® Publishers, Inc.**
P.O. Box 310
Shippensburg, PA 17257-0310

*"Speaking to the Purposes of God for This
Generation and for the Generations to Come"*

**For a complete list of our titles,
visit us at www.destinyimage.com**